T0324408

Folk Horror

Folk Horror
Hours Dreadful And Things Strange

Adam Scovell

First published in 2017 by
Auteur
24 Hartwell Crescent, Leighton Buzzard LU7 1NP
www.auteur.co.uk

Copyright © Auteur Publishing 2017
Designed and set by Kim Lankshear
Printed and bound in the UK

Cover: *Witchfinder General* © Tigon Films; *Whistle and I'll Come to You* © BBC;
The Wicker Man © British Lion; *Kill List* © Warp X/Rook Films

All rights reserved. No part of this publication may be reproduced in any material form (including photocopying or storing in any medium by electronic means and whether or not transiently or incidentally to some other use of this publication) without the permission of the copyright owner.

British Library Cataloguing-in-Publication Data
A catalogue record for this book is available from the British Library

ISBN: paperback 978-1-911325-22-2

ISBN: cloth 978-1-911325-23-9

ISBN: ebook 978-1-911325-24-6

Contents

To Jan and Keith, for finding a copy of The Daemons *on VHS*
all those years ago when it was rarer than a cursed crown;
and to the memory and work of Mark Fisher.

Chapter I

'Hours dreadful and things strange'

Threescore and ten I can remember well: Within the volume of which time I have
seen Hours dreadful and things strange; but this sore night Hath trifled former
knowings. – Old Man in *Macbeth* (1611)

A Cold Evening In Stockport

In October 2013, my head was being gently jolted against a window to the
rhythm of a cut-price train. I was exhausted from a long spate of writing and
filming but, tonight, I had decided to make the effort and leave my flat in Liverpool for an evening in Stockport. Though the steam on the window had distorted the view outside to a blur of electric lights upon a rich blackness, I had
trusted the last minute rush to the ticket machine and quietly assured myself
that this strange vision was gradually evolving into an industrial town, typical
of those found in the north-west of England. This place of my destination,
more famous for viaducts painted by L.S. Lowry, was drawing me to its streets
for a particularly special event; a certain screening of a certain cut of a certain
film in the presence of a certain director.

The specific place and appointed hour was the Stockport Plaza Cinema; a beautifully restored art deco cinematheque, all angles, blocks of light and patinas gleaned straight from The Overlook Hotel (or maybe vice-versa).[1] The cinema was an unusually busy place that evening, far more so than for its more typical screenings, for the whole building had been taken over by a horror film festival, set to unleash a number of films on an audience ready to lap up the pulp. The walls were covered with black and red paraphernalia of all kinds, and the aisles swam with an excited buzz. I took my seat in one of the period chairs, the shakiness being oddly reassuring rather than worrying. Perhaps, I thought, someone had sat here forty years ago (and two months hence) ready and waiting desperately to see Nicolas Roeg's latest mimetic shard of cinema, the gloriously gothic *Don't Look Now* (1973), but was frustrated at having to first wait through some B-picture, about a wooden man or something. Maybe, just like that evening, the organist would have been doing his utmost musical theatrics, bellowing marvellously on the Compton Organ. The green lights that shone vividly upon its casing made it seem more *Dr Phibes* than Lon Chaney Snr.

There was mention of other films in the program, yet it mattered very little; there was an appointment to keep with one film alone. Suddenly, a name was dropped out of the white noise of information apropos of *Chucky* films and the like. The name was Robin Hardy and, for a brief moment, he appeared at the side of the stage. My seat was too far back for a better view at this point but I could see he had come in his typical costume. Rather like the titular lead in *Doctor Who*, Hardy was a man who seemed to wear the same sorts of clothes in his publicity photos as in real life. Some of my neighbouring viewers looked bemused. Who was this man? And, more importantly, why did the sight of him make certain audience members beam in awe as if in the presence of a papal dignitary? This man in the corner, who looked like the second player from an *Amicus* film, felt oddly anachronistic compared to his audience; double-breasted blue sailor jacket, RP pronunciation, Cushing handkerchief in top pocket. I was one of these beaming subjects, enraptured in a strange sense of Zen as the lights went down and his film began.

Of course, the film was *The Wicker Man* (1973). That film of so many strange amalgamations, of so many elements as to require a book of its own to detail its complicated history. This wasn't simply the widely available version, learned by rote in the intervening years through numerous (excessive?) repeat viewings, but a new, longer cut recently discovered in Harvard's film archives. The extra footage hugely reframed the film temporally from the version I knew well, the drama of poor Sgt. Howie, played by Edward Woodward, being taken in by the counter-culture pagan window dressings of the community of Summerisle, now feeling very much like taking place over a set number days. The film was fleshed out, somehow impossibly better, a whole new set of cinematic grammar and rhythms to take on board. The exhilaration reached its peak at the final sound of Paul Giovanni's score, its last horn being both mournful, fateful and celebratory. The head of the wicker man fell into burning flame, giving way to a vibrant sun at dusk, sinking away behind the horizon of film history; an impossibly perfect final shot whose colours are drenched with the dying embers of the British counter-culture itself.

The ever recognisable logo of the Summerisle sun came up as did the house lights, as if it had lit up the auditorium with its rays of the past. Perhaps we would all leave as pagans in its warm glow. Like the jubilant villagers of Summersle, the audience was in equal rapture, clapping as if Hardy himself had sacrificed Woodward in a frenzied ritual of fire for the benefit of horror cinema as whole. Like a distant cousin of Lord Summerisle, Hardy's gentlemanly aura was free to behold as he was asked onto the stage for a brief, seemingly unplanned, Q&A. A few heretics rustled in their seats, impatient for the next film to start. Hardy was rushed through a handful of anaemic questions, those routinely asked of a man sadly only famous for one seriously classic film: a drawn out archaeology of the film's cutting history; where the version just screened had differed from the previously existing copy; what was still missing; all answered with the brief but polite hyperbole brought about through years of rote answering, polished to perfection like a pebble.

Before having time to delve deeper than trivialities, Hardy was rushed off stage. It seemed unfair, or perhaps I was as taken in and brainwashed by his film as the antagonists who inhabited it. I knew instantly that, rather than watch the rehashed horror about to follow, I instead would give chase, meet him, somehow at least attempt to convey the importance his work had played in my own, oddly isolated, viewing life. The second film was due to start, the lights dimming again. In the growing darkness, I could make out the bob of his walk, the sailor-jacketed shoulders sticking out from the black T-shirted crowd of horror fans, as he made his way with a small entourage up the slight incline of the cinema aisle, as if mimicking Howie's final journey. My decision was impulsive, as if a determined race memory had alighted, possibly born all of the way back to when Martian insect aliens crashed a ship under the tube station near Hobs Lane. I was about to spin down the aisles in a way that would have made Duncan Lamont's chaotic skip and jump to a nearby Kensington church seem calm and composed in comparison.[2]

In my moment of possession, I had failed to realise that the ancient seat of the cinema had a dual purpose of trapping coats within its metallic teeth. I was unable to move, and became more frantic as I could see Hardy getting further and further towards the exit. I was as trapped as a sound in the brick walls of *The Stone Tape* (1972) and close to giving a reaction similar to Jane Asher's. My fear was not of a pair of fuzzy, floating red dots, however, but of missing this opportunity to meet the director who had made *The Wicker Man*; a far more terrifying prospect. I escaped the Stone Seat but it required an appropriate hecatomb. My sacrifice was not of blood for the land but of my coat itself, which violently tore down the back as I tugged it out from the seat's jaws. It was only missing the presence of Bernard Hepton purring away and quoting Sir James Frazer's *The Golden Bough* to be worthily counted as a sacrifice: 'Always Robin. Such bounty there was, such fruitfulness, Miss Palmer, from the blood that drained from Robin Hood the old stories say. But they are only stories, of course...'[3]

Now unimpeded, I staggered up the aisle after Hardy. The foyer opened out before me and the entourage had momentarily left him alone, simply waiting there as if dallying impatiently for some local villagers to send a dinghy to him. Several other people had had the same idea yet, despite the efforts of my seat, I had somehow made my way to being two from the front of a makeshift queue to meet him. The festival organisers, clearly unprepared for the actions of the devoted, began to panic as it was clear that a sizeable portion of their audience was more interested in having a few moments shared with the director than catching the short film now playing.

Upon meeting him, my mind faltered. What is the correct thing to say to the man who directed *The Wicker Man*? It had to be short but it also had to convey a total adoration of his work. It needed to be akin to a powerful incantation, like M.R. James' '*Quis est iste qui venit*' only benevolent and summoning up goodwill rather than a Dunwich demon to ruffle the bed sheets.[4] No ideas were coming, my mind was too taken over by the changes in the new version of the film; it had felt like a new experience, the land reborn, the fields replenished. The lyrics of 'Gently Johnny', the song which now had much more precedence, swirled around my mind. What to say? Christopher Lee's kilt, mating snails, Brit Ekland at the window, 'And she says, do you want to see?' These images were unhelpful, much too powerful. I couldn't do it and singing his film's lyrics to him would have been highly inappropriate, to say the least. I strode up to Mr. Robin Hardy and simply thanked him politely for making his film. There was little else to be said as gratitude and admiration covered the common ground of the film's reception. But I sufficiently composed myself to wish him 'Happy Day!' when taking my leave.[5] Hardy looked slightly perplexed and not only for the fact that it was now some hours into the evening. Did he know what I was referring to, the strange connected movements of culture of which his work was arguably at the forefront? I managed to coerce the impatient person behind to get a photo of the meeting which concealed the tear in my coat, at that point now embarrassingly resembling the object of a tussle from a Laurel and Hardy film. It was a moment captured and one that is still treasured, not simply because I had met someone whose work was hugely important to me, but because it was an occasion that solidified my own interest, my own obsessions, and my total and sheer joy in something so far unnamed.

Wandering down the street and back to the train station, the rain hammered down on the tarmac, trying and failing to find the fields underneath. My shirt was getting wet and heavy, the water seeping through the coat as I meandered through the multiple diversions of glistening roadwork. The Stone Seat was a far more comfortable prospect now that I was out in the glacial air of the Stockport night. My thoughts were aptly elsewhere as I stepped onto the train, lost in several realisations as it gave the melancholic sigh of moving off. The journey had felt more like a pilgrimage, for the bettering and confirmation of something that had been gradually manifesting in the flames; the interests in the ancient, the cursed and the 'wyrd'; the 'olde ways', the daemonic and the occult; the furrows of Robin Hardy, Nigel Kneale, Alan Garner and M.R. James; the obliqueness of the *Spirit of Dark of Lonely Water*, 'the electricity board warns children to keep away from sub-stations'; Bok hopping around Devil's End graveyard;[6] Vincent Price in Civil War garb declaring 'The mark of Satan is upon them!';[7] deceased villagers so moved by the worry of new urban planning as to rise from their own graves;[8] 'You cannot escape the field, Whitehead!'.[9] At that point, I knew for certain that all of these things were connected under something powerful and subtlety ubiquitous. It wasn't simply a coincidence of era or error, a simple warning to the curious, or a longing for yesteryear: it was Folk Horror.

What Is Folk Horror?

Folk Horror is a prism of a term. Its light disperses into a spectrum of colours that range in shade and contrast. Contrary to the handful of images that the term now evokes, arguing for it to represent a single body of artistic work with strict parameters and definitions is conceivably impossible. As will be seen in Chapter 2, even the most obvious and widely discussed examples defy such thematic rigidity when discussed in a wider context. Folk Horror is best seen, not simply as a set of criteria to be read with hindsight into all sorts of media, but as a way of opening up discussions on subtly interconnected work and how we now interact with such work. If anything, its genealogy is less important than its stark ability to draw links between oddities and idiosyncrasies, especially within post-war British culture. When first approaching the term, several ideas initially occur through the simple reaction to the words. On initial analysis, it could be argued that it is the ambiguity of the first part of the term that adds to the fluidity of its canon. 'Folk' could mean drawing upon any number of aspects. Is it the practices of a people or community; the elements of ethno-graphic tradition? Is it the aesthetics of such practices and the natural ances-try of the visual and thematic elements that accompanied them? Or could it simply be a connected link between certain forms that emerged in the popular culture of the 1960s and, therefore, the easy categorisation that led on from it? In one sense, it is all of these arguments combined.

This is not to say that the 'horror' part of the description is a simpler compo-nent. As Bob Trubshaw has argued, horror has often been built upon narra-tives formed with folkloric intention anyway: 'The horror fiction genre routinely draws upon folklore – where would the goosebumps come from without assorted werewolves, vampires, cursed Egyptian mummies, and a multitude of things un-seen that bump, creak or moan at the midnight hour?' (2010: 85). When tilling the fields of Folk Horror, it becomes apparent that the work discussed under such an umbrella form is not necessarily always 'horror' within any straightforward guise of the term, but simply a mutation of its affect. The inherent feeling is broad across other forms such as science-fiction and fantasy, which are often used as a fragmented trait to offset their drama.[10] Therefore, definitions cannot be simply built from the material of its description as each individual work is far too at variance, and it cannot be built from the term itself as each component of its etymology is so open to fluctuating meaning. Giving weight to one part alone negates the discussions of various, more idiosyncratic fiends of relevance.

The very term 'Folk Horror', in the form that is recognisable to discussions of popular culture, is rather surprisingly not the old, ancient term dug from beneath the ground that one would expect. The joining of the two words can be found in older analytical work, for example in James B. Twitchell's book, *The Living Dead: A Study of the Vampire in Romantic Fiction* (1983), where he refers to Benedictine Abbot Dom Augustin Calmet's book, *Treaty on the Apparitions of Spirits and Vampires, or Ghosts of Hungary, Moravia, & c.* as 'an anthology of folk horror stories' (1983: 33). But it appears to be a simple method of describing the more horrific end of folklore and fairy tales, which is only a small part of what contemporary discussions of Folk Horror now resembles. For evidence of this, one need only watch a 1970s British Public Information Film such as *Apaches* (1977) – a literal bloodbath on a farm far removed from anything especially folkloric, broadcast in order to keep curious children safe – to see where such emphasis would over-generalise.

In the modern canonisation of the description, the term seems to have been coined by one of the genre's true proprietor's, director Piers Haggard, in an interview for Fangoria Magazine in 2003 with M.J. Simpson. In the interview, he suggests that he was 'trying to make a folk horror film, I suppose' (2003) when discussing the ideas behind his soon-to-be-analysed key film, *The Blood on Satan's Claw* (1971). The popularisation of the term stems from this one quote being used as a reference point for the 2010 series put together by Mark Gatiss for BBC4, *A History of Horror*. Gatiss uses the term as a way of discussing three key films, of which *Blood* is one; Robin Hardy's singular pagan beast and Michael Reeves' brutal *Witchfinder General* (1968) being the other two. Gatiss suggests that Folk Horror films 'shared a common obsession with the British landscape, its folklore and superstitions' (2010) and this has stuck as the groundwork for its initial cinematic canonisation ever since. From henceforward, the term has spun down several alleyways which only seem to marginally touch upon its descriptive character; where the re-appropriation of past culture, even that which is still within living memory, now attains a folkloric guise and becomes ascribed as Folk Horror.

With this minor diversion into its etymology, it should be apparent that Folk Horror is not one thing alone. In simply looking at the description, miscellanea from the Romantic Gothic to pulp 1970s B-movies have already been touched upon. This book, therefore, aims to cover as many areas as possible and not simply adhere to previous assumptions created from its etymology. With this consideration, Folk Horror in all types of media can be considered a channelling of any of the following formal ideas:

- A work that uses folklore, either aesthetically or thematically, to imbue itself with a sense of the arcane for eerie, uncanny or horrific purposes.
- A work that presents a clash between such arcania and its presence within close proximity to some form of modernity, often within social parameters.
- A work which creates its own folklore through various forms of popular conscious memory, even when it is young in comparison to more typical folkloric and antiquarian artefacts of the same character.

These three points are only generalities and it is the detailed strands within them where the true elementals of Folk Horror lurk. One of the aims of this book is to show that Folk Horror is not simply horror flavoured with a pinch of handpicked folklore; this simplistic conclusion is logical but often incorrect. Because of this, the chapters of this book will not be addressing the genre through these three main points specifically but through the microcosms within them and how they thematically develop. The differences perceivable mean that such thematic traits may not apply to all of the examples analysed, though a sense of many shared themes and ideas should be clear, most obviously when works by the same writers are covered under differing perspectives. The book itself is akin to the plough from the opening of Haggard's film, churning up the various relics and summoning its previous inhabitants. However, like most analyses of Folk Horror, this book will begin by looking at the strange relationships found in its three predominate cinematic examples; the 'unholy trinity' as they are sometimes called.[11] As will be seen in Chapter 2, their own thematic proximity to each other is problematic to explain, not to say difficult to comprehend at first when considering them outside of their obvious surface aesthetics and period of production. However, I will attempt to connect them in order to theorise a template with which a basic form of narrative Folk Horror can manifest and be used to cover a broader range of cinema; namely, through the causational narrative theory of what can be called the Folk Horror Chain.

This means connecting disparate forms of media through their shared summoning of these themes and ideas rather than looking at the commercial reasons behind certain cycles of films and television; it is instead about what is attempting to be unleashed that is at the heart of Folk Horror and not simply the decisions of money men tapping into a lucrative popularisation of the occult, the paranoid or the 'wyrd'. There are numerous threads that can be drawn to discuss the work in question and this also crosses the more typical national barriers that discussions of the genre most typically fall into: every country has its own 'folk', folklore and superstitions after all and, therefore, also has its own Folk Horror potential. By using the chain and its special relationship with the landscape, this will lead on to the topographical ideas presented within **Chapter 3**. This will be set out within the chapter through an emphasis on British cult television in order to highlight such oddities and trends within the genre outside of purely cinematic modes. By addressing landscape in such a way, the groundwork will be laid for Chapter 4 which looks at a concept of 'Rurality'; the name given here to denote the sideways tipping of the diegetic reality of a narrative world through an ironic emphasis on the recognisably numinous rural. This manifests in a number of styles, whether it be the 'anonymous rurality' of British films that crop up in discussions of the genre but rarely seem to be horrific in any sense of the word, the purely British pulp variations of rurality focussing on farming communities, villages and general rural sociology, or in the global rurality found in a huge range of pastoral narratives from around the world, in movements such as Czechoslovakian Magic Realism, Australian Outback films, American Backwaters films, early European silent cinema and Japanese ghost stories.

Moving away from the rural landscape entirely, Chapter 5 seeks to understand the presence of the occult flavoured esoteric content within the genre; where pagan entities evoke forms of devil worship, witchcraft and magic(k). The supernatural plays a large part within many Folk Horror forms, whether portrayed as real and fleshed-out onto narrative bones, or as part of a belief system skewed by a geographical and social isolation. Folk Horror often presents a power-play at work, seeking a pathos whereby the narrative roles that are traditional in cinema are subtly reversed, albeit through heretical means. Its horror is often derived from this knowingness, though deliberately breaks away into its own fallow fields when desiring a greater sense of unease; that unease of being recognisable to an audience and uncomfortably close to our own social reality. By separating this strand and emphasising it as part of a wider trend of occult themes in horror media through its relationship with what is now commonly understood under the term 'Hauntology', the summarising of the social geography necessary for the first part of this chapter can occur. Folk Horror is so often known for its sense of rural location, even sometimes referred to rather simplistically as 'Rural Horror'.[12] This chapter seeks to move away from this element by focussing on examples that use urban locations in order to build in a wider questioning of the nostalgia at work within Folk Horror, assessing the psychological prevalence of work from what is commonly considered to be the British counter-culture of the late 1960s and its twisted, post-counter-culture cousin of the early 1970s. The transition between the two raises questions revolving around the very diegesis of what actually constitutes Folk Horror and the framework of folklore itself; where the violent tearing of the veil of normality surrounding 1970s popular culture, caused by various twenty-first century scandals coming to light, is effectively pre-empted by Folk Horror artefacts produced from the same period. In other words, have we ourselves become trapped on a concrete Summerisle of our own making?

To conclude, Chapter 6 will assess the recent resurgence of Folk Horror in a variety of media and attempt to understand why this has occurred. The numerous quantity of post-millennial Folk Horror constitutes a revival that is telling of our current political climate. Its continued prevalence raises stark questions about the social implications of such manifestations. It is more than nostalgia at work in the rejuvenation of our pagan apple orchards; it is equally the plugging of a definite loss of something of ineffable, intangible importance. The genre's questioning of this loss can heighten more wide-spread notions of nostalgia as well as more political themes and ideas, especially those revolving around class in modern-day Britain.

The subtitle of this book, 'Hours dreadful and things strange', comes from William Shakespeare's most haunting and relevant play, *Macbeth* (1611). It is a line spoken by the character of the Old Man when he is discussing unnerving events from earlier in his life. Aptly, the actions of the play make these trite in comparison; a subtle premonition of future horror techniques. Folk Horror often mimics this idea of looking back, where the past and the present mix and create horror through both anachronisms and uncomfortable tautologies between eras. Taken out of context, the line becomes strangely prescient to Folk Horror, whereby era and temporality are linked by esoteric, inexplicable events; things that unnerve through a sheer recognisability of darker ages that are beginning to reoccur. Folk Horror, the horror of 'folk', is out of time and within time, with strangers in the landscape who have survived the ravages of modernity. In the words of Reverend Fallowfield himself in *The Blood on Satan's Claw*, 'strange folk have been seen to pass this way from time to time'.

Endnotes

1   *The Shining (*1980, dir. Stanley Kubrick).

2   *Quatermass and the Pit* (1967, dir. Roy Ward Baker).

3   *Robin Redbreast* (1970, dir. James MacTaggart).

4   *Whistle and I'll Come To You* (1968, dir. Jonathan Miller).

5   *Children of the Stones* (1977, dir. Peter Graham Scott).

6   *Doctor Who – The Daemons* (1971, dir. Christopher Barry).

7   *Witchfinder General* (1968, dir. Michael Reeves).

8   *Requiem for a Village* (1975, dir. David Gladwell).

9   *A Field in England* (2013, dir. Ben Wheatley).

10 And in purely dramatic examples such as *Winstanley* (1976, dir. Kevin Brownlow and Andrew Mollo), the argument becomes even more complex.

11 Of Haggard's, Hardy's and Reeves' films.

12 See Peter Hutching's article for the British Film Institute's website, '10 Great British Rural Horror films'.

Chapter 2

Trilogy

A Preternatural Paradox

Indeed it is impossible to study any single system of worship throughout the world, without being struck by the peculiar persistence of the triple number in regard to divinity. Whether as a group of deities, a triformed or 3 headed god, a Mysterious Triunity, a deity of 3 powers, or a family relationship of 3 Persons, such as the Father, Mother and Son of the Egyptians, Osiris, Isis and Horus. – W. Wynn, Westcott (1890: 43)

In September 2013, I could see an eagle-eyed view of a green and foggy landmass soon to form into Northern Ireland's capital city. My visit was specifically to Queen's University Belfast for a three-day conference looking into all sorts of different forms of creative media. It was, excitingly, the first of its kind that looked, in the spirit of academic, ontological and hermeneutic rigour, at Folk Horror as an artistic genre. Though the term had been steadily amassing interest in its online iterations – the artefacts and anomalies of yesteryear's culture bolstering steadily onto the new and succinct descriptor like a cultural life-raft – the grounding of the genre in an earnest attempt at an academic framework had the air of a benchmark moment.

The conference was put together under the name *A Fiend in the Furrows*, a perfect summation of the genre's aesthetic proponents if ever there was one, with the name taking its cue from *The Blood on Satan's Claw*: 'It were more like some fiend!' and 'Claims he discovered some deformed anatomy in the furrows!' being popular quotes from the film.[1] Like many lines from its quotable script, these short bursts of Folk Horror imagery act in a similar vein to a haiku, where an ultimate truth is conveyed through a strict, immanent simplicity. The Devil is in the fleshing out of these forms with greater meaning and Folk Horror is no exception. Having arrived in the city the day before the conference, a meander around its streets and the University grounds added to the argument that it really was the best place for such exploration. The most obvious manifestation of this reasoning was in the discovery of a crafts shop behind the Victoria Square shopping centre, named, in the most impossibly apt way, The Wicker Man. It was further telling that the well-received conference booklet came with one of the shop's business cards; if it was a cursed rune in the spirit of M.R. James, the demon would most certainly have caught the conference attendees with ease.

The reason for elaborating on this conference is because, with its various and excellent presentations ranging from a consideration of the writing of Arthur Machen to the oeuvre of Nigel Kneale, it was the first time that the problems surrounding any formal analysis of the genre became apparent. When considering my own paper to present, the main theory of which makes up the majority of this chapter, problems seemed to steadily grow surrounding even the most basic of discussions. Suffice to say, in spite of having to leave the conference a day early, the surface was only scratched, the dust barely abraded, and the (perhaps non-existent) golden egg of Folk Horror theory most definitely remained hidden and guarded by a malevolent presence: 'No diggin' here!'[2]

The feeling that this impossible task produced still lingers on. There is no supernatural incantation to define every aspect of Folk Horror. What there is, however, is a variety of frameworks that can be applied, especially of the narrative kind, that at least begin the discussion. The first of these frameworks deals with the very initial problem that arose during the conference's various presentations; that of accounting for the genre's aforementioned chief trilogy of films. As the first plenary presentation began to unfold, I felt the slow and steady falling away of the floor as the entire talk had gone into great detail surrounding the films *Witchfinder General* (1968), *The Blood on Satan's Claw* (1971) and *The Wicker Man* (1973); the three benchmarks for my own presentation.[3]

Not only this, but my presentation was to be further bookended by another paper that again looked into these three films. We were slowly nodding our way towards a folkloric gestalt, all hypnotised by the unquestionable power of this cinematic unholy trinity, but it was undeniable that they not only represented the genre as a whole but were interconnected to each other. Moreover, it was far from simply the addition of a folkloric aesthetic that built this connection but a range of likened factors that, if isolated, could arguably construct some theory of Folk Horror. The worry was unnecessary as the first problem arose; what was it that really connected all three of these films? Thinking about the conundrum, it is far more complicated than it first appears.

The trilogy were all summoned into existence during what can be called the British counter-culture movement, almost acting as signposts for its tidal high-point of 1968 in *Witchfinder* and the dying, post-Manson embers of *Wicker* in 1973. By 'counter-culture', a term to be used throughout this book, it is referring to the evolution of social popular culture that arose dramatically during the 1960s in the west. In its iteration here, the term is even more specific by looking at the influx of drug culture, the sexual revolution, avant-garde ideologies and other elements that became more prominent in Britain and America in the late 1960s, resulting in a definite collection of counter narratives in the arts to more conservative cultural modes.[4]

As Adam Richards writes, 'The counterculture that developed during the 1960s was an alternative lifestyle chosen by individuals who would eventually become known as hippies, freaks or long hairs. Members of the counterculture held convictions similar to that of the New Left movement in that they wanted to overhaul domestic policy within the United States' (2016). This movement can be coupled with a reversion to older ideas but explored within such new social freedoms, producing interest in this period in a wide-ranging array of areas such as Folk Music and Folklore, Astrology, nineteenth-century Transcendentalist ideals and Wicca Magic. This ties heavily to trends in Folk Horror production as well.

It does not, however, account for how immensely different all three of the films in question actually are to each other, which raises an even starker question: if the three most oft-discussed examples of Folk Horror cannot be properly connected, then what hope is there of uniting work outside of this profane trilogy? Some at the conference argued that a far easier rune to cast was to negate one example, breaking the powerful three into a more simplified two. A few argued for *Witchfinder* to be decanted into a separate urn being that it was more akin to an English Western than strictly pure horror, whilst some argued for *Wicker* to be excluded due to its modern setting and *Blood* for its unique use of a genuine supernatural presence. There was logic to each pathway but they lacked tenacity; Folk Horror at its core is tri-formed in hindsight of this trilogy even if the leylines between them are difficult to divine. They may wind off into all sorts of other valleys to connect with totally differing media, but they are still essentially interlinked.

There is, therefore, an abundant intertextuality between the three films in spite of their differences. If anything, it is the differences that highlight themselves as secondary when taking into account the sheer aesthetic resemblances between the films and, most importantly, their parallel narrative structures. The unholy trinity are capable of both interconnection *and* of standing alone; their themes being permeable and mantra-like in their ease of repetition. This connection is not strictly that of British folklore's purely aesthetic or thematic influence, but is instead linked to certain elements within its narrative happenings; they share a mirrored but ultimately differing birth. The Reader's Digest volume, *Folklore, myths and legend of Britain* – a key text in the weird and various counter-culture paraphernalia of the early 1970s – suggests in its introduction that folklore rises up because men 'baffled by the wonders of the universe, will create marvels of the imagination out of their need to understand' (1973: 11). This instantly provides a subtle but indeed healthy distance between the production of Folk Horror and the creation of folklore.

Folk Horror treats the past as a paranoid, skewed trauma; a trauma reflecting on the everyday of when these films in particular were made, especially when bringing past elements to sit with uncomfortable ease within the then-present day, as in *Wicker*. The theory that I argued for was not one simply born of these three films but *is* one that is most perceivable within their flickering celluloid. I called the theory the Folk Horror Chain: a linking set of narrative traits that have causational and interlinking consequences. Though emphasising narrative, such an emphasis has great and inevitable effects upon the aesthetic style of such films too. The ideas allow for a great range of improvisation in spite of the rigidness that describing it as a chain implies. This was, and is, just one of many ways into what is an incredibly subjectivist and flexible form, but one that is structured through reference to Folk Horror's key daemons;

the table-tipping tri-focus of May-Day mayhem, brutality on the broads, and Angel Blake's antics. Contrary to the notion of breaking up the trinity, there *is* a potential framework within these films. This framework, once deduced, can be seen to act throughout whole swathes of film and television, and creates the solid foundation needed to begin the analysis of such an elusive form.

The Folk Horror Chain

> Grendel was the name of this grim demon, haunting the marches, marauding round the heath and the desolate fens; he had dwelt for a time in misery among the banished monsters, Cain's clan, whom the creator had outlawed and condemned as outcasts. – *Beowulf*, trans. Seamus Heaney (1999: 6).

Before diving into the pool of Folk Horror theorising, it is essential to sketch out the narratives of the three films. By summarising their happenings through key descriptive markers and events, there at first appears to be little to connect them other than outside attributes, for example through the connection between two of them being made by the same British production company, Tigon Pictures. The Folk Horror Chain, however, can be seen as the hyphen between these depicted, horrific events; its descriptor as a chain being more than simply for evocation but specifically to highlight connections and strong ties between cause and effect, idea and action, the summoning and the summoned. It is within these connections that Folk Horror as a form can begin to be conjured as a framework or perhaps even as a narrative template. Below, the unholy trinity are summarised to begin this process in chronological order.

Witchfinder General – In the vast plains of the Norfolk broads during the English Civil War, Matthew Hopkins (Vincent Price), a lawyer now turned 'witchfinder', is ransacking communities in the name of God. He is searching for 'witches' within local communities who, when found, are subjected to barbaric tests, tortures and executions in the name of sanctity. Richard Marshall (Ian Ogilvy), a soldier in Oliver Cromwell's army, has pledged that he will marry Sara (Hilary Heath), the daughter of a parish priest (Rupert Davies) who is unaware that he is under suspicion of witchcraft from Hopkins and his second in command, John Stearne (Robert Russell). They torture and eventually kill Sara's father, as well as forcing themselves upon Sara; Hopkins through blackmail, bartering for the life of her father, and Stearne through sheer physical assault. Upon hearing news of his soon-to-be father-in-law's murder, Richard returns to find a broken Sara, swearing upon vengeance after his duty to Cromwell (Patrick Wymark) at the Battle of Naseby has been carried out. After several brief chases, captures and escapes, Richard eventually catches up with the pair in the Suffolk town of Lavenham where Hopkins is performing his usual acts of atrocity. Richard and Sara are caught by Hopkins and briefly subjected to torture. Richard escapes and disables Stearne before setting to work on Hopkins with an axe. The soldiers he brought with him to the town come upon the scene, shooting Hopkins with a musket to spare him from more pain. Richard, overwrought with anger at losing him so easily, screams repeatedly 'You took him from me!'.

The Blood on Satan's Claw – In a rural clime of seventeenth-century England, a farmer, Ralph Gower (Barry Andrews), uncovers an oddly shaped and furry part of a skull in a field while ploughing its furrows. The uncovering results in an outbreak of Satanism among the nearby village's youth, lead by Angel Blake (Linda Hayden). She is first opposed by the minister (Anthony Ainley) who suspects that something is afoot, finding the young in his care passing around a strange object during one of his lessons in church. She falsely but successfully accuses him of forcing his intentions upon her after failing to seduce him physically. Her group form and gather pace, performing evil rites in the grounds of an ancient but derelict church in order to spawn the furry flesh of Satan upon their own. A local girl and previous friend of Blake's, Cathy Vespers (Wendy Padbury), is lured to the site of rites where she is raped and murdered in a brutal ritual. The Devil is using them to rebuild his own body. A local judge (Patrick Wymark) returns from another town, after being sent for by Ralph, to deal with the skulduggery. After some esoteric research and interrogation upon captured follower, Margaret (Michele Dotrice), he takes some men to the sacrilegious and erotic final ceremony where Blake is killed by accident while the fully formed creature is slain by the judge with a sword.

The Wicker Man – It is 1973. Police Sgt. Howie (Edward Woodward) is summoned to the isolated island of Summerisle off the Scottish coast by an anonymous letter. He is investigating the apparent disappearance of a young girl, Rowan Morrison (Gerry Cowper), from the arable, fruit growing community who enjoy the island's unique climate. Throughout his stay on the island for his investigation, Howie, who is a strict and puritanical Christian, is bombarded by the rites and customs of the islanders who have foresworn Christianity in favour of a liberal, erotic form of paganism. They appear to be hiding something and do their utmost to pervert the course of justice in delaying Howie's attempts at finding the girl. Through contact with various inhabitants, including the island's spiritual leader, Lord Summerisle (Christopher Lee) and the 'landlord's daughter', Willow (Britt Ekland) – who tries but fails to seduce Howie – he suspects that the islanders have kidnapped Rowan to use as a May Day sacrifice to rebuke the failure of last year's harvest. It turns out that the whole visit has been a deception by the islanders to test and ensnare Howie who is the real sacrifice needed for the land, being a pure Christian virgin who came of his own free will. He is burnt to death in a giant man made of wicker, though not before he has effectively lined up Lord Summerisle for the next sacrifice if the crops fail again the following year. The film ends as the sun sets, mixing with the flames of the sacrifice.

This section opened with a quote from Seamus Heaney's translation of the text of *Beowulf*, the epic odyssey of Old English poetry detailing ancient battles and Anglo-Saxon drama. The translation captures much of the essence of Folk Horror but it is in the particular quoted segment where ideas of the Folk Horror Chain are forged. Like the descriptions of the films above, this fragment of *Beowulf* begins by setting out its landscape and its inhabitants. Grendel is portrayed as a demonic creature but, more importantly, he haunts the marches and spends time 'marauding round the heath and the desolate fens...'. Within this description is the first link in the Folk Horror Chain: that of **landscape**. This isn't merely just scene-setting or the obvious logic that all narrative art has to have somewhere to act out its drama. The landscape is essentially the first link, where elements within its topography have adverse effects on the social and moral identity of its inhabitants. This isn't to say that Grendel would have been an amiable character, keen for a drink down at The Cloven Hoof[5] if housed in a more social climate, but it's difficult to imagine his character being anything other than malevolent when confined to his usual haunts of 'desolate fens'; the landscape, in spite of being a punishment, augments and defines his character as well as actually being a character itself.

The landscape is, therefore, key to the second element of the Folk Horror Chain: that of **isolation**. The landscape must in some way isolate a key body of characters, whether it be just a handful of individuals or a small-scale community. Creatures are 'banished' to this landscape but the implication is actually that it is an inhospitable place because it is in some way different from general society as a whole and not simply because of a harsher topography. Isolation in a specific Folk Horror context is even more extreme. The people who inhabit Folk Horror are not in the places of their dwelling because of some particular banishment like that of 'Cain's clan' but because of a natural enforcement through circumstance, situation and the landscape itself. This isolation, it must be stated, does not necessarily need to be of a rural character as in our core trilogy and, as will be seen in later chapters, it can occur viscerally in more urban forms as well. As long as people are cut off from some established social progress of the diegetic world, the Folk Horror Chain can continue in its horrific domino effect.

The halting of social progress can have a number of names but, for the sake of simplicity within the main chain, it is best to refer to it as skewed: that is, of **skewed belief systems and morality**. This moves a little outside of *Beowulf*'s furrows in that the reading is from a post-Enlightenment perspective that assumes folklore, superstition, and even to some extent religion, form through this very physical but also psychical isolation. This is also skewed within the context of the general social status quo of the era in which the films are made coupled with the diegesis of the cinema itself. For example, if *Wicker* was somehow set during a far earlier period in history, the final execution would perhaps not be so shocking in the context of that earlier era's normality, but perhaps only within its distanced reflection; when Howie travels to Summerisle, he is travelling physically away from a more established society but also travelling culturally back in time because of that context.[6] Folk Horror narratives need this plateau away from such modern eyes whether it be a Gulf stream-exploiting isle off Scotland, a village unfortunate enough to be away from and outside of progress in East Anglia, or even a derelict London tube station long since forgotten about by the bustling society above it.[7]

The final link in this chain is the resulting action from this skewed social consciousness with all of its horrific fallout: that of the **happening/summoning**. The huge range of possibilities within this description perhaps makes it the weakest link in the theory to argue, but the solidity of the previous factor often highlights a duality of such beliefs; that these ideas will manifest through the most violent and supernatural of methods. The violence can be theological in origin, perhaps even territorial as in *Beowulf*, but is often at the very least primal and raw; Folk Horror is often about death in the slowest, most ritualistic of ways, occasionally encompassing supernatural elements, where the group belief systems summon up something demonic or generally supernatural. There's a sense that, in many Folk Horror examples, this chain has already established itself by the time of the film's narrative, the protagonist uncovering the results of this summoning on some isolated plain without the need to go through the motions of the chain itself. *Blood* is a good example of this but so are many stories by Nigel Kneale and M.R. James.[8]

Sometimes in Folk Horror, there is a desire to paint the narratives as being very simply a clash between 'the olde ways' and modernity.[9] Whilst in some sense this is true, it most often stems from these final, violent actions speaking to a modern audience in a non-diegetic way, or found at least in the previously mentioned, implied status quo of the narrative worlds as in *Wicker*. *Witchfinder* is most definitely the strongest example of the former, whose clever grounding in supposed real events lends its various culminations of violence (still produced through the structure of the chain) a genuine sense of shock as it shows the (British) audience a recognisable version of its superstitious, misogynistic itself. *Wicker* fits snugly as an example of the latter, not only because of its modern day setting, but because modern authority appears to confidently impose itself upon the 'olde ways' yet is in fact deceived by them.

With the chain now set out in detail, the devilish tri-force of our Folk Horror unholy trinity can now be shown to fit within its esoteric schema. All three films aesthetically bask within their settings, almost in contrary to various other, more claustrophobic horror exploits of the era. The horror is plainly set in motion by both their varieties of ruralism and, in the case of the recent cut of *Wicker*, very much *because* of leaving the safe sanctity of the Christian church of the mainland which opens the film. Contrary to this, *Wicker*'s original opening (before the reinstating of such deleted scenes) earnestly began with Howie's plane journey towards Summerisle. This opening effect would simply not have been the same if he was perhaps flown there by another pilot or had some other form of more communal transport been available. Howie is alone, solitary in his plane, which aesthetically juxtaposes the sheer scale of the landscape into which he is venturing.

Blood opts to open with an even stronger interaction with the landscape than simply a journey into it. Along with *Witchfinder*, the majority of the people of the film are locals, not outsiders like Howie. Their status as such is denoted by a confident relationship with such landscapes, upon which they are divested and shown to live by. *Blood* instantly places a malevolence upon its soil, highlighting its perspective view of farmer Ralph from a deliberately low angle, as if the earth itself is glaring at him. Haggard has him ploughing the land, an endless, sticky mud covering his lower legs and machinery, giving the landscape a palpable, clawing sentience and agency. As Matthew Sweet suggests in his documentary on occultism in popular culture, 'In this picture, the land literally contains evil' (2015). The vastness of this plain is shown by the momentary acknowledgement of Cathy, seen shouting greetings from an adjacent field some way away. Ralph is instantly isolated by such a context, ready for the scene of the uncovering of the first scrap of the demonic creature. With Marc Wilkinson's music introducing a descending motif (implying a downwards movement) and the low camera angles providing a ground perspective, it's perhaps unsurprising when Ralph eventually finds the evil under the top-layer sludge. It is, however, the landscape that sets the film; even being extended over its opening credits as the evil is given an avarian symbolism over a landscape montage.

Witchfinder opens in a surprisingly peaceful manner by comparison, at least at first. The very first shot is a beautiful capture of sunlight glare refracting through the leaves of a tree.[10] This cuts to the open Suffolk countryside, its pleasant pastures only given the air of menace by the sound of an unexplained hammering in the distance. The sound becomes louder before it is revealed to be that of a hangman's scaffold being constructed on a rustic hill in the gaze of a vibrant sky, pockmarked with John Constable clouds. The narrative then follows the journey of a condemned woman being lead from a nearby town to the hill to be executed. Ian Cooper writes of the importance of this opening, whereby 'The first image, of the English countryside, introduces the importance of landscape in *Witchfinder General*, a landscape which is at once familiar and alien, a beautiful backdrop to inhumanity' (2011: 60). It is telling that Reeves creates this relationship at the very beginning of his film; that, unlike later on in Lavenham where this will deliberately be reversed, the awful murder of the (no doubt innocent) woman must take place upon a more isolated vista and not in the inhabited climes of the town. This sense of landscape also gives the feel of space required for the rest of film; where civilisation is isolated in small pockets and are too far apart and too separated by Suffolk's winding and bucolic idylls to morally stand against the film's small-scale atrocities.

The sense of isolation that results from all of these various landscapes is steadily apparent. A pertinent question to ask at this stage would be how this differs from the more general isolation found in many horrific forms. In some ways the isolation present in Folk Horror has been set in concrete, the viewer being allowed to peer into the worlds of the films momentarily rather than in more typical horror scenarios, which are often about following a character into isolation only.[11] Even though Howie is isolated upon Summerisle in this way – first by the sheer distance of the location from the mainland, secondly by the islanders sabotaging his plane – the real effect of the isolation has already happened by the time the viewer comes upon the film. The isolation in question is affecting the islanders themselves, being a product of an extreme locality and localism. In many ways Folk Horror is simply the hyper-extension of localism down a dark, parallel footpath; 'A local shop for local people'.[12] The isolation and its desired effect has, therefore, already happened, creating the right environment for the antagonists and their belief system to spring forth and propagate.

Though *Wicker* requires both the islanders and Howie to be isolated (albeit in separate manners), the latter is simply to aid the narrative: it is the process of creating the former that the Folk Horror Chain really accounts for. The same cannot simply be said for *Blood*, partly because the isolation works similarly in regard to the effect upon Sgt. Howie, preventing help from being close at hand until much later on in the film, but also because there is little that is technically skewed outside of the Devil's main gestalt; the supernatural within this film is as real as the landscape that it inhabits. (This issue will be addressed later on when dealing with films of a similar supernatural ilk.) Yet the isolation is still present, the characters and their small groups only really communing on a larger scale when engaging in theological practice (either of Christian *or* occult flavour). This isolation is still potent, however. Consider the scene of Cathy's luring to the sacrilegious site for the ceremony of sexual assault and murder. She is lead away through empty fields, through forests and pastures as if playing in some Enid Blyton jaunt; an innocent game that ignores the gradual journey towards a more isolated location. Not only does this macabre meander prevent any social relation or context for the gestalt to see what they are committing, it is also away from any moral barriers being put upon them by society; there are no authority figures to save Cathy or prevent the barbarity. It is interesting, then, to consider that *Witchfinder* breaks this rule, quite deliberately in terms of the isolation. If anything it begins by following *Blood*'s relationship but deliberately inverts it to create an even starker, more troubling form of horror.

The emphasising of landscape that opens *Witchfinder* is one that is away from the scattered communities of Suffolk. The most stunning use of this isolation, however, occurs during Hopkins' journeys and chases through the county. Reeves fills his film with long roads, endless fields, and a landscape altogether devoid of people. The inversion comes when the horror happens within the towns, especially later on in Lavenham, but also earlier in his torture of the priest and various other sham witch trials. Both forms of this isolation are on show, as if the lonely East Anglian broads breeds the menace like a virus which can then spread to the larger towns. This isn't a social critique of the era in which *Blood* and *Witchfinder* is set; on the contrary, such forms of belief didn't need the isolation and one need only peruse any literature on the Pendle witch trials in Lancaster to see evidence of this (and perhaps a strange parallel to its virus-like ability to spread as well).

Instead, all three films produce these varied forms of isolation to breed the desired belief systems and moral attitudes needed for the horror to occur. Whether they reflect the eras in which they were set is immaterial (at least for the time being) as the aesthetics on show provide the linkages for the sociolog-ical make-up of many of the characters. The belief systems in question are not necessarily theological either. In fact, in many cases the theology is used as an excuse to hide the greater sense of sadism under a black veil of piousness. Religion in these films is skewed in every sense, though the most important is the context of the worlds within the film. This accounts for the strange feeling of unease upon first encountering *Wicker*, the society it portrays, its beliefs, and its subsequent actions. Hardy and screenwriter Anthony Shaffer make it sur-prisingly difficult to dislike the Summerisle-anders and far easier to side with them than is comfortable. As Hardy himself suggested in an interview in 2013, his desire was to build a link between the older pagan beliefs and modern day society:

> …we have a right to think that our Pagan ancestors were very much like us, they liked to dance and sing and get drunk, tell jokes and also have a laugh. So recreating (as we tried to do) that sort of society, all those aspects of normal life should be there. They were not inhibited by things like sex, which really only came in with Christianity, so one needs to show it and we do, I think, but not to excess. (2013)

Folk Horror is equally about muddying the morals of community as it is about portraying them. Summerisle's theology is a mixture of imagery from Sir James Frazer's ethnographic work *The Golden Bough* (1890), of eco-fetish botany and pagan sexuality, distilling neatly and effectively the tail-end of the coun-ter-culture social-scape in which the film was made but taken to an extreme. The system skews the morality of the islanders to the conclusion of their final enactment upon Howie, manifesting in the most obvious of folkloric motifs. As Trubshaw suggests, these motifs are easy to spot and actually frame the happening in a more modern heritage by making them obviously far from any potential pre-Christian ceremony:

> The folkloric and mythic elements that have been borrowed to make up the pagan festivities of Lord Summerisle in *The Wicker Man* are easy enough to spot – a beheading game at the culmination of the morris dancer's sword dance; naked girls jumping over a fire in the middle of a stone circle; and the eponymous burning effigy. If this suggests an 'unbroken pagan tradition', then the film itself informs us that these rituals were reconstructed by a Victorian botanist with anthropological interests. (2010: 86)

This is not, however, a comment upon their general social mores. Indeed, it has been said on various occasions (including at the Belfast conference) that there is great potential in Summerisle's more liberal elements; the skewed morality is their blindness and complicity in the pointless final murder, not in their sexually open culture, free from the guilt-ridden, puritanical worldview of Howie and his like. With the inclusion of the opening church elements in its later cuts, Hardy does ground the Summerisle way of life as overtly 'other', if only by comparison. Even if the values of counter-culture Britain were in some way akin to Summerisle, it was still against the backdrop of Ted Heath's Conservatism. This was the breeding ground for the sort of tyrannical opposition to counter-culture/Summerisle ideology, manifested in the likes of Mary Whitehouse with her equally impassioned gestalt.[13]

Witchfinder has an interesting parallel in this sense as it is the overall set of superstitions from the period in question that are effectively barbaric in the cold light of a modern day context. Reeves highlights this further in showing the unnerving effect of such absurd beliefs by breeding it in rural climes before letting it loose upon Suffolk's small towns. This outburst of violence is, according to Rob Young, 'presented as no fairy tale, but an eruption of terror in a community of working people' (2010: 418). Hopkins and his own morals are a slightly different matter. There's a knowingness to his actions, brought out further by the performance of Price; clearly the infamously tense working relationship between actor and director paid off. Whilst Hopkins' actions are indeed morally reprehensible, there's little doubt that he is also acutely aware of it. Unlike the villagers in the towns that he pollutes with his ideology of fear and misogyny, he is an evil seemingly born of some other force. The same otherness can be found in *Blood* but for an entirely different effect overall.

As the superstitions are shown to be very much based in truth, the skewing of morality and theology must be read through the presence of the Satanic faction itself manifesting within the puritanical era. If proof be needed, imagine if the skull had been unearthed in London like the Martian ship is *Quatermass and the Pit*.[14] The effect of the Devil's power and the social mechanism it uses to rebuild its body would not function in a more populated realm. The Devil would need power akin to the giant Martian at the end of *Quatermass* to achieve its goal as it would be dealing with a generally more enlightened, questioning and larger community. *Blood*, therefore, plays upon the lack of education – morally, spiritually, and in general – within its rural zone. These shortcomings within the group of young heathens are tied to the landscape and its isolation. Though the same potential is possible for other reasons in more populated, urban locales,[15] it works in *Blood* explicitly through this mechanism in the context of the Folk Horror Chain. The final part of this chain can be generally surmised in the three films through describing their outbursts of violence. Though the chain is causational, this isn't to say that these moments only occur at the very ending of all three films. In *Witchfinder*, this violence manifests very earnestly and literally from the outset because the chain has already taken effect before the porous barriers of the film's beginning and end have been set in stone.

Blood also has momentary spurts of violence rather than just the ritualistic lead-up to one, all-consuming moment, though the supernatural summoning does act with a sense of ending in its final confrontation. The violence spreads again through the youth within the film but the summoning takes the entirety of its running time to occur. The chain works to enhance this build-up of dread, with the stark moments of brutality appearing to be part of the film's total ceremony in conjuring up the Devil. The final heathen celebration is itself the teleological outcome of the film's themes; a natural cadence, handily ending before any sort of addressing or tidying up of the morality of the subsequent massacre can occur.

With the application of the Folk Horror Chain, it is *Wicker* that comes out most evenly in its defining incident. Whilst many macabre happenings occur during Howie's investigation, it is not until the very final moments that the real violence of the film occurs. With its false beheading 'chop!' ceremony, the film sets the tone for a potential sacrifice but does not fulfil the final outcome of the chain until Howie's demise. There is no return for Howie once the chain has been enacted and lived through, its conclusion of primitive violence or summoning of evil inevitable; like the demon on the London to Southampton line, it cannot be simply called off until it has quenched its blood lust:[16] it must fulfil its runic promise.

Beyond The Runes

> He supposed that the men whom the Druids burned in wicker-work images represented the spirits of vegetation, and accordingly that the custom of burning them was a magical ceremony intended to secure the necessary sunshine for the crops. – Sir James Frazer (1912: 658)

There's little use in arguing totally for any one theory to cover all of the work that by now sits within the discussions surrounding Folk Horror. The chain covers some reasonable ground but, unlike other genres, with their relatively compact themes and scenarios, Folk Horror is intuitive even once, as has just been attempted, its narrative core has been broken down. As Andy Paciorek poetically notes in his introductory essay to *Folk Horror Revival: Field Studies*: 'So in a bid to answer "What is Folk Horror?" one may well attempt to build a box the exact shape of mist; for like the mist, Folk Horror is atmospheric and sinuous. It can creep from and into different territories yet leave no universal defining mark of its exact form' (2015: 8). In constructing such a theory as the chain, much of the horrific mist has escaped the constructed box. This begs the question, then, what context has previous analysis of this trilogy of films been constructed within? Like the analogy suggests, even attempts at solidifying readings of the films on their own terms requires a rigidity which undermines their recent placement at the top of the Folk Horror canon.

Paciorek goes further in elaboration of the Folk Horror Chain theory, high-lighting a key point in its discourse. He shows that it is more than the causa-tional narrative effects but, essentially, the entire ethos that the films are shot through that characterises a work as Folk Horror:

> Some of these chain links may be also found in a variety of films that seem to bear no relation to Folk Horror, and this difference may simply be a matter of delivery, because as mentioned before there appears to be a 'Folk' ambiance and aesthetic that more often can be felt intuitively rather than defined logically. (2015: 11)

It is on this point that exploration of other analyses of the three films in question is, therefore, called upon. In 2010, Rob Young penned perhaps the most important analysis of a variety of Folk Horror material. In the essay for the August issue of the magazine *Sight & Sound*, 'The Pattern Under the Plough', Young builds his chief argument (whilst not using the term 'Folk Horror' once) on concentrating on material solely from the British Isles. He suggests a likeness to British architecture within the work in question (which earnestly includes all three films as chief examples), writing that:

> But perhaps it's time to admit that certain indigenous traits have been ignored by mainstream film critics for too long. Britain's cinema is comparable to its architectural heritage, in that both, by and large, have proved less good at incorporating avant-garde tendencies and forms but very good at adapting past glories (Gothic, mock Tudor, neoclassical, etc. in terms of architecture). (2010: 17)

In his article, Young is most definitely talking about Folk Horror. There is virtually nothing within the essay that isn't now included in the Folk Horror canon, even connecting work outside of cinema to his arguments in spite of being written for a film magazine. By restricting the work to British examples alone, Young identifies a key trait in the cultural sociology of the counter-culture period and streamlines the argument as to be one of a national cultural trait rather than a narrative, causational one; Folk Horror as public expression of both optimistic and pessimistic collective historicism. In doing so, however, whilst the argument fits more neatly in regards to the unholy trinity and their interrelationships, it becomes problematic when the work in question then moves towards the description of 'Folk'. Every country has a conception of 'Folk', as already argued. Perhaps there is something in the British iteration of Folk Horror, within these three films especially, that is explicitly specific in its psychological workings. It must be assumed, therefore, that it is within the aesthetic aspects of these works where this occurs rather than simply the folkloric processes and race-memory-like facets that they play upon.

To take a similar aesthetic approach to such analysis has often been a way to put these films within their cultural place, and has also provided a range of unique insights and readings. The better of these analyses are often outside the detailing minutiae of production histories; a common bedrock to many analyses in spite of actually having questionable influence on the films' themes as such. The Reeves/Price feuding, *Witchfinder* getting Alan Bennett in a huff, the troubled production and complex disarticulating of *Wicker*'s various cuts, and Christopher Lee insisting that it had been buried as landfill under a motorway: all entertaining but with little bearing on Folk Horror as a whole. Perhaps the exception to this is how this very information in general begins to resemble the films' initial reception. In other words, all of the films struggled either in production or afterwards and none of them took off properly until finding their way into homes through television screenings, VHS releases, word of mouth, cult film fan blossoming, and other (aptly folkloric) methods of popularity production.

Cinefantastique's 1977 issue proudly proclaiming *Wicker* as 'the *Citizen Kane*' of horror may have begun this re-evaluation, which created the labyrinthine odyssey of finding the actual original cut of the film, but it's only in recent years – in the post-millennial fascination with the old ways – that the sort of thematic analysis required for such an intangible genre of film has begun to appear. Young finished his defining article on the subject of *Wicker*, suggesting two interesting points. The first is relating the film to the social climate that it evoked and was made in, suggesting that:

> The alternative ritual society that draws the Christian Sergeant Howie into its web on Summerisle, led by Christopher Lee's magus character who was elected to 'reverence the music, and the drama and the rituals of the old gods', exists in an Eden of its own making (clue: its chief export is apples). (2010: 22)

The point being that, no matter what theological reading of the film is taken, it was essentially a product of a time when a commune mixing esoteric belief systems with free love eroticism was entirely conceivable (the eso-erotic film?). The film's horror was in showing the natural mutation of counter-culture idealism in the early 1970s *and* the older signposts of pre-Christian Britain. The former had effectively opened the gate for the latter. This plays more heavily upon the paranoid topics to be covered in Chapter 5, though it arguably affects all of the British Folk Horror made during this period; where, no matter what theology was portrayed in the films, they still spoke over a backdrop of confident optimism disintegrating impossibly quickly into a nihilistic pessimism. In a sense, Young's other point touches upon this by arguing that Hardy's film readdresses this balance:

> *The Wicker Man* daringly broaches the casket of Anglo-Saxon tribal memory and, in the battle between the old gods and the Judaeo-Christian cult which supplanted them, declares the pagans victorious. (2010: 22)

Young's point is that the horror comes from the confusion of feeling towards this inversion, where history follows another route baring similar window-dressings to early 1970s sociology and culture, but with an added dose of violence (as if violence actually needed to be added to early 1970s Britain). The tribal memory invoked may be that of a violent, pointless death at the hands of a deluded religious cult but it is fundamentally questioning 'What could have been?' through the disturbing context of an 'It can be, right now, if you want it' immediacy. This is providing, of course, that the society in question has spent some time loving it up and growing apples on an isolated but enjoyably warm island off the Scottish coast. Or maybe simply providing the society has listened to enough Pentangle, read enough Aleister Crowley, and dropped enough acid. Both bear a stark and potential believability in the context of the genre.

This sense of social mimicry is one of *Wicker*'s defining features though may also perhaps be the easiest way to misinterpret its actions. Vic Pratt suggests as much in his article celebrating the 40th anniversary of the film in *Sight & Sound*, writing that:

> ...*The Wicker Man* was not a simplistic film which depicted counter-culture free spirits as heroes and uptight authorities as fools. Lord Summerisle – trendily polo-necked, down with the kids, but still, ultimately, landowning gentry – is out for his own ends, his propagation of pagan belief a handy tool for the control of his islands serfs. (2013: 31)

The unconscious social hierarchy in the film hints towards the non-diegetic reality and politics of the period of when the film was made, and also builds upon one of the Folk Horror Chain's chief ideas; that an intellectual awareness of the skewing power of isolating landscapes can be used to control and manipulate people into doing the most terrible of things. This is whether you're a malevolent lawyer seeking a few violent kicks and power, a dominant land owner creating an atmosphere of pagan free-love for a cheap workforce, or a demonic entity attempting to rebuild your body, one piece of skin at a time. Pratt also asserts that the film 'seems so real because the "old ways" sit like vivid fissures on the surface of modernity' (2013: 27), which is an excellent, if perhaps unintentional, summation of its delayed affective response. Was 1973 already culturally canonised as an ancient by-gone era by 1977's *Cinefantastique* hyperbole? It's impossible to truly say but interestingly Pratt also responds to the criticisms of its blanket appropriation of folklore which are overtly born in an age of repeat viewings within a canonised era:

> Some critics have complained that they're not *that* authentic – the sword-dancing comes in for particular tut-tutting – but if this is not how the customs were carried out, it is surely how they should have been. (2013: 27)

This is a key point. Folk Horror, whilst often appropriating various aspects of folkloric themes and aesthetics (as well as history itself), is never all that fussed with a genuine, accurate recreation of folklore. It instead plays it through broad-stroke ideas which, in a populist medium, often build into genuine forms of rewrites of history and culture. It doesn't matter how nuanced the theological implications were around the genuine use of wicker images, gleaned by Hardy and Shaffer from *The Golden Bough*, as well as elements from the novel from which the narrative is adapted, 1967's *Ritual* by David Pinner. The fact is, with the effective and exciting narrative representation of a sociological system such as the chain, anything could effectively be put into the mix of practices and customs, and still come out looking relatively authentic. As long as it retains just enough essence of recognisability to work, it can be both an uncanny revalidation in the Freudian sense and an enjoyably horrific realisation.

The sense of this as a theatrical notion has been dissected in John Harrigan's essay, 'The Sacred Theatre of Summerisle', where the aesthetic performance of the islanders (parts of which may or may not be true depending upon what is read as being put on for Howie's benefit) is inevitably tied to the landscape:

> Summerisle's grand ritual exists across the whole island, because perhaps the greatest and most vital role is that of the island/landscape itself. We witness its materialisation as Howie explores Summerisle, from the songs sung in the tavern to the skyclad women who jump through the fire in the stone circle in the grounds of the manor. (2015: 323)

Because of this, Harrigan calls *Wicker* 'perhaps the most authentic of all British horror films' (2015: 320). This is in contrast to the folkloric commentators upon the film who, as Pratt suggested earlier, sit in frowning disapproval at the conglomeration of broad-stroke folklore, historical plagiarism and unquestioning recreation of colourful, nineteenth-century ethnographic theory. Mikel J. Koven suggests, in a critical essay in his book, *Film, Folklore, and Urban Legends*, that 'the film attempts to diegetically revive an un-self-consciously Victorian perception of Celtic paganism' (2008: 25), further elaborating that 'it is this interpretation of Frazer, of seeing *The Golden Bough* as *historical* rather than a folkloric description, that colors the entire film's folkloristic discourse – the film's "folkloristic fallacy" as I have termed it' (2008: 26; italics in original). It is worth noting how critical folkloristic scholars can be towards the more overt Folk Horror material, perhaps because it enjoys such open freedoms with the history that they take great pains to contextualise, and it plays mischievously with various (heavily mythologised) interpretations for the sheer hell of it. In other words, 'This is private property. You can't land here...'[17]

Unlike *Wicker*, *Blood* has acquired less in-depth analysis, perhaps because of the longer period needed for it to gain its heathen heritage. It is telling that the DVD release of the film was in 2010 as this appears to be the year that all things Folk Horror really solidified; the undercurrents of curiosity rising up into a full blown field. In the notes accompanying the DVD, Darius Drewe Shimon is rather upbeat about what is another brutal entry in the Tigon Studios film canon, but also acknowledges the framework of the film's slow but steady rise in popularity: 'As is often the way, its true fan-base came not from box-offices but from television, in the living-rooms and bedrooms of 1970s and 80s Britain where ardent cults are formed' (2010: 2). This is a theme more relevant to our penultimate chapter but it's worth noting that even Folk Horror's most popular examples are born from cult receptions, formed extensively through late night television repeats: 'See how these old superstitions die hard.'[18]

Essentially, *Blood* follows on from *Witchfinder*'s themes and aesthetics, almost undoubtedly because of the studio latching on to Reeves' surprising success. Kim Newman acknowledges the links between the two films, suggesting that 'Haggard's witchfinders are more righteous than Reeves', but *Blood on Satan's Claw* finds just as much cruelty running riot in the picturesque English countryside' (1988: 31). The point is that the horror isn't just anywhere but specifically in this landscape, such an idea being quietly ubiquitous in British horror but treated with renewed interest once noticed. Cooper even aligns *Blood* as a natural successor to *Witchfinder* in his book dedicated to the latter, describing the relationship with an enjoyably parallel character to the earlier idea of the evil being virus-like in its spreading: 'Both films present violence not as escapism or aestheticised spectacle but as contagion, a contagion so virulent that it may spread beyond the screen and infect the unwary viewer' (2011: 75). Notably, Cooper charts the genuine paranoia surrounding screen violence and censorship during this period of British cinema; the era of Droogs, sexually possessed nuns and uncomfortable ambiguities around Susan George's flirting.[19]

Cooper further makes the connection between the fictional realms and reality that, with such thoughts in hindsight, may explain the birthing of *Wicker*. In *Blood* there are 'inescapable parallels between Angel's gang and the Manson family' (2011: 90); horror acting as modern social commentary but also drawing upon the increasing post-war notion that reality is always a rich source of genuine brutality, oddness and horror – ready to be tapped or, more aptly, unearthed from the thin layer of furrow. Unearthing, whether diegetically or non-diegetically, is uniquely one of Folk Horror's key themes after all, and Young makes an interesting connection between *Blood* and *Quatermass and the Pit* because of this.[20] He suggests that:

> Like the *Quatermass* film, its plot turns on a sinister object churned up from underground; a gruesome skull unearthed by a farmer's plough that turns the young people of a 17th-century village into a wood-dwelling pagan cult with a penchant for erotic blood sacrifices. (2010: 22)

The object that was already there begins the horror, reminding us again of previous confluences of unseen Folk Horror Chains; the isolation that lead to the Devil being originally summoned but then buried in some undoubtedly pre-Christian era being similar to both the unearthing of a dormant alien ship and the isolation (on Mars) perhaps inherently needed as a reason for the insects of the film to kill, purify, and manage their own population. Young draws the lineage of such an idea back to literature, conveying the influence of the weird fiction writers of the *fin de siècle*:

> This common trope in British cinema – the sudden unearthing of a long-buried object, and the disquiet and havoc it inflicts on its surrounding – lies squarely in the macabre literary tradition of Arthur Machen, Algernon Blackwood, M.R. James, etc. (2010: 22)[21]

Blood's manifestation is, however, far more simplistic than *Quatermass* in terms of its themes. As Young succinctly suggests, 'erotic blood sacrifices' mixing with a general sense of pervading evil seems as far as the film willingly pushes its ideas without the context of the counter-culture sociology it is ultimately commenting upon. As Haggard himself admits when being interviewed by Mark Gatiss in *A History of Horror*, 'We were all a bit interested in witchcraft... We were all a bit interested in free love...' (2010). But the same social commentary cannot be simply applied to *Witchfinder*, which brings along, with its own ground-breaking desolation, a whole host of cultural and historical resonances to bear upon its narrative, largely thanks to its maverick yet tragic director. Newman calls *Witchfinder* 'one of the most down-beat movies ever made, a ninety-minute negation of every moral precept horror films have stood for' (1988: 31) and this begins to portray its creation as a watershed moment, reflecting horror through the actions of Albion's occupants; the very real horror of our history.

Reeves' own cinematic obsessions have often meant that the readings of *Witchfinder* in particular of his three complete feature films, have been largely discerned through the lens of admiration he had for the likes of Don Siegel, Sam Peckinpah and the more violent films of the Western genre.[22] The emphasis on reading *Witchfinder* as akin to a type of spaghetti Western set in England is useful in highlighting the uses of landscape within the Folk Horror genre, but also means subtle differences get left behind when too much attention is paid to scenes of horse chases and musket draws. Iain Sinclair, a close friend of both Reeves and the film's script writer, Tom Baker, relates Reeves' obsessions and their effect on *Witchfinder*:

> I believe that the film's success lies in the tension between Baker's Utopian permissiveness, his feel for the countryside, and Reeves' demonic fatalism. The film, a loose account of the career of Matthew Hopkins, a hunter and punisher of witches at the time of the English Civil War, finds its way into the dictionary of horror films – when, in truth, it is nothing of the sort. It's a Suffolk western, a British cowboy picture: with extreme and painful scenes of mutilation, torture and execution. (1997: 293)

Newman echoes this sentiment, suggesting that Reeves 'shot *Witchfinder General* in Suffolk and Norfolk not to bring horror out to the country but because he wanted to make a kind of British western in horror-film disguise' (2013: 50). Later, however, he argues that the relationship is subtly inverted because of the nature of the English landscape: 'But the American West's scenery complements the harshness of the western, whereas the English countryside counter-points the horrors with black-clad figures on horseback, splashes of blood on greenery and authentic recreations of witch-torture on the precise sites where the historical events took place' (2013: 50). This element of counter-point in the reading is in the aesthetic sense alone, and there's little doubt that the landscape itself does more than just provide a pleasant juxtaposition to the extreme levels of violence. As suggested earlier, it aids them.

When Matthew Hopkins casts sentence upon three condemned witches in the film (one of whom is Sara's father), his final judgement is a simple 'Take them to the tree...'. Outside of Folk Horror, this simple sentence has a far less malevolent character than it does within Reeves' film as the topographical elements of the landscape are providing the very means for people to be killed, as well as providing the isolation that is required to skew their moral systems enough to partake in such killings in the first place. Cooper hints at this within his reading of the film's opening scene: 'The combination of shots suggests that the gallows is as much a part of this corner of rural England as the trees, sheep and sun' (2011: 60). The scenery may be beautiful in *Witchfinder* but its landscape, even if Reeves intended to simply transplant the Western onto a Suffolk vista, creates a far greater sense of omnipresent evil within the air; unseen and at risk of infecting the small communes of East Anglians.

Cooper also generally aligns with this landscape-as-Western reading, writing that 'Landscape and history are two of the key elements of *Witchfinder General* and they are used in such a way as to consciously evoke the Western genre' (2011: 57). Where his reading differs slightly is how the landscape plays its role in the film. Newman believes it creates a juxtaposition but Cooper finds that this juxtaposition is more specifically creating a sheer indifference to the atrocities: 'At best, the rural backdrop of *Witchfinder General* is a striking blank, as indifferent as the faces of the good folk of Lavenham, as they watch a woman being burned to death. At worst, it's a malignant world, distorted and nightmarish, governed by dark forces...' (2011: 63). Even Young's brief summation of the film recalls its 'Westerness' rather than looking beyond the aesthetic relationships that the landscape provides:

> In the open fields and fenlands of East Anglia, Reeves and his cinematographer John Coquillon (later to shoot Sam Peckinpah's *Straw Dogs* in a remote village in Cornwall) discovered the wide open skies that marked the Westerns of the era. (2010: 18)

If there is anything that the analysis within this chapter has shown, it is that the landscape provides far more than a backdrop, either as a contrast or as a nod to other cinematic influences. As we shall see in the next chapter, the landscape can be used in more ways than simply as a causational starter, but for a huge range of thematic palates of exploration. Newman arguably summarises best the overall reasoning behind the three films' relative success since their release, and though his reasoning is mentioned to perhaps ground this academic analysis back down to some sense of earth, it is also worth noting that, alongside the likes of a general quality of filmmaking, great casting and musical scores, it is the landscape – the starting factor of the Folk Horror Chain – that is displayed as a key element within the trilogy: 'Frankly, they're all good – they share a reliance on music and landscape, have a sense of the rooting of horrors in British history, feature lasting cult performers and build suspense well' (2015: 25). The 'fiend in the furrows' indeed.

Endnotes

1   The conference was organised by Eamon Byers, the University's School of English, and The Institute For Collaborative Research in the Humanities. More information can be found at www.blogs.qub.ac.uk/folkhorror/.

2   *A Warning to the Curious* (1972, dir. Lawrence Gordon Clark).

3   From henceforth known as *Witchfinder*, *Blood* and *Wicker*.

4   This can be traced further back to the 'Beat' movements in the 1950s and the alternative culture that seemed to build almost immediately in the post-war period.

5   *Doctor Who – The Daemons* (1971).

6   And perhaps potentially forward too, depending upon your politics.

7   *Death Line* (aka *Raw Meat*, 1972, dir. Gary Sherman).

8   Who knows what horrific rituals and societies initially brought the devil to lie in an English country field?

9   Or often vice-versa with the blame being put upon modernity for venturing into ancient territory. See M.R. James for examples.

10   A visual trope that Ben Wheatley would borrow in *A Field in England* (2013).

11   The isolation is also often created by a vastness of landscape rather than an enclosure of space.

12   *The League of Gentlemen* (1999 – 2002).

13   Mary Whitehouse was part of the Nationwide Festival Of Light movement which opposed various forms of social liberalism in the British media and arts.

14   Full analysis of *Quatermass and the Pit* is found in Chapter 5. For an entertaining and amusing comparison for this point, see *The Skull* (1965, dir. Freddie Francis).

15   See Chapter 5.

16   *Night of the Demon* (1957, dir. Jacques Tourneur).

17   Spoken by the Harbour Master in *The Wicker Man*.

18   Spoken by the Judge in *Blood on Satan's Claw*.

19   References to Stanley Kubrick's *A Clockwork Orange*, Ken Russell's *The Devils* (1971) and Sam Peckinpah's *Straw Dogs* (1971).

20   For more on this film see Chapter 5.

21   This is a trend that also extends to fiction from the period in question, from Alan Garner, Susan Cooper and Susan Hill to name only three.

22   Reeves' other two films are contextualised in later chapters due to their total difference to *Witchfinder*.

Topographies

On Lands Untouched

There *are* combinations of very simple natural objects which have the power of affecting us, still the analysis of this power lies among considerations beyond our depth. –
Edgar Allan Poe, *The Fall Of The House Of Usher* (1839: 129)

In March 2015, I found myself ambling along the busy, bustling streets of sunny Cambridge. My visit was yet again ordained by a Folk Horror pilgrimage
in the guise of an academic event, but the perspective of this particular iteration was different in emphasis. I was visiting a one-day symposium at Corpus
Christi College, evocatively named *The Alchemical Landscape*.[1] Unlike *A Fiend
in the Furrows*, the emphasis of investigation for the event and its various presentations was not strictly Folk Horror but instead was addressing the elements
of landscape; how such a theme can be linked to forms of media, art, and the
practice that goes into their production. This meant that aside from analysis of

well-known examples of Folk Horror, presentations also looked into tangential fields such as Psychogeography, Hauntology and Nature Writing. It wasn't so much the specificity of one particular presentation that began trains of thought towards the variety of roles for landscape in Folk Horror, but instead opened up ideas of the genre to other perceptive angles. Folk Horror can amalgamate many forms and ideas into its methods of producing drama and horror, the emphasis on landscape being far more multifaceted than solely the lowest common denominator within the previous chapter's Folk Horror Chain.

In hindsight, the naming of the conference aptly accounts for this analytical exploration of Folk Horror. Because landscape can be so nuanced, and almost infinitely variable, there's almost an ease in mythologising it; to drawing out its already folklorically contained mystery and heightening its speculative character, to the point of inducing fantastical and terrifying apparitions. The landscapes discussed in the presentations, which traversed both rural and urban varieties, were not in themselves uniquely alchemical; all landscape sits within a potentiality of 'alchemicalness', with a natural transmutation of its base material into something more manifest with horror and an agency.

The use of rural landscapes especially became a prominent theme in the presentations, and links began to build between place, space and to many examples of Folk Horror. In the lunch break, I wandered through Cambridge's many cobbled alleyways and found an impossibly old bookshop down St. Edwards Passage, just a minute's stroll from the symposium; one of the few shops on my brief visit that looked organically grown. It was aptly named The Haunted Bookshop and my attention was drawn not simply by its cottage-like appearance but by a specific book in its window, a first edition volume of M.R. James' *Ghost Stories of an Antiquary* (1904). Though a prominent academic, and variously Provost of King's College Cambridge and Eton School, he is arguably now best remembered for defining and honing the English ghost story, in a variety of effective volumes, to its highest creative peak. This volume in particular has great importance in its mixing of folklore with horror (and, ergo, Folk Horror) as Bob Trubshaw writes: 'Some of these blends of folklore and literature were sophisticated. M.R. James (1862–1936) raised standards far higher when he published *Ghost Stories of an Antiquary* in 1904' (2010: 85). Connections were forming as this was James' old territory after all; the place where the stories of vast, unnerving landscapes – usually East Anglian – were bestowed upon a lucky few at the Chit-Chat society of King's College whilst quietly snug in a fire-lit study at Christmas time.

Landscape can be used to isolate but, especially in British Folk Horror, the realms of possibilities opened up by an aesthetic and thematic emphasis on landscape leads to a huge range of complex functioning. As Reggie Oliver notes of James' work, however, isolation does play its part, revealing a stark fugue on the ideas of the Folk Horror Chain. He writes of James' typical protagonist being 'that of an isolated, and therefore vulnerable, figure somewhat at odds with the world, who is taken to the edge of madness by a series of inexplicable events' (2012: 8). This occurs to some extent in British film, as well as other national cinemas, but the strongest, most powerful examples occur in British television. It essentially works through a contrast; between the vast, windy vistas of many dramas with the warm living rooms of winter-time – a quick, eerie trip out to the endless beachscapes of Seaburgh, the stone circles of Milbury and Bascombe Moore, or an isolated Welsh valley a few miles from Aberystwyth.[2] Audiences in the 1960s and the 1970s seem, in hindsight, to have been spoilt for choice with drama focussing on different forms of ruralism, producing the eerie, the uncanny and the horrific. Folk Horror delves into all of these territories and produces such heightened effects through building upon a general, modern unease towards the familiar vistas of the countryside.

The British relationship with landscape is a complex one that is intertwined within the history of its artistic practice, and Folk Horror builds heavily upon this practice by sitting obtusely within its context, simultaneously turning it upon its head. It is in some ways heightening the Romantic ideal of embracing darker emotions towards the landscape but doing so to such an extent that is only conceivably possible in the post-mechanised age of the twentieth century, when wars calcified any such simplistic notion of an escape within rural climes. Folk Horror finds much within the initial ideas of Romanticism, especially in its admiration and use of landscape, but it instead forcibly uses its anti-rationalist disregard for Enlightenment thinking in various, extreme ways to show an inherent danger in such self-indulgent abandon. Enlightenment here is used in the sense of Immanuel Kant's definition, interpreted by Michel Foucault as 'the moment when humanity is going to put its own reason to use, without subjecting itself to any authority' (1984: 38). Folk Horror often denies reason and embraces new forms of, often theological, moral authority; it just so happens that this is linked almost consistently with the topographical location of its societies. In a sense, Folk Horror frames itself in such landscapes to evoke the awe-inspiring terror embraced in such a period of artwork, but also ironically suggests that such terror be derived from a more primitive set of ideals; the sort that Romanticism seemed to equally embrace but at a comfortable, lofty distance. Many examples of Folk Horror are, therefore, contradictory because of a circularity; where the cycle has jumped backwards a number of rungs rather than forwards. A progressive backwardness, perhaps. This act of look-ing/travelling back has a nostalgic sense akin to Romanticism but Folk Horror also takes great pains to subvert these perceptions, almost always showing this nostalgia to be a way up many a moral blind alleyway.

Unlike the cobbled Cambridge alleyway, decorated with expensive but tempt-ing volumes of M.R. James, Folk Horror's alleyways have an unnerving attrac-tion in spite of their many dead ends. This is often reflected as such through its landscapes. Modernity often tends towards forward movement because it implies a definite sense of progression, whereas Folk Horror, mimicking aspects of such landscapes, is far more cyclic and socially static. Again, modernity here is best described by Foucault who writes that it is 'characterized in terms of consciousness of the discontinuity of time: a break with tradition, a feeling of novelty, of vertigo in the face of the passing moment' (1984: 39). Folk Horror is the violent rejoining with tradition which, on paper, seems almost conservative, yet it even subverts this reading by often summoning up pre-Christian values rather than more purely traditional ideologies: a strangely progressive form created through a conservative mechanism.

Folk Horror brings the people of the city out to the places supposedly of rest, exploration or holiday, and shows a vast tapestry of permutations of landscape interactions; almost alien in comparison to the everyday bustle of the urban. The danger can be from those who work the soil or those who want to kill for the soil, from things excavated from under the soil, from objects that sit confi-dently but uncannily upon the soil, or indeed from the very soil itself: 'Forces of the earth. Forces in the earth. Forces from the earth and below the earth. You who made me manifest...'.[3] Folk Horror has its own idiosyncratic rela-tionships with topography and landscape, channelling a sense of the uncanny through subverting our pre-existing relationships with such recognisable types of place. An unmappable shadow-landscape, fluctuating to the point where only a searching alchemical topographer would dare to attempt a plotting of its many ley lines.

'Whether it was the wind....'

Bleak and solemn was the view on which he took a last look before starting homeward. A faint yellow light in the west showed the links, on which a few figures moving towards the club-house were still visible, the squat Martello tower, the lights of Aldsey village, the pale ribbon of sands intersected at intervals by black wooden groynes, the dim and murmuring sea. The wind was bitter from the north, but was at his back when he set out for the Globe. He quickly rattled and clashed through the shingle and gained the sand, upon which, but for the groynes which had to be got over every few yards, the going was both good and quiet. – M.R. James, *Oh, Whistle And I'll Come To You, My Lad* (1904: 128-129)

A man in Edwardian walking attire strolls slowly but confidently along an East Anglian coastline. The image is in black and white, a tonic choice that highlights the long, wooden groynes that segment the beach, the flecks of marram grass sprouting in barren clumps as an oddly unrealistic sun sets at dusk. As the man approaches closer, a voice tells the viewer that what they are watching is 'a tale of the supernatural', that it is by M.R. James, and that it is the 'darkest' of his many ghost stories as it is one 'of solitude and terror'. There is no music as the man approaches; instead there is a simple emphasis on the wind blowing with a gentle but strangely sentient persistence which dominates the soundtrack. A man is about to be haunted by his own beliefs shattering upon a twentieth-century floor, by strange objects and figures stalking his perambulative journeys, and even by his own bed-sheets rustling and forming into some sort of demonic, Freudian presence. He is, however, to be most chiefly at the mercy of what is seen within the first segment of this television play; he is the psychological and hauntological plaything of something malevolent within, and almost indistinguishable from, this vast landscape. It may eventually manifest in the tangible likenesses of containable forms and objects but the whole of this play presents a topographical area that has its eyes squarely and calmly watching over a lonely figure; an academic disintegration mirrored heavily by the transient elements of his walking destination.

It is 1968 and the writer, director, scientist and general polymath, Jonathan Miller, has been given effective free reign over the BBC's art documentary series, *Omnibus*.[4] The show is barely over a year old before it reverts to more experimental forms as was common for many anthology programmes on the BBC during this daring period of television.[5] Miller has been given the opportunity to adapt M.R. James for a Christmas slot and has chosen to psychologise the story, '*Oh, Whistle And I'll Come To You, My Lad*' (1904) as *Whistle And I'll Come To You*. The story is ambient, taking James' narrative of conservative worry over the costs of scientific and academic progress, and replacing such themes with its atavistic polar; turning the tables on James through modernity, showing the potential truths the writer had let slip about his own psychology, and all unfolding upon the backdrop of a landscape horror. As a Cambridge science graduate himself, Miller is clearly doing some personal exploration of his own, recapitulating the original writer's logic into a subversive form of biography and taking pleasure in how far away he is from the cosy comforts of an academic fireside.

James as a writer is an intriguing figure and though his stories do not all fit into the categories and characteristics of Folk Horror as a whole, almost all of their subsequent adaptations do; programmes and stories which loom large over all other Folk Horror in some guise, especially upon British television. One aspect consistently crops up when discussing James, however; that of the role of landscape in his work. In hindsight, it is perhaps the way this landscape unfolds in these television adaptations that plays equally heavy on the minds of those interested in the darker elementals of Christmas rituals. James may have imbued his stories with many a malevolent landscape but it is clearly their visualisation in the latter half of the twentieth century that solidifies their aesthetics totally. Mark Gatiss, in his wonderfully personal documentary on the writer, *M.R. James: Ghost Writer* (2013), suggests one of his principle themes to be of 'horrors that lurk in the idyllic English countryside'. In terms of their television appearances, this is their chief meme even when stories remain stubbornly in dusty rooms, libraries and churches; the outside still somehow always seems to find its way in. Miller's play explicitly builds on this and a narrative breakdown follows.

Whistle And I'll Come To You – Professor Parkins (Michael Hordern) is on a walking holiday in an undefined East Anglian locale.[6] He is shown to be a fettered individual, socially awkward, unknowingly arrogant in his beliefs, and deeply sceptical in the most modern of ways. Turning down offers of playing golf (contrary to James' original story), he trots off to the woods and beaches for a good 'trudge' as he describes it. On his walks along the crumbly cliff tops and beaches, he comes across a Knights Templar graveyard falling into the sea (most probably hinting at being Dunwich on the Suffolk coast). A grave opened by the land falling away reveals what he later discovers is a whistle which he takes back to his lodgings, though not before noticing a distant figure watching him some way down the beach. Upon cleaning it, he discovers the words, 'Who is this who is coming?' engraved upon the whistle in Latin, before foolishly blowing upon it: unleashing some, as yet unseen, power. A wind is conjured and builds, giving the professor a rough night's sleep. His second night produces nightmares of being chased along the beach by a commutable presence resembling his bed-sheets. He opts to stay in his hotel during the evening of his second day's walk out onto the plains after the nightmare culminates in his waking terror. His final night is eventually disturbed after a day of reading up on various forms of supernatural interest. He awakens to find the sheets of a second bed forming into an entity, pre-empting their earlier ruffling; the sheer shock seeming to precipitate some sort of mental attack. Before anything else can happen, a fellow lodger in the hotel, whom he had condescendingly conversed with several times during his stay about the potential existence of ghosts, enters the room to find Parkins broken, muttering unconvincing denials as to what he has just seen. The play ends with his final denial, a shattered 'No...'.

Whistle And I'll Come To You is often attributed as starting one of Folk Horror's most intensely studied and popular forms; the televisual Christmas ghost story. Whilst this is true to some extent, the history of the ghost story as a television play, especially the type that derives its horror from the English landscape, is perhaps slightly rewritten due to the practice of wiping programmes from the archives. M.R. James had been adapted variously before and even during the year of Miller's production, with stories such as *The Tractate Middoth* being adapted for the NBC television series, *Lights Out!* (1946–1952) under the title of *The Lost Will Of Dr. Rant* (1951). This episode would lack the landscape elements that would solidify the ghost story's general affect, but is important in being both the first non-live broadcast attempt to adapt James for any sort of audio-visual medium and the only American televisual attempt at adapting his work to date. The first British attempts at James for the small screen would again come in the form of *The Tractate Middoth* (1966), produced two years before Miller's film, for the anthology horror series, *Mystery And Imagination* (1966–1970). The series would produce a further three adaptations of his work, adapting versions of *Lost Hearts* (1966), *Room 13* (1966) and *Casting the Runes* (1968), a short fragment of the latter being sadly the only remaining excerpt in existence from these productions. Perhaps if a similar series, such as *Tales Of Mystery* (1961–1963), had survived in any form, discussions of television ghost stories would in fact be more closely aligned with the writing of Algernon Blackwood[7] instead; archive television wiping greatly alters the perspective of such spectral evolution.

Miller's film therefore seems to be the first key note only by default but this is unfair as its influence over all sorts of Folk Horror forms is still undeniably vast. Essentially, *Whistle* ties the visuals of this ambient form of Folk Horror with images of the English landscape. Mark Fisher points out two key points about this story in both of its existing forms. The first is linking back to the ideas of Romanticism, but essentially showcasing the relationships between the enlightenment thinking and primitivism mentioned in the previous section, as geographically created when present in Folk Horror. He suggests that:

> The contrast between the urban world which Parkins has left behind and
> the empty heathland over which he wanders is also a contrast between
> enlightenment knowledge and ancient lore, and Parkins' estrangement consists,
> in large part, in his finding the modes of scholarly explanation which work so
> well in university libraries suddenly having no purchase on what he encounters
> in the Suffolk landscape. (2010: 1)

The argument is of a questioning of moral philosophy manifesting in the play through topographical symbolism. Whilst this varies in Folk Horror depending upon the example, Miller's film is the purest vision of this ideal, upon which most other examples of Folk Horror appear to be some variation.[8] Fisher also ties an idea of Reza Negarestani's to the play, with the concept of the 'inorganic demon' playing as a Jamesian narrative device; an essential and common tool in the arsenal of James' story-telling as well as Folk Horror as a whole. These are the objects of possession, whose discovery often jump-starts the narrative of the protagonists because the evil is often contained within them, whether it be a lost Anglo-Saxon crown, a bag of alchemist's gold, or the cursed wooden stall in a cathedral. In this case, it is the whistle itself, but examples can be found in most other James television adaptations as well as many examples in the writing of Alan Garner, Nigel Kneale and Susan Cooper, and the previous chapter's *The Blood on Satan's Claw*. The most essential aspect to this idea, however, is not the sentient-made essence of these objects, but the process of their discovery. In *Whistle*, it is the curiosity enlivened by Parkins' walks within the landscape that effectively leads to the whistle. In other James adaptations, such processes of unearthing and excavation of the landscape play an even more key role.

After Miller's first effective episode in the ghost story for Christmas slot, the BBC gave documentary director and producer Lawrence Gordon Clark an equal amount of free reign in producing one play per year. This lasted from 1971 right up until 1977 with Clark at the helm, producing a string of important and immensely effective Folk Horror plays. Staying true to Miller's model, Clark began with an adaptation of James' *The Stalls of Barchester Cathedral* (1911), renamed to simply *The Stalls of Barchester* (1971). Though the majority of this narrative is filmed in Norwich Cathedral, the spectre has specific ties to the landscape even though the narrative is oddly sealed-in to both this building and a library further ahead in time. The play begins in some ambiguous present-day (perhaps the present of the original story) with the cataloguing of a university library by an academic, Dr. Black (Clive Swift). He discovers a locked casket in which details are kept of the scandalous and haunted life of the Archdeacon Haynes (Robert Hardy). Detailed within the documentation is evidence of the scandalous story of Haynes having plotted the murder of the man (he eventually succeeded) with a maid he had been secretly courting; the subsequent haunting is caused by his hand coming into contact with a cursed stall at the cathedral, unleashing a cat-like demonic presence when touched by the hand of a murderer.

The landscape of this play is largely in the detailing of the cursed stall, the inorganic demon of the play and narrative. As Clark himself suggests, 'James has a genius for imbuing objects, usually from the past, with implacable malignity...' (2013: 18). When Haynes is walking in the woods with a colleague, they venture to the spot of the 'Hangman's Tree', the wood from which was used to make the abominable stall. Similarly to the horrific role of trees in *Witchfinder General*,[9] the tree and the brutality that occurred within the landscape still haunts the main character, even when he is in the comfort of the buildings in which he is the chief executor of power (either the cathedral or his abode). Once knowledge of this place and tree is ascertained, the landscape in *Stalls* has the ability to pervade and haunt the Archdeacon as much as the cat and the hooded figure who eventually kills him. As the parchment that is eventually found in the narrative conveys:

> When I grew in the Wood
> I was water'd wth Blood
> Now in the Church I stand
> Who that touches me with his Hand
> If a Bloody hand he bear
> I councell him be ware
> Lest he be fetch away
> Whether by night or day,
> But chiefly when the wind blows high
> In a night of February. (1911: 35)

The majority of its hauntings may take place within buildings but they are explicitly initiated by an object effectively brought in from the landscape, albeit unwittingly, unlike many of James' other stories that causes the rising of the demonic creature. Unlike Clark, James takes pleasure in keeping a slight ambiguity within his original story: 'The conjecture that it had been cut out of the wood of the Hanging Oak was not difficult, but seemed impossible to substantiate' (1911: 34). The same ambiguity cannot be attributed to Clark's second adaptation of James, 1972's *A Warning to the Curious*, which is far more brutal and nihilistic in tone. The original story was undoubtedly influenced by the waves of large-scale tragedy that the writer bore witness to during the period of the First World War as Adam Easterbrook conveys:

> With many years' writing experience behind him and the loss of both friends and pupils during the First World War, the quiet Cambridge don takes the reader – each step skilfully rendered with a masterful economy of words – deeper and deeper into the terrible heart of East Anglian legend. (2012: 8)

James' ghosts from this point no longer simply scare or warn off those foolish enough to meddle in pre-Enlightenment affairs but become totally unforgiving and murderous; after all, the post-Enlightenment thinking was coming full circle with the industrialised chaos of the twentieth century about to unleash its untold, real-life horrors. *A Warning* is an intensely complex story, both in its original prose and its subsequent adaptation. This complexity is often overlooked by attention being paid squarely to the journeys within the story rather than the nuance that lies, aptly, underneath its surface. A narrative breakdown of the television adaptation (with its numerous changes and additions) follows.

> ***A Warning to the Curious*** – An archaeologist (Julian Herington) is digging in a coastal forest in Norfolk for an, as-yet-unnamed, object. A local, later on to be identified as William Ager (John Kearney), insists upon him leaving the site of excavation alone, killing him in a frantic attack when he refuses to leave. Ten years later, Paxton (Peter Vaughan), a London bank clerk who has recently lost his job, makes his way to the East Anglian town of Seaburgh. With a minor interest in archaeology, he has heard rumours of the burial of one of three priceless Saxon crowns – the sacred crowns of Anglia that still supposedly guard the realm from danger – still hidden somewhere in the area. His research into the crowns is met with some resistance from the locals, though he quickly acquires several pieces of information from a parishioner (George Benson) and various useful artefacts from a local shop. Quickly piecing the information together, he discovers the whereabouts of the last remaining crown though not without arousing the spectre of Ager himself who haunts his journey of discovery, being the last member of the Ager family whose job it was to protect the crowns. Early one morning, Paxton embarks on a short train journey to the burial site and retrieves the crown. This unleashes the presence of

Ager, who pursues him across the land, all of the way back to his hotel. Ager's presence unnerves Paxton to such an extent as to drive him mad. He confides his find and his troubles with another guest at the hotel, Dr. Black (Clive Swift), and together they return the crown to the site in the hope that Ager's ghost will leave him alone. The following day, Paxton is lured out of his hotel by Ager who briefly takes the form of Dr. Black, and chases him back to the burial site. The real Dr. Black follows in pursuit but, upon catching up, he finds that Paxton has been brutally killed in exactly the same manner as the first archaeologist. Black takes the first train out of Norfolk but notices that the train guard opens the door for a passenger who is not there, implying that the ghost is now after Black. The train leaves and Black's fate is subtly sealed.

Clark's rendition of the story is at once refreshingly original and modern, but also direct in its further emphasis of certain elements of landscape present in James' original. The prose of the story, like many of James', is rich in landscape detail owing no doubt to James' own relationship with the counties of Norfolk and Suffolk. Seaburgh is standing in for Aldeburgh on the Suffolk coast which, upon visiting, can be walked from end to end with the detailed minutiae of *A Warning* acting as an accurate guide. Clark's resetting of the story to Norfolk works equally well, being full of typical East Anglian landscape keynotes and filmed variously in the beautiful wooded beaches of Holkham, the sweeping gentle coast of Happisburgh, and the slightly more inhabited fishing town of Wells-Next-The-Sea. A visit to these places opens up readings and impressions of the story greatly, and comes highly recommended as it highlights how dialectical James' sense of place and topography is. Ultimately, if James' writing can be argued to contain such a pertinent relationship with landscape, then it can also be attributed to much of Folk Horror, as he is, after all, one of its key innovators.

Similarly to Fisher's reading of *Whistle*, Easterbrook again ties in the landscape of *A Warning* to temporal instability, suggesting of the setting that it is:

> then, as now, far from the modern world and its sodium-lit scepticism. The cold
> blue skies, autumnal hues and barren, wide-open sands with their wind-bent
> treelines transport the viewer to a place out of time, where the omnipresent past
> is felt only in the ganglia or seen from the corner of the eye. (2012: 9)

The sense that all the thematic material at work in these James adaptations is derived from the landscape pervades. This doesn't simply occur through providing topographies, formations or places for objects to lie in wait for some unsuspecting inquisitive, but by also providing a permeable essence for the narratives to slip between times; the landscapes of Folk Horror are temporal as well as physical. This may seem obvious when discussing stories that use ghosts and hauntological elements (is there a more pertinent embodiment of the past invading the present outside of nostalgia than that of a ghost?) but, as examples later on within the chapter will show, a ghost is not always required in order to perceive the potential pasts under the surface top-layer of the landscape. This is yet another organic example of a Folk Horror theme, one whose only real likeness lies in the occasional art-house film and has little parallel with its other pulp bedfellows.

Clark would continue to adapt James, producing brilliant versions of *Lost Hearts* (1973), *The Treasure of Abbott Thomas* (1974) and *The Ash Tree* (1975). All three stories have various Folk Horror elements, especially *The Ash Tree* with its horror built around a witch trial whose link to the present (then the nineteenth century) is through an ash tree which lies adjacent to the mansion of a gentleman; handy for its horrific and poisonous, spider-like demons to kill the occupants of the supposed cursed bedroom (the story is adapted by David Rudkin, whose contribution to Folk Horror we will return to later). They lack the overt use of landscape of *A Warning* and instead opt for smaller fragments of place to splice up their narratives. *Lost Hearts* does this especially well, placing the ghosts of two children – murdered for their blood by a demented alchemist – often in snatched glimpses within the landscape of the grounds of yet another mansion house. The film is less famous for its landscape motifs than for its use of the hurdy-gurdy, an instrument for which any viewer of *Lost Hearts* will almost certainly grow an aversion. It is played by the long-nailed hands of the smiling ghost of a gypsy boy who displays with glee the empty crevasse where his heart should be during his performance. These three films are still all astonishingly effective, especially *Treasure,* which sees Michael Bryant (a reoccurring Folk Horror performer) as the most arrogant of characters, succumbing to his own greed for an alchemist's gold. They may not be about or use much of the landscape but they are most certainly linked to an almost folkloric alchemy of sorts.

Moving on from James, Clark adapted a final classic ghost text for the BBC in the form of Charles Dickens' *The Signalman* (1976). This example, arguably the strongest of Clark's films, is perhaps more pertinent for later discussions on technology and Hauntology but, suffice to say, Clark still imbues the narrative of a plagued Victorian signalman with a surprising and visually beautiful landscape to sit in contrast with the obvious industrialised cavern in which the majority of the story takes place. The contrast is, however, most chiefly visual and in fact plays heavily again into the Folk Horror Chain whereby the physical isolation causes great psychological distress for the main character. It pales in comparison as a theme to how discerning the play is towards technology, however, pre-empting – via an adherence to Dickens' fear of the industrialised society after involvement in a train accident – the twentieth-century's technological calamities. To bring matters back to topographies, it is Clark's final BBC supernatural drama that opens up discussions on landscape further; that of his collaboration with scriptwriter, Clive Exton, on *Stigma* (1977). The play is more than a ghost story of the pure kind but of the recognisable character of a short form Folk Horror. A narrative breakdown follows.

Stigma – Katherine (Kate Binchy), Peter (Peter Bowles) and their daughter, Verity (Maxine Gordon), are a well-to-do family who have recently moved into a new country cottage, in the standing-stone dominated village of Avebury in Wiltshire. Some workers tending the overgrown garden have uncovered a large stone while cutting back the vegetation and Peter has organised for its removal so he can extend the lawn. The stone is clearly part of a wider circle, continued in the adjacent field by more prominent *menhir*. A digger has been organised and is briefly able to lift the stone which unleashes a strange breeze before ultimately resisting being moved. Soon, inexplicable events begin to occur in the cottage. Katharine starts to bleed from unseen wounds on her body. Peter is also effected by strange experiences, finding unusual activity within the cottage at night. The events culminate as the stone is eventually removed by a bigger crane, revealing a skeleton beneath. At the same time, Katherine is discovered in bed, unconscious and dowsed in pools of her own blood. A local doctor (Jon Laurimore) arrives and escorts her to a hospital but she dies as they are on the road. The workmen find ancient, ritualistic daggers around the skeleton as well as one encased in the ribcage at the same spot from which Katherine bled. They are told by Verity that it was part of the ancient religion of the area who buried their dead under stones. She peels an onion which earlier Peter had found chewed on the kitchen floor by persons unknown.

Stigma has many essential elements that are notable of Folk Horror from this period. The landscape again hides the thing that must not be tampered with. This element is heightened further by being hidden under a *menhir*; a genuine antiquarian object that imbues the narrative's mysteriousness with a sense of recognisability. Because standing stones still occupy a folkloric sense of history and mystery, their use in Folk Horror is inevitable and popular, with many narratives pivoting around the very important role of some sort of monolith, stone circle, or other landform. However, this is accompanied by a refreshing stance in the ghost story slot for dealing with a far more feminised presence and perspective. *Stigma* is the only **BBC** ghost story at Christmas that has a female character playing the perturbed and haunted lead role. This is Folk Horror within a domestic environment, occurring with an emphasis on occult body image that is actually relatively unique in the whole Folk Horror canon. Helen Wheatley describes the play's elements in this regard as a 'synergy between the bodies of the women within the domestic space (Katharine, Verity and another female body as the dénouement) and the house' (2010: 10). Wheatley is correct and it is worth expanding this reading to include how the landscape on which the house resides plays its part. The ground holds the spirit of a victim of patriarchy and seems to spread its curse to enrapture the modern-day equivalent (while it's doubtful that Peter would violently sacrifice his wife for his own masculinity, of course, though this ideology can be shown in other examples in this chapter).

After *Stigma*, Clark would leave the BBC's regular spook slot, allowing for a limp last hurrah in *The Ice House* (1978) by Derek Lister and the usually dependable John Bowen. But Clark would direct a further ghost serial, returning to James in his extremely modern retelling of *Casting the Runes* (1979) for ITV Playhouse.[10] The play highlights just how brilliant the use of 16mm film was in Clark's previous outings and it lacks the overall visual splendour of his other films through being largely shot on video. It does, however, boast a startling opening in a snow-covered edge-land; the demon coming for its first victim out on a frosty reed bed. The adaptation is again openly contemporary in its resetting of James' narrative, moving the drama onto a modern journalist (Jan Francis) living in a house that simply screams 1979, and casting Folk Horror regular Iain Cuthbertson as the evil occultist, Julian Karswell.[11] *Casting the Runes* is an intriguing story and one that highlights James' writing perfectly with its various enigmas, antiquarian mysteries and chilling set-pieces.

It is perhaps more famously known through the Jacques Tourneur film, *Night of the Demon* (1957),[12] which is one of, if not *the*, earliest English language Folk Horror feature film. Tourneur was a directorial protégée of the famous horror producer Val Lewton, and the eerie hallmarks of his previous films such as *Cat People* (1942) and *I Walked With a Zombie* (1943) are ever present. Yet something occurs in *Night of the Demon* that means it stands out from his earlier films, at least in terms of Folk Horror. For one thing, the monster, a wonderfully grinning nightmare, is fully on view in all of its fiery glory. But it is the greater sense of landscape that differs. Perhaps it is an aspect that will always rise up when adapting James' writing, even leading Tourneur to such unnecessary but enjoyable filming locations as Stonehenge; another example of menacing *menhir*. The early death of a psychologist at the hands of the demon in the woods is now iconic: 'It's in the trees! It's coming!' The phrase cannot help but suggest Kate Bush's song 'Hounds of Love', due to its effective sampling in 1985. But the phrase is one that is quintessentially Folk Horror; there is not only something coming – something that is unknown and defies quick description – but it is something that is coming *from* the rural landscape ('It's in the trees!'). The film chooses a pleasing array of locations but builds the horror link between more rural and semi-rural locales such as the garden of Karswell's manor or the railway line at night where he finally meets his demise. It is unsurprising, then, that such a link, one which permeates versions of the story separated by twenty-two years, is forged and repeated; that isolated rural locations are not simply a binary of pleasing juxtaposition but the dwelling place for demons and spirits. This is Jamesian through and through.

Of course, there is still a contrast to this. So many of James' stories were designed to be read aloud to a small, nervous audience in the confines of a space whose cosy atmosphere inevitably created a dialectic opposite; that of the outdoors with all of its demons and spooks. Other James adaptations have sought to rectify this by moving the form back into its original performative character. Series such as *Spine Chillers* (1980) with Michael Bryant,[13] *Classic Ghost Stories of M.R. James* (1986) with Robert Powell[14] and (perhaps most effectively) *Ghost Stories for Christmas* (2000) with Christopher Lee[15] all attempt this authentic guise. The latter raises the same questions about how landscape works within these stories as it attempts an adaptation of *A Warning* (and succeeds admirably), providing a genuinely distorted and creepy handful of Aldeburgh asides with its wintery blue vistas. The episode is easily the strongest *because* of the contrast between the impossibly Gothic, candle-lit room of the telling and the frosty beachscapes of the story.

Adaptations of James halted rather during the intervening years but made a welcome, if haphazard, return in the early 2000s; a prime period for excavation of classic television reboots and retellings that demand greater discussion later on. The first of this new wave of adaptations came in the form of *A View from a Hill* (2005), another perfect example of James in topographical mode. It concerns the finding of an alchemically-altered pair of binoculars which allow antiquarian Dr. Fanshawe (Mark Letheren) a view into the past landscapes surrounding the house whose library he has been sent to catalogue and value. The drama unfolds within these vast realms, unafraid to take its visual cues from the landscape and the exciting ability to effectively split the visual perception between the reality of the play and the temporal vision of the binoculars.

The fear comes from a naivety on the part of the main character, lost within the time-slips of a landscape; the concepts of time and space are endlessly permeable and osmotic within James and within Folk Horror. Robert Macfarlane, on using the story as an introduction to discussing the themes of what he calls the 'English Eerie', suggests in his article for *The Guardian* that:

> A second reason James stays with us is his understanding of landscape – and especially the English landscape – as constituted by uncanny forces, part-buried sufferings and contested ownerships. Landscape, in James, is never a smooth surface or simple stage-set, there to offer picturesque consolations. Rather it is a realm that snags, bites and troubles. (2015)

This sense of the eerie was first explored in the writing of Joe Kennedy for a number of articles for the culture website, The Quietus. In 2013, he charted the evolution of a counter-strain of British arts especially those that tie into this sense of the eerie: 'This, though, is a perversion of a tradition in English art which has long intuited that the countryside is uncanny: a place which seems to offer security, and yet is somehow the location of menaces far more profound than those found in the city' (2013). He further writes of the political element in Macfarlane's own writing where it 'also contests the notion that the countryside can, or should, be a place of simple assurances readymade for co-option by a reactionary politics' (2013). Kennedy applies this criteria to music by the likes of The Caretaker (Leyland Kirby) and Richard Skelton but it has varying simulacra in film and television too.

This summarises both *A View from a Hill* as well as the other examples already discussed; James as the delighted purveyor of landscapes that simultaneously resist and tempt his characters through ghostly machinations and false security. Though the adaptation was filmed in Surrey rather than in the vast Anglianscapes of James' initial inspiration, this lusher, more meadow-enclaved zone of haunting, pays off well. As Simon McCallum notes regarding the forced change of landscape for the adaptation, 'Financial and logistical constraints can sometimes pay unexpected dividends' (2012: 4). The dividend in this case is a refreshing, autumnal ghost story that plays heavily upon such geographical haunts as 'Gallows Hill'; Folk Horror of the past shaping the very perception of space by leaving their trace runically through place-names.

The same, however, cannot be said for the claustrophobic adaptation that followed it, *Number 13* (2006). Though the original narrative is deliberately confined, and in a sense a chamber drama of sorts, it fails to account for the lack of any real moments of Jamesian tension and Folk Horror. This is even more surprising considering the source of the horror within the story which is in itself a spatial one; a hidden, almost sentient room derived from something nasty under the floorboards. The movement of the story's setting from Denmark to an English country hotel of uncertain location is one that, on paper, makes logistical sense, though also deprives the main embodiment of the story of its unique tone from which it fights to realign.[16] A pleasing terror of sorts but with some elements heavily weighed around its neck, *Number 13* lacks the topographical spine of other James adaptations.

At the other end of the spectrum, comes an adaptation that in many ways loses its Jamesian character *because* it spends so much time on its landscape and not enough on its narrative. Andy de Emmony's take on *Whistle and I'll Come to You* (2010),[17] is less of an adaptation and more of a 'best of' collection, removing most semblances of the original narrative and replacing it with visual references to many of James' coastal stories (and their subsequent adaptations).[18] As Reggie Oliver points out, the adaptation is 'more a modern psychological ghost story which makes use of motifs and images to be found in James' original work' (2012: 9). The chief strength of the adaptation is in its subtle inversion of the very concept of the ghost; Parkin (John Hurt) is not being haunted by a ghost summoned purely from some possessed object, but actually the spirit of his wife (Gemma Jones), whose body is still alive in a care-home but whose spirit is now seemingly chasing him down the beaches of their old holiday spot, desperate to alert him as to her presence. Applying this narrative to such an effective use of landscape visually does work well in creating the typical isolation found in Folk Horror, but the programme is hobbled by supposedly being an adaptation of James, where such positives seem to have missed the point; that the landscape and the ghost should be inextricably interlinked. The change of the whistle to a ring makes little sense and further muddies what is an extremely well-directed piece of television.

The most recent James adaptation to find its way onto the BBC brings the ideas, and his role in Folk Horror, around full circle: in Mark Gatiss' short attempt at *The Tractate Middoth* (2013). Coinciding with an extremely detailed and rounded documentary of James (also by Gatiss), the play takes pleasure in the crunching of unknown footsteps upon the gravel paths of country lanes. The visual references of the ghosts are also suitably natural, with the haunted presences often coming subtly in the form of dust and spiders; Gatiss is very much immersed in the inner workings of Jamesian narratives and the earlier adaptations' imagery, even when his story has to return to more confined areas such as sitting rooms and libraries. This admiration is clear in Gatiss' own introduction to a collection of James' stories where he writes that 'Lawrence Gordon Clark achieved a rare kind of poetry with these beautiful short films...' (2013: 6). It is without doubt a poetry of the landscape, the strange beauty of horrific adventures into England's dunes, forests and country paths. As James suggests of such landscapes in his book on Norfolk and Suffolk, catchily sub-titled *A Perambulation Of The Two Counties With Notices Of Their History And Their Ancient Buildings*, 'The marshes and flats about it have a peculiar attraction' (1930: 102).

James and the ideals he represents create the topographical backbone for Folk Horror. Their horrific and terrifying ruralism plays heavily on other television work from the period in which they were popularly adapted, to the point where almost all of the Folk Horror in question has aspects of or, at the very least, some minor facets of the man's work under their soil. As will be seen, the haunted objects, the landforms, the unseen horrors, the ghosts, the demons, the spirits and the very essence of the landscape, all play key roles in the most pertinent and most widely regarded examples of British Folk Horror television. James is the man who honed all of these themes into a body of work perfectly ripe for screen adaptations. He is, therefore, the ever-present protector of the crown that guards Folk Horror's shores from attack and calamity: 'I always saw him with the tail of my eye on the left or the right, and he was never there when I looked straight for him' (1925: 48).

From the Furrows to the Living Room

> This idea is taken up by a cluster of rural-based narratives... that represent ancient landscapes where humans are compelled to repeat actions from a distant history, either real or mythological, in a manner that effaces not just human agency but also modernity itself as a social force. – Peter Hutchings (2006: 37)

One of the dominant narratives surrounding the history of Folk Horror concerns a spate of immensely unusual programmes produced on British television during the 1960s and the 1970s. The interconnections between the programmes are another support to the rigging of Folk Horror alongside the unholy trinity, and usually are analysed almost always in some relation to each other, like a gestalt dependent upon each member being present in order to activate its power. The earliest canonisation of this strange proliferation of heretical heritage comes in Peter Hutchings' 2006 essay, 'Uncanny Landscapes In British Film', where he notes of 'a cluster of rural-based narratives' that take up the idea of 'locating one's actions in relation to a historical past...' where 'repetition of that past can entail a threatening loss of identity in the present' (2006: 36). In Hutchings' group of programmes and films are numerous examples to be examined within this section, interconnected through this slippage of topographical time, and how this highlights the more horrific role that folklore and landscape plays upon the British psyche. As with so many canonisations, however, there are many examples often lost in the furrows, due in part to their rarity. They are here restored to the narrative of landscape-based Folk Horror.

This collection of programmes, which also includes virtually all of the ghostly visions from the previous section, act as a Folk Horror meme in that they are usually called upon to account and contextualise other (and often newer) examples of Folk Horror. In writing about Ben Wheatley's film *A Field in England* in 2013, Kim Newman suggests that the spirit of these programmes are contained in that particular film's pastures:

> ...the film approaches the type of British 1970s television horror – practiced by Nigel Kneale (*The Stone Tape, Quatermass*), Alan Garner (*The Owl Service, Red Shift*) and others (*Children of the Stones*) – in which standing stones are locuses for hard-to-fathom sacrifices and miracles, and deep history is constantly on the point of breaking through the surface, often with gruesome, physical consequences. (2013: 51)

Newman presents most (though not all) of the chief mystics of television Folk Horror that, along with the regular spectrality of the BBC Ghost Stories, are often plotted in chronological order, with *The Owl Service* (1969) and *Quatermass and the Pit* (1956) (or Miller's *Whistle* for that matter) beginning the journey, and the BBC adaptation of *Red Shift* (1978) or the Euston Films production of *Quatermass* (aka *The Quatermass Conclusion*, 1979) for Thames Television aptly often marking its end point.[19] This does, however, ignore the many interesting meanders off this well-worn track, and also cuts off the narrative of British televisual Folk Horror far too early. Though examples of this quality and overall effect *did* largely die down with the painful demise of the counter-culture and the incoming of Thatcherism,[20] it leaves too many interesting examples at the margins; a place where Folk Horror is often found thriving. Again, as it is subtly written and manifested within M.R. James' stories and adaptations, it is the topography that is the most recognisable element in connecting these programmes. It is not simply the counter-culture atmosphere which allowed many of them to spawn and unleash their various narratives of haunted dining plates, the ghost of an old pagan king giving advice to a troubled teenager, or a stone circle being harnessed for its power to remove free will. For the sake of structure, this cycle will not begin here with *Quatermass and the Pit,* due in part to its relevance to Chapter 5's hauntological/urbanity thesis, but also because of how anomalous the programme seems in both its timing of release (far before counter-culture popularisation) and its small-scale, urban geography. There are pertinent examples in the writing of Nigel Kneale, *Quatermass'* creator, that are relevant to this chapter's landscape emphasis but his work is, for the sake of argument, squarely contextualised within the hauntological realm later on. Instead then, we begin at *The Owl Service* and its writer, Alan Garner; an archaeological elder who succinctly defines all that is topographical about Folk Horror.

Cheshire-born Garner is another of Folk Horror's key luminaries. Since his debut novel, *The Weirdstone of Brisingamen* in 1960, he has been mixing folklore, landscape and fantasy into a heady mixture of writing that is suitable for both younger and older readers. His prose is teeming with the folkloric imagery of Cheshire and other nearby areas, where magic and the old ways have not been forgotten; instead lying, James-like, under the earth waiting to be found. The sense of time being malleable within his works is a key feature *because* of the historical and folkloric power of the landscape, recurring consistently to the point where the areas themselves are often mapped in detailed terms of topography *and* chronology. As Garner himself suggests in an ITV documentary about his writing practice, *The Edge of the Ceiling*, 'I did have an intense and emotional understanding of the landscape' (1980).[21] The first television appearance of Garner's fantastical plains did not appear until he had penned some four novels[22] and this was not in the live-action format of later adaptations, but instead came about on the series *Jackanory* (1965–1996), in which Garner's *Elidor* was read over five episodes by John Stride in 1968. The story tells of the adventures of a group of children on a Manchester edge-land, all rubble and dereliction, as they discover a C.S. Lewis-like gateway into the kingdom of Elidor where dark forces are rising. It is a thrilling adventure but perhaps one that has marginal relevance to Folk Horror's more obvious, ritualistic terrain.

In 1969, with much aid from Garner as script-writer, an adaptation was produced and directed by Peter Plummer of the 1967 novel, *The Owl Service.*

Garner's role in the production is great enough to have induced a nervous breakdown, a separate book concocted by his children telling of the production being released in 1970 under the title of *Filming The Owl Service*. Garner writes with a stark honesty of his experiences of making *The Owl Service*, concluding that, 'There are few occupations more tedious than the making of a film' (1997: 106). It is perhaps surprising then to find such a wealth of film work attached to him. The programme is not only the first key production filmed in colour for ITV[23] but is a quintessential piece of Folk Horror in its deft mixture of folkloric manifestations, isolated and increasingly desperate characters, and its extensive location filming in Wales;[24] creating an unusually ambiguous character for the unseen powers lurking throughout the narrative and the valley. This is, after all, adapted from a text that, when not largely concerned with dialogue, refers chiefly to topography and to place: 'Alison sat in the shade of the Stone of Gronw among the meadowsweet. Clive stood in the river' (1967: 88). A narrative breakdown follows.

The Owl Service – Alison (Gillian Hills) and her new step-brother, Roger (Francis Wallis), are taken to the Welsh valleys by their newly-wedded father (Edwin Richfield) and mother to their holiday cottage which resides deep in the countryside. The house is maintained by a groundskeeper called Huw (Raymond Llewellyn), a housekeeper called Nancy (Dorothy Edwards), and her young son, Gwyn (Michael Holden). When Alison hears a scratching noise in the roof above her bedroom, Gwyn goes to investigate and finds a dinner service covered with a strange design, part owl-like, part flower-like. Alison begins to make cut-outs of the flowers, making them into owls before the designs disappear from the plates completely. Eerie events begin to unfold as the ancient Welsh tales of *The Mabinogion*, specifically the tale of Blodeuwedd from the fourth branch, manifest within the household. Blodeuwedd was at the centre of an ancient love-triangle between Lleu (who had her created for him as a wife out of flowers by the magicians Gwydion and Math) and Gronw, with whom she has an affair and plots to murder Lleu. The triangle and its fallout begins to exert its force over the present-day young trio as the spirit takes hold of Alison. Photography of the nearby Stone of Gronw, a genuine *menhir* relic, reveals mysterious figures – a man hurling a spear and another riding a motorbike – highlighting that the love-triangle had previously arisen between Nancy, Huw and Gwyn's dead father. The trio argue and fall out, resulting in several excursions into the hills. The last of these is an attempt by Gwyn to escape the valley as he is being bullied for trying to change his accent with the help of elocution records. He does not get far before he is stopped by Huw who shows him an ancient spearhead, implying that he accidentally killed his father by sabotaging his motorbike over his love for Nancy. After a failed attempt by Nancy to get Gwyn away again from the house, leaving in a tremendous rain storm, he returns to find Alison possessed. She is leaning towards the power of owls; the creature who Blodeuwedd was eventually turned into by Gwydion the magician as punishment for plotting the failed murder of Lleu (who turned into an eagle when Gronw had attempted to kill him with a spear). Gwyn refuses to help her, still falsely believing that she had told Roger about his elocution records to tease him. Roger eventually saves her, talking the spirit down as he inhabits the symbolic figure of Lleu, and forgiving her. The story ends showing three young children, two boys and a girl, through the hole in the Stone of Gronw where the spear was supposed to have penetrated, implying that the rising of Blodeuwedd's spirit will cyclically repeat again and again.

Considering that *The Owl Service* was produced as a children's programme (and marketed, at least, as a book for young adults), its situating of the narrative in a piece of archaic folklore adds a top layer of complexity to an already surprisingly layered story. Perhaps the most intriguing way of perceiving its narrative is by seeing it as cyclic as its landscape; that once Blodeuwedd's folklore is understood, it can then be seen to be manifesting in the isolated landscape and to the isolated people repeatedly. Throughout, there is a sense that this manifestation is happening, not simply because of the powerful magic of *The Mabinogion* (which Alison is shown to be reading), but because of the place itself retaining its magic in the ground. The original story was fittingly inspired by Garner's genuine visit to Bryn Hall in the Mawddwy Valley. The core theme of a place retaining a trace of historical and cultural happening is another key Folk Horror motif, especially when that place is explored rigorously through the aesthetics of its landscape. It can then allow for the slippages in time, the event and its topographical traces being the gateway that allows the past to exist within the present, often fantastically and sometimes horrifically.

Apart from other obvious elements of Folk Horror that *The Owl Service* basks in, such as the landscape, the role in the narrative of a standing stone, the role played by visual analogue technology[25], and its strange sense of eroticism,[26] it is the sheer oddness of its narrative that most connects with Folk Horror themes. The idea of a spirit forcing young people to effectively partake in an almost incestuous relationship is in itself powerful for any sort of drama, never mind one aimed at a younger audience. But the programme is replete with visual oddities to match its themes, not least in its avant-garde opening sequence by Bridget Appleby. Another such element is the complete invisibility of Alison's mother who, like in Garner's novel, is neither seen nor heard. On an earlier viewing, I personally was convinced that this was because the mother had really died, the holiday being a strange exercise in catharsis to help get over the loss for the family by still pretending that she was there; her spirit then manifesting in Alison through the Welsh legend, recreating the narrative with Roger and Gwyn. This, in hindsight, is far-fetched to say the least though tells of the story's multivalent character. Newman calls this decision an 'unprecedentedly daring bit of writing and direction', further elaborating that 'You'd expect this device from an experimental filmmaker like Alain Resnais or Chris Marker, not television professional Peter Plummer...' (2008: 19), though it was, however, an aspect chiefly brought over from the novel.

Stephen McKay describes the series as 'a landmark of British telefantasy and young people's drama in general; it stands out as an exceptional film series, paving the way for Granada's more prestigious works' (2008: 14). Outside of the sheer innovations in colour and film, the programme is, at this point, seemingly unique in being a well-supported, fully location-filmed series, blending perfectly the elements of folklore and fantasy with Garner's deep understanding of the landscape as a temporal and sentient being; full of the ghosts of spurned lovers, the remnants of unseen violence, and the barriers between understanding and superstition. As Gillian Hills recounts of her time working on the show, 'I think all three of us became fairly superstitious during the filming. We slipped into character' (2008: 16). How apt for a programme shot in such an evocative place: fact and fiction blurring just like the temporal lines that separate the legend and the present day of that sunny/rainy holiday in Wales, 1969: 'And the room was full of petals, flowers falling, broom, meadowsweet, falling, flowers of the oak' (1967: 155). The supernatural is still natural-born.

Garner would return to creative hermitage after *The Owl Service*'s stressful production, entering into a period which may be called his 'red shift'; the aptly named point in which his literature changes tack and moves towards less fantastical goals through work on his novel *Red Shift* (1973). Whilst writing it, his ideas were clearly somnambulating through the outer landscapes of Cheshire and the lapsing of time occurring around its topography. His ideas surrounding the narrative were to be noted in an incredibly innovative and abstract form in an episode of the BBC series *One Pair of Eyes* (1967–1984) called *All Systems Go – Alan Garner* (1972). The programme sees the writer exercising creative free reign to make what is essentially an avant-garde essay film concerning his current themes and ideas, which then included the temporability of the landscape, objects which transcended this temporal shifting, and how emotions such as those of amorous or physical fall-out between people could also move between time strands.

Garner labels the latter of these emotions as a 'violence'; a form of energy that he admits builds up inside himself when confronted with emotionally treacherous waters.[27] *Red Shift* deals with this in an almost autobiographical way, though it is in itself already innovative in terms of narrative structure. The book would later be adapted by the BBC for their *Play for Today* strand in 1978 by director John Mackenzie, pre-Thames-side gangster vs. IRA operatives, of course.[28] The play makes the most of this visual and emotional fall-out, naturally making the transition to screen, with its time-slips being easily arranged as simple cuts; the audio-visual form playing with time in a far simpler manner than the written word. The Folk Horror aspect of the story is not in anything specifically horrific but created through the sense that there's an otherness to the landscape of its setting; that of the distinctive tower and hillside of Mow Cop in Cheshire. This is further aided through the context of one of its three interconnected stories being set in that most pertinent of Folk Horror eras, the English Civil War. A narrative breakdown follows.

> **Red Shift** – Jan (Lesley Dunlop) and Tom (Stephen Petcher) are a young couple on the cusp of an awkward period in their relationship. They live in Cheshire and enjoy walking along the M33 motorway, if only to get away from Tom's clinging parents who live in a cramped caravan. Jan is soon going to London to work and the tension creates anxiety for Tom who lashes out at his parents for assuming that they've had sex (and that such a thing would be a bad). Meeting when they can once Jan has moved to London, the pair begin several excursions from the train station at Crewe, cycling to the tower of Mow Cop and its surrounding countryside. They both promise to look up at Delta Orionis at the same time every night so they know they are still together. They also find a strange piece of rock, which Jan calls a 'bunty', lodged in the ground under the castle ruin.
>
> During the English Civil War, Thomas Rowley (Charles Bolton) and his wife, Madge (Myra Frances), are holed up in a church near Mow Cop, in fear of enemy Royalist soldiers after the rebel, John Fowler (James Hazeldine), takes refuge with them. The 'bunty' rock is found by Rowley and he brings it inside the church which is battening down for the siege. The rock is said to have fallen from the stars. The royalist men are led

by Thomas Venables (Michael Elphick), a past flame of Madge's, who commands a successful raid on the church. Rowley is plagued by strange visions of a man in some distress and does little during the raid other than stare out at Mow Cop. After killing most of the men, Venables allows Thomas and Madge to go free. They hide the bunty rock before fleeing.

In the Roman period, an embattled assault unit on the run from both their own army and the natives take refuge on the hill of Mow Cop after being attacked. Macey (Andrew Byatt) is a strange warrior, appearing to be able to tap into some relentless power when need be. His axe head is made of the 'bunty' stone. They find a girl (Veronica Quilligan) on the hill and keep her prisoner in a cave. She looks after Macey who is also plagued with strange visions, apparently similar to those of Tom and Thomas. She poisons the other soldiers after they rape her, causing hallucinations which eventually kill them. She leaves with Macey, who buries the axe-head. Back in the present day, Tom discovers that Jan has been seeing an older man in order to make ends meet in London. They argue in the turret of Mow Cop, Tom admitting that he has sold the bunty rock to a museum to fund coming down to London in secret, where he first saw Jan with the other man. At Crewe Station, their usual farewell of 'Hello' changes to 'See you' implying that they are now breaking up.

On paper, *Red Shift* may seem like an odd anomaly in Folk Horror. Though in some respects it does follow the Folk Horror Chain's causation of geographical isolation, it is only fleeting and too peripheral to instigate the chain's other functions. It also lacks the grounding in more obvious aesthetic and thematic elements of folklore, found in *The Owl Service*, for example. So why exactly does it fit into the equation? It can only be in how it accesses its questions of time and emotion through its landscape. This aspect is broadly shared with many other examples, especially on television. *Red Shift* is, therefore, essentially the connecting of past traumas through two objects that reside in the land-scape; the stone, supposedly fallen from space, and the ruined building/area of Mow Cop. The former could be read as creating the connection between Tom, Thomas and Macey, though the fact that all three also connect through their emotional traumas, linked to the decayed fortress and craggy rock-bed of the place itself, suggests it to be a dual layering. In Mackenzie's adaptation, the cuts in the film act as the paragraph separations do in the novel, and there is a great feeling of cascading back-and-forth between times that burnishes the journeys with a geographical feeling; that time, in *Red Shift*, and Garner's writing as a whole, actually has a topographical quality.

David Rolinson believes that 'The play's complex engagement with time is, therefore, connected with its engagement with adolescence' (2014: 3). This is true to some extent, especially within the context of Garner's explorations of such themes in *All Systems Go!*, but if this is true overall then both aspects are still under the shadow of the very landscape itself; both are morphed and tied explicitly to its terrain. The absence of folklore is also somewhat of a misreading as *Red Shift* itself is a melding of a historical, hyper-local folklore with a canonisation of Garner's own life experiences into that folklore. He writes of the true historical events of the nearby town of Barthomley and the genuine disappearance of the Ninth Legion being influences on the story as well as some real-life graffiti found near the monument: 'I had known about the massacre of Barthomley for many years. Four months after hearing about the "Spanish slaves" I was reading graffiti on a wall. One, written in chalk was: "Janet Heathcot = Alan Flask. It is true." Then the sky, and *Red Shift*, fell in on me' (2013: 7).

Garner's own admission in the documentary that the acting couple reminded him of painful memories in a faux-Jan/Tom fight (to the point where he has to go off camera), suggests that *Red Shift* is using folkloric methods, especially in regards to landscape relations, to replay and situate autobiography into a wider temporal frame, but simultaneously into a reduced geographical frame as well. As Garner writes in an essay analysing the concept of 'Inner Time', 'The crucial point is that an author's characters are all to some degree autobiographical: and the time of a film or a play is Now; dangerous as it ever was. The distance has gone' (1997: 112). *Red Shift* is both maverick-like and deeply imbued in the mechanisms of Folk Horror because of this. As the character of Randal in the novel suggests, 'You can't be everywhere. There's many another day at the back of Mow Cop' (1973: 74).

Garner would work on several other television projects, including the essay film *Images* (1981),[29] the short drama *Lamaload* (1981),[30] an episode of the *Dramarama Spooky*, *The Keeper* (1983), and finally a live-action version of *Elidor* in 1995 for the BBC. The latter, whilst having the potential to tap into the same elements as *The Owl Service* (being a serial adaptation told over six episodes and directed by TV regular John Reardon), is hamstrung by its video aesthetic and pales in comparison to earlier Garner adaptations shot on celluloid. Instead, the last example to mention of Garner's presence on television[31] is a little-seen episode of the anthology series *Leap In The Dark*; a rarely spoken about (and barely existing) series that ran between 1973 and 1980. Garner's episode is in the final 1980 season and its title is the enigmatic, *To Kill a King*. Garner's drama is again explicitly autobiographical, following an author plagued by writer's block who just happens to live in Garner's distinctive Blackden Cheshire property next to Jodrell Bank and its Lovell Telescope.[32] His creative block brings about folkloric and ghostly visions, as well as awkward meetings with his literary agent. Brian Baker suggests that the play questions the role of the writer as some sort of receiver, just like that of Jodrell Bank's scope – 'The conception of artist as receiver, a poetic of transmissions, is crucial to Garner's work' (2015) – and it is evident that the landscape is the node through which this information travels through. Though perhaps excessively autobiographical, *To Kill a King* is such an effective collection of contrasts – the ancient obliqueness of the building and area with the modern obliqueness of the scope and the railway – that Garner is virtually admitting and accepting ultimately that the landscape of Cheshire is the pure source of his creativity; not simply the muse, the backdrop or the palette, but the very conductor of his artistic energy.

With the signposts of televisual Folk Horror marked by Garner, its more frag-mented and isolated elements can now be filled in; the furrows marked but the detail currently lacking. Elements found in Garner and James persist in British TV but some examples also tap into themes that are equally connected to the era of production as to the topography. Themes such as malevolent uses of magic and occultism, social power plays and moral discrepancies, filter subtly into many programmes. These react to the social interests and worries of the period through using older mechanisms to set in motion their respective dra-mas. The best example of this came in the year following *The Owl Service*, not in the form of a children's programme, but in the guise of a very adult and provocative episode of *Play for Today*; John Bowen and James MacTaggart's enigmatic and highly influential play, *Robin Redbreast* (1970).

Bowen had several writing credits under his belt before *Robin*, including the previously mentioned *The Ice House* and an episode of *Mystery and Imagination*, adapting M.R. James' ghostly forefather, J. Sheridan Le Fanu, and his story, *The Flying Dragon* (1966). Yet, with this clear interest in more esoteric matters, *Robin* still comes as a shock to the system, even with the knowledge of the occult and pagan interests of the period being taken into account. The play is nihilis-tically cyclic as well as ritualistic; subtly mundane in its slow-build horror which makes its conclusion and dénouement an intensely eerie and unnerving expe-rience. Newman has written of cinema's need to often move drama further north in the UK (often towards Scotland in particular) when looking at esoteric communities, writing that, 'Often when it comes to locating magical, savage pockets of rural lore, British cinema overlooks England entirely and imagines Scots islands...' (2013: 48). *Robin* is the first of a number of strong examples that show television to be the opposite of cinema in this sense. A narrative breakdown follows.

> **Robin Redbreast** – Norah Palmer (Anna Cropper) is a successful TV script-editor who has recently been dumped by her long term partner. To get away from things, she takes residence in a rural barn she has had converted some way out of London to spend some time away from her lecherous and snide friends. Having restored the barn and employed a housekeeper, Mrs Vigo (Freda Bamford), she is paid a strange visit by the local 'lay-reader' and thinker, Fisher (Bernard Hepton). He enquires about finding artefacts (sherds) in her garden and tells Norah of the predilection that the local birds have for the property. She finds a cut marble on her window-sill and brings it in, marking some unsaid significance to both Fisher and Mrs Vigo. Having a problem with rodents, Norah is recommended the local vermin controller, Rob (Andrew Bradford), who has a penchant for karate and Nazi history. Norah lusts after him but his awkward personality puts her off on a dinner date, though she is intrigued as to why the locals refer to him as Rob rather than his real name of Edgar. She is frightened by a bird appearing unnaturally down the chimney, and Rob, who was sent away earlier, mysteriously returns and helps her. They sleep together, though Norah notices that her contraceptive cap is missing on the night, oddly reappearing the next day. She discovers she is pregnant with Rob's child and returns to London. He visits her, encouraging her to keep it and to return to the village where she is gradually made a prisoner in her own cottage. One night, Rob visits just as her house comes under attack from Fisher's men, Peter (Cyril Cross) and Wellbeloved (Robin Wentworth). She accuses Rob of being involved in some pagan cult, but before blacking out she hears his screams and realises that he is as scared as she is. She awakens in the cottage to find everything as normal, with Fisher paying her visit. He tells her that Robin has finally managed to emigrate to Canada but, in discussing the practices related in Sir James Frazer's *The Golden Bough,* he insinuates that Robin has been part of some complex ritual involving her pregnancy and his own role as 'Fisher King'; for Robin has been killed for the benefit of the land. She is allowed to leave as the ritual is complete – with Fisher hinting that her child will be a future sacrifice – and, as she turns back, she sees the four members of the cult, not in their everyday clothing, but in strange, ritual clothing from an older England.

It's difficult to adequately convey the eeriness of *Robin Redbreast*. So much of the atmosphere comes from choice phrases of dialogue and potential double meanings. The play builds on the rise of interest in certain esoteric belief systems and culture during the period (the subject of Chapter 5), and uses the rural isolation of an urban character to almost pitch-perfect Folk Horror effect. Often denoted as a precursor to the happenings of *The Wicker Man*, *Robin* is in fact far ahead of that film in terms its of script. Unlike Hardy and Shaffer's loose play with texts such as *The Golden Bough*, Bowen's script seems to be interested in the genuine detail of the past and its folklore as opposed to only the elements that would be dramatically effective. Fisher's dialogue especially is characteristic of an array of references and detail; his is the very language of Folk Horror, being the absolute pinnacle of the genre's villainous forms. It also benefits from its mixing of these more questionable forms of historical folklore with genuine events, basing the narrative loosely around the Lower Quinton murder of farmer Charles Walton in 1945. Walton, unlike Robin, *was* found gruesomely murdered (with a pitchfork), the actions and directions of which lead to rumours that he was killed upon Candlemas Day[33] because of his ability to cast the 'evil eye' upon fellow locals, being that he was a witch. Its proximity in history makes its appropriation in *Robin* both disturbing and incredibly effective, lending an air of believability to what could have been a quite farcical play.

The role of pagan sacrifice is emphasised here, moving away from simply the landscape, and expressing another facet of Folk Horror; that of the re-emergence of interest occult themes and imagery in the late 1960s and early 1970s. It has been a thematic spectre lurking since analysing the unholy trinity and though it is more pertinent for later arguments, there's a poignancy to this element here. Whilst the complexities surrounding the interest in various characters of belief system are socially complex, its other definite contributing factor is that of its relationship to the landscape. It is not just free love and drugs that brings such occultism to the fore, but an embracing of the rural in its various cultural guises. Vic Pratt notes in his essay, 'Hunting for Sherds: *Robin Redbreast*' (2013), that Fisher's beliefs, perhaps even his unseen violent actions, are not in themselves out of character for the period but are, startlingly, very much in keeping with the era: 'And his beliefs are not quite as unusual as all that. *Robin Redbreast* reflects a cultural moment when witchcraft and the occult were no longer ludicrous' (2013: 2). Fisher is only a slight twist on the typical counter-culture guru, dressed as a country gent akin to Lord Summerisle, but more ready for a trudge through fields looking for 'sherds' rather than a flower-child sage heading to a happening. He could easily have shared a stage with Allan Ginsberg, R.D. Laing *et al* and hardly seem out of place.

The Folk Horror Chain becomes relevant again in *Robin* as it is a virtually perfect example of its landscape mechanism; the isolated village in the vast rural landscape, harbouring an old, cultish religion that requires a violent sacrifice for social appeasement. *Robin*, however, highlights that the chain can be circular; the sacrifice leading back into the landscape and, in a sense, *for* the landscape. This is brought about in the play by a subtle emphasis on the aesthetics of such a topography. Apart from several fragments of effective location filming, the place is largely expressed through the soundtrack which is dominated by a soundscape akin to Miller's *Whistle*, where an eerie breeze constantly haunts the drama. The belief system, like in *The Wicker Man*, is parallel to the landscape; the happening is for the crops, for the ground and for the soil. It's telling that the play shows very little of Norah's urban life, her London career as a television script-editor never seeming to exist outside of her slightly cramped flat. The contrast is built, if only to show the irony of the big country cottage and its vast rolling topography having the ability to equally trap her, an aspect she realises all too late.

Bowen would produce several other works related to Folk Horror, a key example being an episode of *Dead of Night* (1972), yet another horror anthology series, of which only half of all its episodes now exists. *A Woman Sobbing* shows the trapped female protagonist to be a recurring theme for Bowen, as Anna Massey plays a mother who is driven over the edge by the unexplained sound of weeping emanating from her attic. Lisa Kerrigan calls the episode a 'feminist tale', writing further that the whole series offered 'highly personal takes on psychological disturbances, often related to contemporary social anxieties' (2013: 1). Also connecting to *Robin* is Don Taylor's *Dead of Night* episode *The Exorcism*, which sees Anna Cropper yet again being perturbed in a converted country abode, only this time being gradually possessed by the spirit of a previously wronged woman during a typical 1970s dinner party. The Folk Horror connections tighten further as Clive Swift, aka Dr. Black from Clark's James adaptations, plays one of the guests. Knowing Norah and Dr. Black's luck, it's unsurprising to find that the wine turns to blood, though it's a wonder that anyone was brave enough to take a country cottage at all in the early 1970s, when television consistently showed them to be forbidding zones of esoteric horror. This is a trend that continues into the modern day, with *Midsomer Murders* screenwriter Anthony Horowitz suggesting as much: 'English villages are special places where hatred and mistrust and suspicion and anger and bitterness have a natural place to grow... I love the fact that in an English village everybody is hiding something and people are far more curious about what is going on behind their net curtains' (2016).

Bowen would even write a part follow-up to *Robin* in the form of another *Play for Today* episode, *A Photograph* (1977), seeing Mrs Vigo living in a caravan and again up to no good, though it fails to fully tap into that same sense of 'wyrd' arcania. *Robin* channels elements of a culture prevalent in Britain during the 1970s, and begins the decade in earnest with its propensity for rural-based, isolated village-horror. Even Adam Adamant and Peel & Steed were facing such dangers in the mid-1960s in the *Adam Adamant Lives!* episode *The Village of Evil* (1966) and *The Avengers* episode *Murdersville* (1968). In other permutations, this aspect can be interchangeable with the isolated research establishment (or occasionally even contain both), but the landscape comes to the fore in many post-*Robin* examples with just as much vitality. A number occur in that ever-hungry genre absorbing programme *Doctor Who* (1963–1989), which tapped into the same veins of Folk Horror topography in the 1970s and, arguably, even into the 1980s as well. The first wave of Folk Horror's themes began to emerge in the Jon Pertwee-era, due to producer Barry Letts and script editor Terrance Dicks exiling the Doctor to Earth. Arguments can be made that stories dealing with prehistoric reptilian survivors, such as *Doctor Who and the Silurians* (1970) and *The Sea Devils* (1972), delve into elements of Folk Horror; pre-history and its monsters inducing regressions to primitivism and folklore in both stories.[34] But there are stronger, more overt examples in the series.

The first real and pure example of Folk Horror in *Doctor Who*, however, comes in the form of the 1971 season finale, *The Daemons*. Written by Letts and Robert Sloman under the pseudonym Guy Leopold,[35] the story is an effective distillation of British Folk Horror. The small isolated village of Devil's End is subject to an archaeological dig. The Doctor, recognising that something is amiss on the live broadcast of the excavation, arrives too late as the dig at the barrow – known as 'The Devil's Hump' – unleashes the power of Azal (Stephen Thorne), a devil-like alien from the planet Daemos, whose species has been guiding man for centuries. The Master (Roger Delgado), the Doctor's regular Time-Lord nemesis in the season, is summoning the power of the Daemon in the crypt of the local church while posing as the local vicar. With possessed Morris dancers, a stone gargoyle that comes to life (Bok) and a variety of black magic and occult references, *The Daemons* actually canonises Folk Horror's tropes into one neat package that arguably never happened in quite the same, succinct fashion again. These elements did, however, manifest further into the programme's run in various, often alien fashions.

In Robert Banks Stewart's *Terror of the Zygons* (1975), now with Tom Baker as the Doctor, the legend of Loch Ness is used as the basis for a group of shape-shifting aliens (Zygons) whose ship is hidden under the loch. Set in a creepy Scottish village, the story is crammed with the sort of evocative faux-folklore that lends what is a simple narrative an incredible atmosphere. Tales of people disappearing over the years persist, some being driven mad by something that appears when the mist rolls down upon Tulloch Moor; which, without fear of spoiling the atmosphere, is really filmed in Sussex. The role of the rural village is undoubtedly used most effectively in Terry Nation's *The Android Invasion* (1975), where an eerily empty English village (near a rural space defence station) turns out to live up to its ambience by actually being a test centre for an alien force using duplicate androids to infiltrate Earth. Tom Baker's era, perhaps because it is the longest, boasts the most examples of Folk Horror ideas and almost always expresses them through location filming and topography. In Chris Boucher's *Image of the Fendahl* (1977), the haunted pasts of Nigel Kneale are evoked, as a research facility in the middle of a haunted woods (built into a gothic mansion) is plagued by the unleashing of a myth-ological being. Again its implications are that mankind has been twisted and evolved to allow for this moment to happen, but the story is deeply shrouded in faux-folklore as well. Salt is used to fend off the summoned creatures, with the mineral being an ancient defence against such things, while the local vil-lagers are yet again part of a cult who unwittingly help the creatures achieve corporeality. This is even before acknowledging that the skull at the centre of the mystery has a Pentagram naturally built into the bone; our whole folklore and belief system being derived from its power first asserted millions of years ago (a theme also considered in *The Daemons*).

The same themes occur in *The Stones of Blood* (1978) but manifest through more typical Folk Horror methods, with its setting being a stone circle on Boscombe Moore near Cornwall (actually filmed at Oxfordshire's atmospheric Rollright Stones). The story is chiefly about the Doctor's attempt to find a segment of an object known as the Key to Time, with the whole season being dedicated to this story arc. The segment has, however, fallen into the hands of Cessair of Diplos (Susan Engel) who is masquerading locally as the Druidic god of war, the Cailleach, for the Druid research group who are getting a little carried away with their practices. The landscape takes centre stage as the alien menace turns out to be the Ogri; stone creatures who drink blood and happily inhab-it the stone circle when not murdering weekend campers. There are numer-ous references to folkloric ideas and even research, with names such as John Aubrey being dropped by the Doctor. Though the story descends into an enjoy-ably farcical trial in hyper-space in its final episodes, it is Folk Horror through and through; the characters isolated by the landscape,[36] which has allowed a confident trend of Druidic sacrifice to return to the moors. Even alien stones are left in peace to wander and kill in the English landscape.

Doctor Who would leave such themes behind in the 1980s, its landscapes becoming more alien than in the 1970s. However, several examples did slip through. Peter Davison's era has two in the form of Eric Saward's *The Visitation* (1982) and Eric Pringle's *The Awakening* (1984). The former follows a band of renegade aliens stuck in seventeenth-century England who spread the Black Death and scare the local woodsmen with an android dressed as the Grim Reaper; while the latter follows an alien which is manifesting through the psychic energy of a village currently re-enacting an English Civil War battle. Both bask heavily in their leafy vistas. Sylvester McCoy also has several Folk Horror elements in his era, chiefly in Ian Briggs' *The Curse of Fenric* (1989); a story about an ancient Viking curse, an inter-dimensional foe trapped in a jug, and vampire-like creatures (Haemovores) coming out of the Dorset sea to attack a local church and army base. The Lulworth Cove location is pivotal to the story's effective and complex examination of the horror of war. Perhaps certain moments from *Silver Nemesis* (1988), with its initial Elizabethan skulduggery, and *Battlefield* (1989), with its Arthurian madness, witchy villain and demonic evil, could also be said to be at least conveying a strange, pulpy sense of Folk Horror even if it isn't in its purest or most recognisable form. Landscape does, however, fall largely to the wayside in these latter examples.

The programme's many writers did also produce other strands of Folk Horror,. notably in the guise of Bob Baker and David Martin, most famous as the creators of the Doctor's robot dog companion, K-9. In the same year that the pair wrote the Tom Baker story, *The Sontaran Invasion*, they also penned an HTV series which, arguably, is more landscape-obsessed and ecologically minded than any other example of televisual Folk Horror. The series was *Sky* (1975), a seven-part drama mixing science-fiction, fantasy and horror into a unique blend of Folk Horror that seems almost impossible to conceive being produced today. The series follows the arrival of inter-dimensional being named Sky (Marc Harrison), who has accidentally slipped in time into a rural part of England. His presence is unnatural and heavily fought off by the very foliage that surrounds him, attacks from tree roots and leaf storms being common throughout the series. The natural world eventually conjures a being known as Goodchild (Robert Eddison), a humanoid form to combat and destroy the anomaly of Sky. The series is replete with eerie moments, entering into some intensely dark territory, with Eddison's wide-eyed stalking of children through forests, schools and hospitals, but its message is clear; that the planet is under threat from our own lack of education in how to responsibly live upon it.[37]

Sky returns through a portal, located at Stonehenge, the implication being that such forms and objects – named 'Juganets' in the series – were designed as messages for man to take heed of and to remember the influence of Sky's race and their earlier visitations. The ground is sentient and is shown to be hurt by man, though why it cannot conjure more creatures like Goodchild to fend off humanity's general follies is never quite answered. *Sky* presents a journey through peril but it is the programme's imagery that most resonates in Folk Horror analysis. In Tim Worthington's excellent essay examining cult programmes from this era, 'Completing The Circle: A Retrospective of HTV's Cult Children's Programming', he writes that '*Sky* benefited greatly from the skill and enthusiasm of its cast and crew, not least on the account of the effective contrast between the wide open and panoramic location work and the cramped, claustrophobic studio sets' (2011: 7). The obvious landforms are all there and the direction makes the most of various location filming, mixed with the cosmic elements of the narrative in similar fashion to *Red Shift*. The pair would make a fitting double bill because of their linking of space and time with effects upon topography; the Goodchild character's 'Forces of the earth' quote (**see page 38**) is one of the most important as it shows its creative hand to be immersed in the temporality of the terrain. Three of *Sky*'s episodes were directed by executive producer Patrick Dromgoole, who would dip into Folk Horror territory throughout his career; producing such relevant series as *Arthur of The Britons* (1972–73), *King of the Castle* (1977),[38] *The Clifton House Mystery* (1978) and *Into the Labyrinth* (1981–82). His most important contribution to Folk Horror, however, is not his role in these varying and effective series, but in producing the most definitive of Folk Horror examples aimed at a young audience, HTV's *Children of the Stones* (1977).

Alongside *The Owl Service*, *Children of the Stones* is key to discussions of Folk Horror, whether the perspective be focused on landscapes, folklore, ties with the cosmic, or even sociological relevance to Britain in the 1970s. Following in the mould of the seven-part series format that HTV honed, *Children* builds an unease within its landscape, again making the link between the temporal and the astrological; the past rituals being allowed to repeat with horrific inevitability. Written by another creative writing partnership, Trevor Ray and Jeremy Burnham, the series encapsulates all that is most earnestly recognisable about the genre, boiled down into the purest of examples. A narrative breakdown follows.

Children of the Stones – Professor Adam Brake (Gareth Thomas) and his son Matthew (Peter Demin) arrive in the small town of Milbury. The town is dominated by its stone circle, and Adam is here on research leave from his university to conduct a number of tests and gather data about the stones. They also bring with them a strange painting which details a powerful ritual bearing an unusual resemblance to the village and its stones. The village is a strange place, its occupants seemingly divided into those who are 'happy' and those who are not, the former greeting people with the unnerving salutation 'Happy day!'. In his temporary school, Matthew finds that the split is also recognisable in the children, the happy ones being of immense and uncanny intelligence, the normal ones being more typical in their attitude to school. Adam's housekeeper Mrs Crabtree (Ruth Dunning) and the local village leader Hendrick (Iain Cuthbertson) are also seemingly a part of some sinister plot involving the ancient power of the stones, further heightened by the energy which now traps them all within the village. Matthew befriends Sandra (Katharine Levy), one of the normal children, whose mother Margaret (Veronica Strong) runs the local museum detailing the history of the area. He also discovers Dai (Freddie Jones), a local man who has seemingly been driven mad by some unnamed force and now lives in a protective cave outside of the circle of the stones. After several uncanny experiences and hallucinations, it is revealed that Hendrick is using the power of the stones, derived from its connection to a black hole, to empty the minds of his villagers of all of their evil thoughts. Gradually, all of the remaining villagers succumb to this power, the conquests becoming apparent at the village's May Day festival. With only Adam and Matthew left, they let themselves be taken to Hendrick's mansion from where he controls this power from a stone antechamber. The circle's power depends upon the precision of its time of activation, and the pair foil Hendrick's plan by putting his atomic clock forward, allowing them to escape the mind-wipe process. The power breaks down, unleashing the energy of the circle which turns several of the villagers into stones and forces the whole village back through a time-loop to a point to where Adam and Matthew are leaving the village while a much younger Hendrick is seen prospecting the initial purchase of his mansion.

Children's eeriness is in part derived from the filming location of Avebury itself. Several narrative themes, including one of a man crushed and found under one of the stones, are taken from genuine folklore from the area, imbuing the story with a surprising believability. When I interviewed Burnham about using Avebury as a location, he spoke of its natural eeriness: 'But I remember our research visit to Avebury before we started writing – we always knew it had to be Avebury – and seeing a large crow alighting on the back of a ram, after which both of them remained motionless. We knew then that this was the sort of place where strange things happen' (2015). He also tells of a pleasing moment that symbolises the mixture of the false with the real in terms of the landscape: 'As the whole story was based on the Avebury Ring, we followed both the geography and history of the village, which meant that the incomplete stone circle had to be completed with false ones. Veronica [Strong] told me that some Japanese tourists who were watching the filming stared open-mouthed as a member of the crew picked up one of the false ones and carried it away' (2015). This is the basic inner mechanism behind *Children* and Folk Horror; the horror of a false reality being used as a springboard that taps into a half remembered past.

When discussing the prevalence of megalithic objects in *Children*, as well as in several *Quatermass* serials, Hutchings adds to this temporal reading, suggesting that 'these stories depict scientists, the creatures of modernity, investigating mysterious phenomena only to find that science is unable to save them in the face of an immensely powerful compulsion to repeat long-past events' (2006: 37). *The Stones of Blood* and *The Owl Service* could equally be added in some way to this sense of invasion and entrapment of figures of enlightenment. For Worthington, *Children* 'is built around the sinister rural themes of closed communities and ancient traditions and superstitions prevalent in British horror films of slightly earlier in the decade, notably *The Wicker Man*...' (2011: 11). It is this combination of ideas that makes the series such an effective and compelling watch, but there's little doubt that all of these elements are rooted in the Avebury landscape itself. Whether it's the aesthetic principles of the programme or its narrative themes – those such as power, control, entrapment, ancient history and astrophysics – boiling all of them down still brings it back around to the village's rolling green fields, its stone avenues and its gravelly country paths.

Time and space is folded in and accessed through the portal of oblique stones sitting quietly but powerfully within the landscape. These same configurations, highlighted by *Children of the Stones* and in the writing of Garner, are reproduced with alarming consistency in 1970s television. The most effective of these slippages, however, comes in the writing of David Rudkin and his subsequent work for television. The playwright is most noted for a number of works which have a role to play in discussions of Folk Horror; notably the 1974 *Play for Today* episode *Penda's Fen*, as well as experimental series such as *Artemis 81* (1981) and the previously discussed M.R. James adaptation *The Ash Tree*. This is in spite of the writer dismissing the label in a recent interview when confronted with the suggestion that *Penda* is a piece of Folk Horror: 'It's a bloody political piece,' he observed, before adding, 'I've always thought of myself of a political writer' (2016: 6). *Penda's Fen* is, in spite of Rudkin's suggestion, a key example of the genre. Its legal rights wrangle has largely delayed analysis of its workings, being only viewable on YouTube and subject to a handful of 16mm screenings at contemporary gallery spaces until its 2016 DVD release by the British Film Institute.[39] If there's anything that provides evidence that Folk Horror concerns complex academic questioning, it is the natural presence of events in contemporary spaces, such screenings being an ode to the refreshing intellectualism of the drama found on television of this period.

Penda's Fen follows similar lines to Garner's work but concerns an older, teenage protagonist; the result is that a more complex element of sexuality and politics is present. John Coulthart writes of a resemblance with some of Garner's adaptations, suggesting that, 'Stephen in *Penda's Fen*, Gwyn in *The Owl Service* (1969) and Tom in *Red Shift* (1979) are all intelligent teenagers compelled to face deep truths about themselves by contact with the history interred in the British landscape, what Rudkin calls the 'layer upon layer of inheritance' (2015: 65). Stephen (Spencer Banks) is the lead character in *Penda's Fen* and Coulthart is right to compare him to Garner's characters; if not for his own initial staunch conservatism as a character, then he could effectively slot easily into any number of Garner's worlds. But Rudkin's landscape variations differ slightly from Garner's in the sense that the trauma is more deliberately exposed and heightened because they are undoubtedly far more fictional than Garner's autobiographically cathartic characters. Yet Rudkin's process of creation is indeed similar in detailing reactions to genuine places as the following quote from the writer shows:

> There had always been in me a very vague sense of wanting to write and deal with my feelings about England, whatever that might mean, and that inevitably derived for me from the landscape because my work is pretty strongly landscape-based very often. And I've always been much more a country man than a town man. (2014: 15)

This idea is presented most strongly in *Penda* as it is a landscape which effectively breaks down the main character's ego, unleashing his sexually complex id through contact with the ancient as well as the surreal and the supernatural. A narrative breakdown follows.

Penda's Fen – Stephen (Spencer Banks) is the son of a clergyman who lives near the Malvern Hills. He is about to finish school and is precocious in his philosophical and nationalistic beliefs though is a social failure due to his inadequacy at sports. He has obsessions with the music of Elgar and his Christian faith, which hides a darker conflict between his outward beliefs and his inner knowledge of his own homosexuality. Information of a secret military base being built at the fen site nearby emerges as someone is hurt badly by unknown experiments near the fen itself. Throughout the final days of school, he has visions of angels and demons, of meetings with Elgar himself (Graham Leaman), visions of two conservative parents who won a battle against a controversial television drama, and finally King Penda (Geoffrey Staines) himself, the last pagan king of England. With each vision, his false identity is chipped away at until he is told on his 18th birthday of his own adoption; finally undermining his own belief in conservative ideas of belonging. His final meeting with the king forces him to drop his own conservatism, represented by the false perceptions and romanticisms of the landscape around him, and to venture into the unknown, to cherish the 'sacred demon of ungovernableness' as King Penda puts it.

The above description can hardly convey the full effect created by Rudkin's script and direction by Alan Clarke. The play functions as a collection of images bombarded onto its main character as a form of emotional development. The link between the images is the landscape, and the gradual change in perspective towards it signifies a shift in the very psychological makeup of the perceiver. *Penda* is, therefore, akin to *Red Shift* except that its shifting emotional tectonics are being forced upon the shoulders of a single individual rather than an interconnected trio. The results are darker, partly because of the initial sociological state of the character in the first place (a nationalistic conservative), but mainly because of such a pressure being confined to one person; such a personality cannot survive intact when misreading such a landscape for so long.

Similar themes can be found in other works by Rudkin. His first, sadly missing, television play, *The Stone Dance* (1963) is an obvious example from its title alone, but the play concerns the goings on surrounding yet another Neolithic circle and the barriers of a repressed sexuality within an isolated, religious community. Coulthart notes of the casting coincidences within the play, with roles taken by Michael Hordern and John Hurt, both of whom would play the lead in future adaptations of James' *Whistle,* and notes Rudkin's realisation that the play was 'probably the first treatment of same-sex desire in British television...'

(2015: 61). Of most interest to this section, however, is a little discussed play of Rudkin's that features in the *Leap in the Dark* series, *The Living Grave* (1980), the same series and season that produced Garner's *To Kill a King*.

The play follows Pauline (Lesley Dunlop, a further connection to Garner through *Red Shift*), as she is regressed under hypnotism to Kitty, a girl who suffered a great trauma in the 1700s and whose body lies in a grave in the fork of a country roadway. The most essential element is not the potentially supernatural incursion of reincarnation that the narrative implies, but the way that the story builds such an implication through the perception of landscape. The story is solidified with a cross-cutting of the psychologist, Joe (Ian Hogg), visiting the places that Kitty speaks of: the preternatural connection solidifying when confirmed by the landscape and the detail in such things as the rural buildings in which Kitty is supposed to have hung herself. The disparity in the play is created through a sense of the two aspects of the human form – the mind and the body – where the former is supposed to have transferred to a new body while the other becomes cyclically part of the soil yet again. Rudkin treats landscape and personality in the same vein. As he himself suggests:

> And you can see the different anatomy that's underneath just as you can look at an old village and, with a bit of training, can subtract the modern buildings and you can see the old ones. Or you can look at a road and you can see where the old road was. So I began to feel in that way about the landscape, looking at the surface as though it were a filter through which you could just glimpse a previous layer. (2014: 16)

There is the temptation to cut-off the chronology of landscape-infused Folk Horror here but, if any of the tributaries explored within this chapter have shown, the 1970s did not hold sole monopoly upon either Folk Horror television or its varied and terrifying uses of landscape. Already, several examples have found their way into the following decade and beyond, but it is their context that differs, not just their effectiveness as artefacts of Folk Horror. The connections may be less esoteric and less interested in the mystic as a counter-culture ideal, but the 1980s did produce its own Folk Horror topography that consistently tied in various ways to the Folk Horror Chain. The first of these is the four part 1981 series *The Nightmare Man*, scripted by *Doctor Who* writer and script-editor Robert Holmes. The series is adult in tone, verging on dystopian, as it follows a spate of violent killings on a lonely and isolated Scottish island. The killer is seemingly inhuman, though the narrative evolves into Cold War territory, as experimental weaponry is found and a group of

Russian commando soldiers arrive disguised as the British army to take back their experimental fiend.

Douglas Camfield's direction takes full advantage of the rocky outcrop in a similar fashion to his *Doctor Who* episodes; in many ways *The Nightmare Man* feels like a *Doctor Who* story, but one aimed solely at an adult audience with its level of violence and politics raised to a more complex and disconcerting level. The Folk Horror Chain comes into full effect with the fog cutting off the island, isolating the people and rendering them helpless as they lack the capabilities to deal with the augmented, demon-like creature who quite literally tears the inhabitants apart. The sense of the indoor realms being warm and safe is palpable, the outside being rewilded by the presence of a demented experiment gone wrong. The result is surprisingly morbid for the BBC in this period. The idea touches on another trend of fighting against the coming of experimental zones and bases within rural communities, elaborated on in series such as *Raven* (1977), which follows a borstal boy (Phil Daniels) attempting to stop the development of a historically relevant and supernaturally powered cave by an oil company.[40] *The Nightmare Man*, on the other hand, is not an accurate gauge of tone of the Folk Horror from this period, however, and the majority of the definitive 1980s examples are still aimed at a much younger, family audience.

Series such as *The Witches and the Grinnygogg* (1983), *The Box of Delights* (1984), *The Children of Green Knowe* (1986) and *Moondial* (1988) all contain effective elements of Folk Horror as well as an emphasis upon the landscapes in which the narratives occur. The English village is the key to them all, their variations coming largely in the weather and the mystery; for example, the fields of John Masefield's *The Box of Delights* are enjoyably snowy vistas for the characters to traverse at Christmas time (whilst on the run from an evil presence after a magical box is given to them by an old Punch & Judy man).[41] On the other hand, *The Witches and the Grinnygogg*, based on the book by Dorothy Edwards, basks in the gentle summertime of a village church as its museum is reopened by a group of children who find themselves at the centre of a strange mystery involving a stone ornament that their mother picked up from the back of a lorry. Whilst the horror is negligible in these series, their fantasticalness lends them to Folk Horror categorisation because of the period of production in which they sit. This is not the period of counter-culture freedom or a highpoint in magical interest; this is 1980s Britain and the pastoral weird has taken a dive underground. That these series exist in such a climate at all perhaps overemphasises their Folk Horror, especially in contrast to their vibrant counterparts from a decade earlier, but their place in the conversation is still deserving.

The last example to consider is one that ventures back into familiar territory; that of Jamesian ghosts, evil marsh landscapes and a sense of genuine terror. In 1989 Herbert Wise directed an adaptation of that most Jamesian of more recent novels, Susan Hill's *The Woman in Black*. The narrative will perhaps be more familiar than other examples here because of its remake and sequel, made as feature films by the renovated Hammer Studios in 2012 and 2014 respectively. What marks the 1989 ITV version in terms of Folk Horror is how much its moments of terror are derived from ideas earnestly associated with M.R. James; curiosity being punished, figures in the landscape, and the past fighting back against the modernity that invades it. Script-editor Nigel Kneale creates a hauntology of dread in the bogs of Eel Marsh House; the landscape is similarly malevolent to those landscapes discussed in James' adaptations earlier. The crux of the narrative is the connecting of two Jamesian events; the required documentation of past paraphernalia and paperwork, and the encountering of a landscape that is haunted by a violent and uncanny trauma.

The fact that its setting is genuinely in flux in terms of its accessibility gives its horror a great sense of rising and falling away, as if the story and the land is in fact breathing.[42] Though other examples made after this play could be brought into the argument[43] it seems fitting to mark an end point in Folk Horror television topography on an example in the same vein as we began. For it marks an interesting evolution: beginning with M.R. James, through to writers such as Alan Garner, David Rudkin and others, but still finishing on a period ghost story in spite of the various splits and narrative forms in between. The form is one so often aligned with more Gothic (rather than folkloric) traditions, and yet, even when setting work in the era of such Romanticism, the relationship with the landscape still has a psychological focus that is easily recognisable as being a trait of Folk Horror. This may seem purely cyclical in character but, having the finalising element of the chapter finish on a connection to Nigel Kneale suggests its own haunting; a figure who has yet to be properly explored yet whose work hangs heavy over Folk Horror in an entirely unnerving furrow all of its own. The past rising in a multitude of ghostly visions, not simply to scare or punish us, but to do something far more unnerving: to warn us off the very landscape itself.

Endnotes

1   Organised as an ongoing research project by Yvonne Salmon and James Riley. More information can be found at www.thealchemicallandscape.blogspot.co.uk

2   Seaburgh – *A Warning to the Curious*; Milbury – *Children of the Stones*; Boscombe Moore – *Doctor Who – The Stones Of Blood*; the Welsh valley – *The Owl Service*.

3   As spoken by the character Goodchild from *Sky* (1975).

4   Running from late 1967 intermittently until 1993.

5   See any of Ken Russell's contributions to both *Omnibus* and *Monitor* for more extreme examples.

6   In James' original story, the narrative is set in a place called Burnstow, a fictional substitute for Felixstowe.

7   The show produced a whole 29 episodes worth of Blackwood adaptations and perhaps cemented John Laurie as the ultimate teller of terror; a role which he would reprise satirically in his many comedic stories told as Private Fraser in *Dad's Army* (1968–1977).

8   It may be said that many Folk Horror ideas are in fact variations upon James' paranoid narratives rather than purely Miller's visual interpretation of one of his stories.

9   And James'/Clark's *The Ash Tree*.

10   The Network DVD release of this version also brings to light two interesting James curios. The first is a short adaptation of *Mr Humphries and His Inheritance*, created as a guide for an educational programme on the use of music in film. The second is the rather ponderous documentary on the man, *A Pleasant Terror: The Life and Ghosts of M.R. James* (1995). Presented by Bill Wallis, perhaps better know in Folk Horror terms as Rat from *The Box of Delights*, the documentary features some intriguing explorations of James' landscapes and fine interviews with Christopher Lee, Ruth Rendell, Ronald Blythe and, most usefully, Jonathan Miller.

11   Cuthbertson finds his way into a surprising number of key Folk Horror roles including performances in *The Stone Tape* and *Children of the Stones,* as well as episodes of *Survivors*, *Ripping Yarns*, *Doctor Who* and *The Ghosts of Motley Hall*.

12   Released in America as *Curse of the Demon* in a slightly altered cut.

13   Produced by the same team behind *Jackanory* and adapting *The Mezzotint*, *A School Story* and *The Diary of Mr Poynter.*

14   Adapting *The Mezzotint*, *The Ash Tree*, *Wailing Well*, *The Rose Garden*, and '*Oh, Whistle and I'll Come To You, My Lad*'.

15   Adapting *The Stalls of Barchester*, *The Ash Tree*, *Number 13* and *A Warning to the Curious*.

16   A tone which sits alongside *Count Magnus*, a Scandinavian-set story which Clark himself had wanted to adapt.

17   Adapted by Neil Cross, writer of the *Doctor Who* episode, *Hide* (2013), which is an earnest if flawed homage to both *The Stone Tape* and *Sapphire & Steel*.

18   The title is now called upon simply as the song of that title, shared lovingly between the elderly couple; the inorganic demon now pointlessly becoming a ring which may, or may not, have been left behind by the couple when younger. The story makes little sense either way and would have worked far better if simply being its own thing rather than an adaptation of James which it ultimately fails at.

19   Aptly because Kneale finally kills off Quatermass in the programme's conclusion.

20   After all, if Folk Horror depends on society as a core concept, it's likely to have little horrific effect if such a concept is being forcibly abandoned.

21 The title refers to Garner's troubled childhood with various illnesses rendering him incapable of leaving his bed; the ceiling acting as a canvas on which to play out narratives and create landscapes of the mind: 'The daily landscape for me was a bedroom ceiling in a brick cottage, with a porch' (1997: 9).

22 *The Weirdstone of Brisingamen* (1960), *The Moon of Gomrath* (1963), *Elidor* (1965) and *The Owl Service* (1967).

23 Though it was sadly first broadcast in black and white due to industrial disputes regarding the changeover to colour, it was repeated in colour in the mid-1970s.

24 Though the main house used in the production actually sits in Bromborough on The Wirral.

25 The story itself seems stretched out at times to cover the full process of Roger's 35mm photography of the stone, revealing both Gronw throwing the spear and Gwyn's father riding the motorbike which Huw had tampered with, leading to his death.

26 After all, Gillian Hills had been the first onscreen totally nude female three years before in Michelangelo Antonioni's *Blowup* (1966) and would do so again two years after *The Owl Service* in *A Clockwork Orange*.

27 An example of this blows up unexpectedly in the episode, not so much in his dramatic experiment with two young actors, but when the programme reveals what Garner's relatives are doing to his relatives' house down the road in Alderely Edge. The encounter is one that is genuinely raw, with Garner almost unable to contain his anger at the changes being made to the cottage.

28 Mackenzie is most noted as the director of *The Long Good Friday* (1980).

29 Directed by Edward Joff.

30 Directed by Matthew Robinson.

31 Excluding *The Keeper*.

32 The scope plays a definitive role in the finale of Garner's *Weirdstone* trilogy, *Boneland* (2012).

33 The link to pagan beliefs being that this is the same day in the calendar of Imbolc, the celebration of the Spring Equinox in certain Gaelic theologies.

34 The Silurians seem to induce people who come across them into a caveman state though the idea is largely discarded some episodes in. Likewise, the almost folkloric element of the Sea Devils, aquatic cousins of the Silurians, is largely abandoned once the military action starts. Both stories also have isolated locations, the former being a nuclear research centre built into the very rock of the Derbyshire moors, the latter being set on a fictional prison island off the coast which is largely and typically rural.

35 Due largely to contractual reasons whereby the producer could not also work as a writer.

36 Notice the character of De Vries (Nicholas McArdle) as he amusingly moans '... Plymouth!?' as a suggestion of a safe haven away from the trouble.

37 The theme is equally taken up in the Children's Film Foundation short *Haunters of the Deep* (1984), which sees the development of Cornish tin mining prevented by ghosts.

38 Also written by Bob Baker and David Martin. See Chapter 5 for more details on this surprisingly Ballardian series.

39 These screenings were initially small-scale gallery events at the likes of The Horse Hospital and Whitechapel Gallery in London. Since the comprehensive season of Alan

Clarke's work curated by the British Film Institute, *Penda* has become incredibly popular, with its own DVD and Blu-ray release. At the time of writing a one-off symposium is being organised for 2017 at the BFI dedicated to exploring the play and its many complexities.

40   See Chapter 5 for more examples of this form of narrative.

41   Played (and criminally underused) by Patrick Troughton.

42   A stronger example of this is found in the next chapter in Roman Polanski's *Cul-De-Sac* (1966).

43   For example, *The Green Man* (1990), *The Demon Headmaster* (1996-1998), *Aquila* (1997), *Jonathan Creek* (1997–2004), etc.

Chapter 4

Rurality

Reality As Rurality

> The sense of the past lying just behind the present – 'the pattern under the
> plough', as the folklorist George Ewart Evans put it – is a key feature of
> British, especially English, art of the past century. Let's call this tendency the
> 'antiquarian eye'. – Rob Young (2010: 18)

> The Plough was used, too, on a ritual occasion: on plough Monday, the
> Monday after Twelfth Day, the end of the medieval Christmas holidays...
> It has been suggested that the ritual ploughing on Plough Monday
> anticipated the real ploughing which was to take place later. –
> George Ewart Evans in *The Pattern Under The Plough* (1966: 135)

In May 2015, I was sitting in a cafe in Liverpool attempting to promote a film
whose screening I had organised at a recently developed cinema co-operative.

Due in part to the film's relative obscurity, it was requiring an extra burst of effort.[1] The relevance of the screening to Folk Horror is quintessential as the film in question explores a number of the genre's key features; some that are built upon ideas found within the unholy trinity, whilst others being expansions into areas of its own accord. The film that was demanding such effort was the 1976 experimental feature *Requiem for a Village*. The film's complexity and small-scale distribution had led to its obscurity and the screening required posters to be screen-printed, content to published, and other such usual methods of promoting events in the fight against unfair invisibility.

Briefly checking my phone, I noticed that I had missed a call from a number that I didn't recognise. Playing back the answerphone message, a gentle, older male voice spoke, almost sounding like a more mellowed Professor Yaffle from *Bagpuss*. The voice belonged to *Requiem*'s director, David Gladwell: sometime member of the Free Cinema movement, editor of Lindsay Anderson's *If....* (1968) and *O' Lucky Man!* (1973), and a director in his own right. He was concerned that some interview questions he had answered for the article I was writing had not come through properly and was now experiencing difficulty in making contact again because of his questionable Suffolk internet connection.

I had emailed Gladwell with the interview questions out of the blue, and it had felt like a shot in the dark; in many ways the director seemed to have shrouded himself in an obscurity equal to his wonderfully eerie films, both of short and feature-length variety. And now, on this sunny day, in an urban landscape miles from the luscious Suffolk of his most ambitious and poetic film, I was listening to his voice on my phone. It was a surreal moment but one that suggested all sorts of ideas about the film in question; its complex, non-linear narrative about the invasion of rural village England by urban and suburban dwellers: the moment reversed this briefly.

One way of viewing the unholy trilogy from Chapter 2 is by connecting their relationship to their rural setting, and this idea has many potential effects. Gladwell's film questions the logic of such location-bred violence by looking into darker aspects of the rural. This isn't simply through emphasis upon the topographical difference between urban and rural areas[2] but more akin to the accoutrements of rural living and lifestyle; the aesthetics of farming, and other practices that are required to live off the land have a dual character of violence and history. Perhaps, in its purest of examples, it could even be described as an 'occultivation' of the land though the narratives here are about a huge range of aspects besides farming. Folk Horror regularly builds its sense of the horrific around societies and groups of people that have very specific ways of life, and it is not by sheer chance that these often happen to be rural rather than urban. This sense of divide between the two accounts for what was earlier called 'skewed belief systems and ideologies' but there is more to it than the allowing of pulp forms of paganism and occultism to grow; Folk Horror uses the otherness that can be attributed to rural life to warp the very reality of its narrative worlds and often for its own explicit means.

Gladwell's film is a perfect example of this as the urban-to-rural clashes melt down the barriers of logic, physics and time in the film; as if the setting of its rural village – one which is slowly mutating into a suburban outlier – twists and augments what can happen in its zone whilst still retaining some essence of believability. This twin effect of bringing in historical and cultural memorabilia from British ruralism is, for the sake of simplicity, named in this chapter as 'rurality'; the simultaneous grounding in the real world rural and the mythologising effect it also creates, where fantastical, surreal and horrific events can spring forth. In other words it is the mixing of reality and the rural (in the conceptual sense) to produce a symbiotic effect of eeriness. In terms of the Folk Horror Chain, it is moving its causational elements into the non-diegetic realm, where the directors and writers are playing on our, often incomplete but still in-part existing, knowledge of the rural realm and playing it much to their own aesthetic, thematic and narrative advantages.

This goes some way to explaining and critiquing a large number of films that prevalently appear in discussions surrounding Folk Horror yet which do not have a strict horror sensibility or even have any horrific events of recognisable guise at all. In fact, rurality can be said to account for many examples of film and television that often crop up in discussions of the genre but rarely conform to its most basic of definitions. This does not mean that they should be ignored but, on the contrary, should be seen in a wider context of esoterica as a whole. This book does not argue for a rigid Folk Horror canon because of the need to discuss these examples, with the awareness that various factions of cinematic and genre academia would typically overreact to such a shift in genre for many of the films in this chapter. Luckily, a film such as *Requiem* defies most genre descriptions in the first place, as do many films contained herein.

Requiem depicts a small Suffolk village whose edges are gradually being scratched at by the development of the outlying suburban estates. The potential calamity that such a development is to the local ways of the villagers conjures strange images of the dead rising from their graves to attend emergency village council meetings. Meanwhile, the new ease of access to the countryside has lead to a local biker gang invading the peaceful vista of the meadows, their violence culminating in a number of scenarios that disrupt the agricultural harmony. Yet the film also shows the slight hypocrisy of such a paranoia. Unlike its poetic equivalent, 'Going, Going' by Philip Larkin (1972), which is equally dismayed at the death of the country village – 'And that will be England gone' (Larkin 2003: 134) – *Requiem* recognises the violence already present in the rural zones.

The film is perhaps most infamous for an extended montage of sexual assault, slipping in its perception between the motorbike gang and the workers of the land, both forcing themselves upon women. Perhaps neither area nor its people hold sole monopoly on the skewing of morality. Rob Young's quote that opens this chapter raises the question of the influence of rural-based ethnographic and agricultural practices. Later in the same essay he describes *Requiem* as 'an essay film that slips into reverie and fantasy' (2010: 19) and there's certainly a connection between the idea of slips into the fantastical, the violent and the 'past lying just behind the present'. Indeed, Gladwell, in our interview, cited the same book that Young mentions (as a marker of the films of 'old, weird Britain') as a chief influence on his film:

> I had harboured the wish to try and incorporate some ideas of the English artist, Stanley Spencer, and his paintings of a churchyard resurrection, in which previous generations of villagers are united with the present; and when I came across the documentary books of George Ewart Evans, 'The Pattern Under the Plough' and 'Ask the Fellows Who Cut the Hay', for example, I realised I had found a way of depicting the subjects which could represent those previous generations. (2015)

There should now be a sense of the character of rurality and how it influences Folk Horror; where films represent previous generations and their practices, either in period where the films take on a sense of the uncanny, or in the present where tradition itself becomes a source of unease and anachronistic horror. Gladwell uses this notion as more of a surreal social commentary on the topographical developments occurring in mid-1970s England, but other films delve into the territory for purely pulp means. Both *The Wicker Man* and *The Blood on Satan's Claw* tap into this sense of rurality as they both follow communities whose livelihood is derived from the land and whose belief systems are based around it (even if only manifesting in superstition in *Blood*). The former is an example of the anachronism of traditional practices, using them as a thematic gateway to bring other associations back through to the 1970s (i.e. a pop-paganism and its potentially violent window-dressings). The latter uses the grounding of its rurality to both set in motion its narrative and to bring a sense of recognisability to its macabre happenings; the past being as tangible as the mud of its fields with its hinting at Charles Manson-like group violence.

Gladwell's film, along with several of his shorter works,[3] is the epitome of the former type of rurality; the modern day colliding with a past, an urban/rural divide manifesting physically and psychically in both place and people: the film's image of a farmer violently throwing clumps of earth at a commercial digger is one of the most profound in all of Folk Horror.[4] On its release, Elizabeth Sussex argued that it was essential to see Gladwell's work as a reaction to the present rather than purely as nostalgia for something lost, writing that, 'It is important, I think, to know that what started him off on this was not nostalgia for anything familiar to himself. It was, on the contrary, the sight of the new towns spreading across the country and in their progress replacing, burying – what?' (1975: 3-4). The horror in this sense is not a feeling of terror but more of a pressurised frustration at the old ways being bulldozed and tar-macked into the byways.

The essence of rurality can create a huge number of differing narratives and relationships once embedded into the very soil of a film. Gladwell's rurality forms around more avant-garde mechanisms, but a general rurality can be seen in such narrative tropes as the insider/outsider, the modern city dweller entering the zone of the countryside and being shocked by its differing ways of life, an old magic being derived from the landscape, the rural becoming the testing area for scientists with their experimental urbanity, and where places are subject to a cultural form of violence; these are all potentially derived from the sideways tipping of reality through an emphasis upon the rural.

The screening of *Requiem* at the Liverpool cinema co-op went marginally better than expected. Trying to market a film that uses traditional farming aesthetics as a violent, surreal protest against topographical post-war development was never going to be an easy sell. Yet Gladwell's film deserves to be more widely seen and discussed because it exemplifies a key theme in Folk Horror; the breakdown of the everyday normality that occurs through an obsession with the seemingly normal. It may not have done it in such a populist way as to achieve the cult and pulp popularity of other films that use the rural to augment their narrative worlds but, as an example to begin the analysis of the concept itself, there is no better, more visceral, or more hypnotic starting place. Gladwell concluded in my brief interview with him by suggesting in regards to *Requiem* that, 'It was probably the fragmentary quality of this story which attracted me – including, again, the bringing together of different worlds' (2015). Little could he know how much his film reflected the clash of such worlds in cinema from all corners of the globe; the clashing of realities with the rural, the agri-aggressive, and the eeriness of rurality with all of its pastoral horror.

Tilling The Trauma – British Rurality

Pulp Rurality

British Folk Horror cinema saw a wealth of films emerge from the shadows of the unholy trinity, largely blossoming in the 1970s. It could, however, be argued that such trends started even before the counter-culture had got into the full swing of land-worship and paganism, with a number of films sprouting in the mid-to-late 1960s. The connecting element of these films is arguably their sense of rurality, in that they often delve into surreal and fantastical narratives which connect overtly to rural lifestyles, places and aesthetics, as well as outsiders venturing into such rural worlds. British director John Gilling produced a number of films in this period that deal overtly with Folk Horror themes through the prism of a varied and oddly amalgamated rurality; where the supernatural is tied to either industrial potential in working the land or folklore on the loose within the very landscape itself. Gilling had already been dipping into horror in the early 1960s with such Gothic films as *The Flesh and the Fiends* (1960) and *The Shadow of a Cat* (1961) before committing fully to films with more interest in landscape (his equally relevant English Civil War film, *The Crimson Blade*, is analysed in the next section).

In 1966 he made two early forms of Folk Horror film for Hammer Studios, clearly on a modest budget as they were filmed back-to-back and with shared crews. The films were *The Reptile* and *The Plague of the Zombies*. Their (admittedly visually flimsy) setting on the Cornish coast sets their tone apart from other Hammer films of the era. In the former, a married couple inherit an isolated cottage in an area seemingly over-run by a mysterious disease. The unfriendly locals add to the tension as it becomes clear that some venomous creature is on the loose, attacking and killing the inhabitants. It turns out that it is the local Doctor's daughter (Jacqueline Pearce) who is afflicted with a deadly curse that turns her into a vicious reptile creature. The rurality of the film manifests, not so much within the main narrative or even the general aesthetic (it was clearly filmed on the usual Surrey back-lots of other Hammer films), but in the hostile attitude of the locals to the newly arrived couple. The tension between outsiders and insiders is defined well by Gilling, filling the film with dreamlike moments of dizziness and paranoia; the faux-Cornish emphasis skewing reality into a fiendish, surreal mixture.

The same queasy elements can be found in Gilling's other Cornish horror film as well, though it is heightened even further by some of the studio's most grue-some dreams sequences. *Plague* is far more industrialised, taking inspiration from early zombie films such as *White Zombie* (1932) whereby the living dead are given an Orientalist hue, mixing with some vaguely continental voodoo, and using the resulting monsters as a slave force to work the land, specifically down the mines.[5] Young emphasises this aspect, suggesting that *Plague* 'car-icatures the English capitalist aristocracy as voodoo-practicing slave-masters, zombifying their workforce to increase the production rate in a Cornish tin mine' (2011: 418). The film's sense of rurality comes from this bizarre scenario, mixing a multicultural (but ultimately still colonially-tinged) folklore with a ba-sic rural industry. Perhaps the Folk Horror Chain can also be linked to both sto-ries; the lack of morality behind both hiding a daughter's dangerous capacity to kill and the revival of the dead for free labour are arguably only conceivable in an isolated rural zone (and both subsequently solved by incoming townie in-terlopers). *Plague* could even be seen as a subtle inversion of Lord Summerisle's business plan, only he has to cast a false magic over the living rather than a real magic over the dead.

Certain other Hammer films from the 1960s also touched upon vague elements of rurality, the most relevant to Folk Horror outside of the occultist films of Chapter 5 being Peter Graham-Scott's *Night Creatures* (aka *Captain Clegg*) (1962), which sees an illegal smuggling racket functioning by playing on the old tales of the local marshland. Hammer's period films, however, largely moved far into the Gothic and away from either rurality or Folk Horror connections generally. Some elements did still appear, including the sadistic fox-hunting opening of Terence Fisher's 1959 take on *The Hound of the Baskervilles*. The same narrative ploy, as well as a stunning East Anglian landscape, would also be used with equal effectiveness five years later in Roger Corman's Edgar Allan Poe adap-tation, *The Tomb of Ligeia* (1964). Yet the most overt example of British rurality from this period comes not from Hammer or even from horror cinema at all, but, surprisingly, in the form of Roman Polanski's *Cul-De-Sac* (1966). The film was the third feature for the director, after an equally rural debut in *Knife in the*

Water (1962),[6] soon followed by its opposite in the urban paranoia of *Repulsion* (1965).[7] *Cul-De-Sac* feels more in line with the former rather than the latter, being a film where its characters are at the literal mercy of its landscape and also because of their total lack of experience within a more rural environment. *Cul-De-Sac*'s position in Folk Horror is a strange one, where the overt folklore of the film's setting is hidden under layers of psychological torment and drama. A narrative breakdown follows.

> **Cul-De-Sac** – George (Donald Pleasence) and his wife Teresa (Françoise Dorléac) live in the isolated vista of Lindisfarne Castle on Holy Island off the north-east of England. The pathway and road to the island is flooded regularly by the sea, and the impression is given that George wanted to move there to escape, especially from his friends. A pair of runaway criminals, the burly bully Richard (Lionel Stander), and the injured Albie (Jack MacGowran), arrive on the island for sanctuary after a botched job. They take control of the castle, subjecting George and Teresa to a series of psychological torments while they await help from their gangland boss who they contact via phone. The married couple's relationship begins to break down under the strain when the pair have to accommodate George's horrendous friends and their family who visit them. Albie eventually dies of his injury, further sparking tension and breakdowns in the trio who are forced to deal with the body. The married couple eventually attack Richard and shoot him dead. Fearing reprisals from his gangland boss, Teresa hides in a cupboard where she is later found by one of George's friends. George's fragile psyche is fragmented to the point of madness, the film finishing with him in a foetal position on a rock as the tide around the island gently ebbs around him.

Though Polanski's film uses little of the aesthetics of rural life, it taps into another other key part of rurality; the inability of city-dwellers to properly acclimatise. The reasoning behind George's initial decision to live in the castle is made all too clear by Polanski, showing his friends to be utterly unbearable. The isolation of the castle plays against George's own desire to be there and the fact that he is unable to leave it at the end of the film is a poignant point. Rurality highlights the strange and misconceived urban notion of retreating to the countryside to rest, to escape, and to leave behind the hustle and bustle of city life. *Cul-De-Sac* subtly points out the fallacy of this ideal by pushing a character to the very limits where he eventually acknowledges that there is no running away and no place to hide. The only real place left for him is his mother's womb, which he attempts to recreate in the final shot, waiting for the natural amniotic fluid of the sea to cocoon him once again. Death or return to the womb are the only escapes in the world of Holy Island. There may be no agricultural practices depicted in Polanski's film but the rurality is palpable as it comes to its disturbing, paranoid conclusion.

Polanski would follow this rurality to its logical conclusion in his 1971 take on *Macbeth*; possibly most Folk Horror-infused of the play's many cinematic adaptations. Rebekah Owens has written specifically of why Polanski's *Macbeth* can be easily situated in Folk Horror, suggesting its use of landscape and horror are very much akin to the films of the unholy trinity but also because of the film's '...realisation that its horror is very much earthbound and human' (2017: 84). Owens' analysis is apt for the discussion of rurality and its sense of the real blurring with surreal horror, her concluding thoughts summarising the likeness perfectly: 'It shares with those films the idea that what you see on screen is not the result of an intervention with anything supernatural' (ibid.). Or, to put it another way, the fantastical becomes so absorbed into the real that the two are unnervingly difficult to tell apart.

One of *Cul-De-Sac*'s producers was Tony Tenser, the executive producer of both *Witchfinder General* and *The Blood on Satan's Claw*. Tenser was the founder of Tigon Studios, the company responsible for both of these films as well as numerous others of note, though many have often been under-represented in more general horror discussions. Perhaps the way rurality haunts both Polanski's film and these other two films is merely a coincidence but, looking back through Tigon's back catalogue of films, the studio's output is replete with examples of Folk Horror; where such forms of rurality are used in the most pulp, violent and exploitative of ways. If there is one thing that drives Tigon's many horror films, it is the sheer madness and violence which flows forth when at the mercy of the countryside and the free-pass on morality that it often diegetically secures.

Tigon's films are split in terms of their horror output; some use very clear concepts of rurality for exploitation purposes whilst others use more modern-day ideas to present an almost oneiric vision of present-day, counter-culture Britain. Both facets have some sway on Folk Horror but examples of the second type will be more useful when looking at the occult and urban examples in Chapter 5. Therefore, films such as Michael Reeves' *The Sorcerers* (1967) and Vernon Sewell's *Curse of the Crimson Altar* (1968) are set aside for later. Before making *Crimson Altar*, Sewell had made the admittedly terrible *The Blood-Beast Terror* (1968) for Tigon, which hints at a more rural setting and imbues the narrative with interesting details such as making the victims of the monster work in en-tomology; even the *study* of more rural interests spells disaster in Folk Horror. The same unintentional amusement can be seen in *The Beast in the Cellar* (1970), written and directed by James Kelley. Pre-empting, albeit poorly, such modern films as *Dog Soldiers* (2002), *Beast* is another flawed film, though one that at-tempts to express its horror through aspects of rurality. Two elderly sisters are keeping a secret in their basement that, since finding ways to regularly escape, is now causing the violent deaths of the soldiers who are training on the moor. It is perhaps the only Folk Horror film that has T.P. McKenna speak the line, 'A leopard? In Lancashire?', which rather comically highlights one of rurality's dead-ends.

Two other films released by Tigon open up aspects of landscape emphasis that represent a parallel strain to Folk Horror; that is, films set on what could be called the Strange British Coastline. The later of these is the underrated and eerie drama *Neither the Sea nor the Sand* (1972) by Fred Burnley.[8] Though laced with 1970s paraphernalia, the film's supernatural happenings and, most re-freshingly, the emotional impact they have on the main character, makes it far more art-house than is typical for the genre. Its zone of weirdness is around the beaches of Jersey (and later Scotland), where Anna (Susan Hampshire) falls in love with a local lighthouse-keeper, George (Frank Finlay). George dies under strange circumstances on the beach but is then in part re-incarnated back into his own body. The film dwells on Anna's torture, unable to mourn as the body of her lover is still technically alive, driving her slowly mad. The visuals of the film emphasise the beach, to the point where readings seem to suggest that it is something unseen about the place, and George's relationship to it, that gives him his living purgatory; the beach as a reincarnatory force, the sea symbolic of life's ebbing and flowing, physically and emotionally.

Tigon's other coastal film is Peter Sasdy's filmic version of the BBC series *Doomwatch* (1972).[9] *Doomwatch* is the culmination in the trend of modern out-siders entering rural realms for experimental reasons that was arguably started by Nigel Kneale in *Quatermass II* (both the television serial and the Hammer film, though the rural vista is meadowland rather than coastline). *Doomwatch* follows the tragedy of an isolated island and its local village which is plagued by physical and psychical deformities. The Doomwatch team are sent in to investigate an oil spill but find that an illegal dumping of hormones has led to the village's plight. The film and series chimes with the era's generally green eco-message, as the horror comes from the commercialised science industries. Such ubiquity and the normality of science establishments entering and then putting up boundaries between the locals and their previous land is typical of this short movement, though *Doomwatch* plays somewhat loose with this and has the industry doing its dirty work unbeknownst to the local inhabitants, rather than in open conflict.

Quatermass II (1957), directed by Val Guest, plays the most on this idea, as its Cold-War-infused paranoia turns the rural vs. modernity trope to the advantage of interplanetary aliens. This is, however, aided by the invasion of a more human modernity, forcing many of the inhabitants out of an original rural place. Peter Hutchings' description of the geography of the narrative is telling in this case:

> The rural area surrounding the refinery is bleak, denuded and festooned with 'No Entry' signs; when a working-class family ventures in to picnic at their usual site, they are ruthlessly machine-gunned to death by the guards. (2006: 30)

The film, whilst watering down this scene, is still brim with such strange, geographical contrasts as villages on the cusp of existence, fenced boundaries of secretive research establishments, and the very edge-lands that they create; if *Quatermass II* has anything to do with rurality, it is attacking the modern interpretations of it, venturing slowly out into the fields and the forests. The local workers, once aware of what is happening in the establishment, mimic Gladwell's scenes of the local man throwing earth at the digger; the journey temporally between *Quatermass II* and *Requiem* is poignant and deeply ironic in its repetition and lack of progress. Hammer Studios would explore this territory again in Joseph Losey's *The Damned* (1963),[10] once the slight sub-narrative of teddy-boy mischief is gotten out of the way. Again, industrial powers use the aesthetics of rurality to hide its experiments that, in more publically accessible places, would be under fire from modern-day morality. The exact same set-up is even found in Terence Fisher's *Island of Terror* (1966), which comes under attack from meat-eating creatures called silicates – the accidental product of the island's research establishment – and in the *Doctor Who* story, *The Green Death* (1973), where an oil refinery's pollution of an old mine shaft in Wales (rather than the coastline) has created a deadly breed of giant maggots.

The coastline is also a place of general violence, as if its jagged topography creates an equally jagged reaction from its dwellers. In Freddie Francis' *Paranoiac* (1963), this relationship is aesthetically grounded to the point where it seems the narrative only progresses because the bourgeois city-dwellers simply don't return to London. The same ideas are present in Ted Hooker's *Crucible Of Terror* (1971), Jim O'Connolly's *Tower Of Evil* (1972) and also in *The Wicker Man*; the ultimate Folk Horror film about a coastal rurality giving every hint to the modern interloper that he should leave before something bad happens at the hands of the isolated locals. Yet if this model is applied to film more widely, then the most disturbing and effective example is not Hardy's 'hippies-gone-wrong' fable, but a joint UK/American production set in Cornwall: Sam Peckinpah's *Straw Dogs* (1971). This may be the supposed same hunting ground as Gilling's zombies and cursed reptile woman but the horror is far from the fantastical; rurality rarely comes in such a controversial guise.

Straw Dogs follows the fate of a recently married couple, David and Amy Sumner (Dustin Hoffman and Susan George), as they return to the latter's home turf to live on the Cornish coast. The village of her past is of a typical, isolated type, the locals starting out as simply passive-aggressive towards David's Americanisms and his supposed taking of one of their flock. David is also educated and a threat being an academic. Their cottage is being renovated by a group of local builders, one of whom was an old flame of Amy's. They persuade David to come on an early morning shooting trip in order to lure him away from the house and lose him while Charlie Venner (Del Henney) goes back and forcibly seduces his wife.[11] However, another of his lackeys, Norman (Ken Hutchison), appears and forces Charlie at gun point to hold her down while he rapes her. The film becomes even more problematic when, after returning early from a night out a few days later, forced in part by Amy's reaction to seeing her attackers again, they help a disabled man, Henry (David Warner), who has earlier (but unbeknownst to them) strangled a girl who was flirting with him. Her father (Peter Vaughan), in a drunken rage, leads a siege on David's house, where Henry is hiding for his own protection until the authorities can arrive. The local Major (T.P. McKenna) arrives but is accidently shot. After several stand-offs resulting in beatings and killings, David finally kills Charlie with a bear-trap, though not before Charlie has himself killed Norman. Even Amy herself is forced to shoot one of the locals to defend David. With the battle over, they put Henry into a car and quietly drive away from the massacre.

Discussions of *Straw Dogs* are often contextualised by the shock content and the horrific lack of moral finitude behind camera. This is fitting for Folk Horror, though little in the way of theory can account for the film's lopsided perspective. Peckinpah's Cornwall in part resembles the East Anglia of Reeves' *Witchfinder General*, where violence and misogyny are daily occurances and the law is often taken into the inhabitants' own hands. The fact that they were both shot by cinematographer John Coquillon also partly explains the likeness. Whereas Reeves manages to stay relatively distanced in his drama, Peckinpah's moral stance becomes more problematically fixed, especially in the treatment of Amy. As Christina Newland writes, the film 'provides a neatly and offensively retrograde attitude toward women's roles' (2013). Yet there is Folk Horror and rurality amidst all of this misogynistic turmoil, especially in regards to the Folk Horror Chain. The village, and especially the Sumners' cottage, are isolated enough to breed the lapse in morality and its subsequent violence, with such an accurate causation as to function almost as a case study of the chain's workings. But Peckinpah complicates things with his depiction of the actions of Henry; another violent, if accidental, expression of misogyny, yet one caused purely by a crass portrayal of disabilities by David Zelag Goodman's screenplay.

In terms of rurality, the whole film could be said to be some twisted form of excuse for ultra-violence, using rural inhabitants as an easy ploy to explain away such happenings. The violence can be seen as an effective pre-empting of Gladwell's own interpretation of such events later on in *Requiem*. However, Gladwell's thematic line would recede to just the right length of morality rather than fall into the exploitative territory that Peckinpah does. It is fitting that, of all of the ruses that the men could have used to lure David away from the house, they use the shooting of birds on the moorland. Such rural interests seems to have bred in Peckinpah's film a sense of skewed morality far outside the fantastical realms of Summerisle. *Straw Dogs* is one of the films that Andy Paciorek calls 'Backwoods Horror', involving 'a principle character or characters finding themselves amongst people who do not think or act the way they do, often with dire consequences' (2015: 11). It is a fitting term with its homonymic character hinting at the word 'backwards'. Rurality is, in another sense, all about context and, therefore, setting narratives such as *Straw Dogs* in the modern realm (even one that is hyperactively rural) provides a temporal stunting where things seem to morally regress. They're not literally backwards; the discomfort actually comes from their recognisability, from a zone that has not apparently moved forwards from an earlier period. Like on Summerisle, only more viscerally, the rurality is functioning as a stark looking-glass. Is the realm of *Straw Dogs* some outlier that simply hasn't moved on from less enlightened times or is it a magnification of something more permanent that refuses to go away?

The same flavour of littoral lawlessness (albeit with added supernatural tendencies) can be found in the final film in our tour of the Strange British Coastline,

Jerzy Skolimowski's *The Shout* (1978). Based on a short story by Robert Graves, the narrative happens in flashback, from a mental asylum where two patients connect and seem to surreally integrate into each other's pasts. A patient named Crossley (Alan Bates) and a visiting medical officer, Graves (Tim Curry), are keeping score of a cricket game, in which another patient, Anthony (John Hurt), is playing. Crossley relates the story of how he came to be in the asylum. Anthony and his wife, Rachael (Susannah York), live in a sleepy coastal village in Devon. Anthony is an electronic musician of the radiophonic variety who uses inspiration from the wildness around him, as well as the paintings of Francis Bacon, to produce avant-garde music.[12] He also plays the organ for the local village church and it is hinted that he is having an affair with a local woman. He meets Crossley, a travelling man who claims he has learnt the power of 'the shout'; a form of death cry taught to him by an aboriginal tribe that has the power to kill. Intrigued, Anthony is taken to the lonely sand-dunes of coastline and witnesses the shout with his ears plugged. Crossley moves into the couple's house and sleeps with Rachael, who herself appears to be under Crossley's spell. Anthony tracks down Crossley's 'key-stone' out on the dunes, which is supposedly the source of his powers, and smashes it, causing a breakdown of reality and Crossley's subsequent arrest by the police. Back in the asylum, a storm brews and further magic occurs when the shed from which Crossley and Graves are watching the cricket is struck by lightning, killing the former. But the latter, who escapes, is implied to still be able to hear Crossley's shout after his death, as if his magic has somehow lived on.

One of the most striking moments in all 1970s cinema occurs in *The Shout* when Crossley demonstrates his shamanic powers for Anthony. The cutting is slow and hypnotic as the noise overwhelms the character and there appears to be sheep on the dunes that are killed by the noise, as well as their shepherd; rurality implied through power and destruction of the traditional ways at the hands of an even older tradition. It is fitting that Anthony seems ill at ease walking the rural landscape, complaining of a stitch as Crossley confidently strides the dunes ahead of him. Though the magic again has a colonialist slant, there is a natural fit between the landscape of the film and the eerie nature of the preternatural; where the narrative quite earnestly fragments leaving only the landscape and the rural nature of the setting stable while the characters try to recapture who they really are. Kim Newman writes of *The Shout* that, 'The story also reflects an interest in whether or not the soul is bound to the body during every moment of life – perhaps prompted by a wish to explain the phenomena of the shared dream, premonitions, and also ghosts' (2007: 5). This partly contextualises the narrative where the sense of a collapsing reality in the film develops from a dangerous curiosity akin to the likes of M.R. James. Alan Bates is also quoted in Newman's article with an intriguing stance on the character of Crossley:

> There is credibility in *The Shout*, however mysterious, however removed from the everyday. Crossley's story is within the realms of possibility, but it touches on the unknown. People are mystified by it and, most of all, they are forced to question... With Crossley the death shout is something mystical – it is magic. (2007: 7)

Bates rightly recognises the credibility though it is the very grounding in the most aesthetically reliant form of the everyday – that of the rural – that imbues the film with its *unheimlich* mentality. David Thompson has said of Skolimowski that 'his self-generated ideas almost invariably turned out better than his attempts at literary adaptation' (2011: 40), but rightly points towards *The Shout* as an example that goes against this general pattern for the director. *The Shout* is an intensely effective drama because its source material builds a mythology through an ambiguous, unreliable narrator, but allows it to manifest in the guise of a rural context; where, for either supernatural *or* psychological reasons, strange events can occur but still seem wholly real or at the very least credible, as Bates points out. *The Shout* is an unearthly exploration to find the human soul either way, and, that such a journey is undertaken on the comminuted Devon ridges, highlights rurality's more surreal edges: 'Has the human a soul and, if he has, where does he keep it?' In the film, the answer is arguably hidden under the sand on the nearby coastline.

Back at the beginning of the 1970s, rurality was spreading itself around more than just Britain's coastal areas. In Don Sharp's *Psychomania* (1973),[13] undead bikers come back to life around a stone circle, and go on to wreak havoc in nearby Walton-on-Thames. Bikers can also be seen to connect with Gladwell's *Requiem* as a symbol of urban power, one also used by Dracula in *The Satanic Rites of Dracula* (1973) (he has them kitted out in matching sleeveless, sheep-skin jackets). *Psychomania* also links to *The Beast in the Cellar* through the presence of Beryl Reid, only she has swapped hiding a mad, animalistic brother for sharing a camp apartment and occult powers with George Sanders. Though the film has many hang-ups in regards to clearly cashing in on the last of the hype around Dennis Hopper's *Easy Rider* (1969), it is also visually and thematically unique; young motorheads killing themselves on outer London motorways only to be reborn as immortal through the portal of a stone circle, specifically The Seven Witches circle. The site where the circle was shot is now boxed around a garden centre and, on the other side of the M3, a golf course; the strange landscapes of the undead bikers now replaced by undead retirees.

Other rural strangeness abounds in the Amicus portmanteau film *Tales That Witness Madness* (1973), where Michael Jayston's passion for gardening takes a turn for the macabre. Though only one of a number of stories in the film, it is the most memorable and the most amusing. The segment is called *Mel* and is written by Jennifer Fairbank. At first, the story seems to simply be about a man's (Jayston) obsession with a strange looking tree he has brought into the house. His wife Bella (Joan Collins) is not amused by such eccentricity but puts up with it. The tree bears a strange likeness to a woman and very gradually it takes Bella's place in the man's affections until he eventually kills his wife and literally replaces her with the tree. If there need be a symbol of how ridiculous rurality can be as a concept, then it is this segment's final moment; where a curvy tree lies in erotic anticipation under the sheets of an unmistakably 1970s bed. Wider malevolence is hidden in the landscape in Robert Fuest's *And Soon the Darkness* (1970), an adaptation of a script by Terry Nation and Brian Clemens. Though set in rural France, the film explores one singular stretch of country road, following two young, British cyclists as they venture into the empty fields and meadows. The rural zone becomes increasingly unnerving as one of the girls, who had stayed behind after an argument, disappears; rather like a more leering, lonely take on *The Lady Vanishes* (1938) but with little of that film's joviality.[14] David L. Rattigan argues that the film's 'air of malevolence' is because of its reversal of typical horror topographies, where it 'relies on the openness of the landscape' (2012), a common Folk Horror theme. The film also connects more generally to the genre with the presence of Michele Dotrice, who has taken time out from the mud of *The Blood on Satan's Claw* for warmer, albeit no less dangerous, landscapes. The film uses a similar technique to that of the more anomalous examples of rurality found in the next section, where the countryside is emptied of its people so that even the presence of one person brings forth a surprising sense of dread. All who are seen in the warm glades of the film's landscape are henceforth under suspicion of something terrible.

Also worth mentioning is Robert Altman's underrated thriller *Images* (1972), which stars, and is in-part written by, Crossley's lover, Susannah York, whose then occupation as a writer is incorporated into Altman's script being based on York's novel. In many ways the film plays as a prelude to *The Shout*, where the psychological reality of the film is seemingly skewed simultaneously by mental illness and the rural landscape. Like Anthony's scepticism of Crossley's powers, the main character, Cathryn, is unsure who is real and who is not in the isolated cottage where she is staying. When she takes to violently murdering all who appear (as they effectively bully her), the tension mounts regarding what is actually part of the delusion. The fantasy comes full circle as she begins to witness herself wandering around, as if haunted by a duplicate.[15] She shouts at herself by a waterfall and the image of a distant silhouette is revealed to in fact be Cathryn watching herself leave the house. It is a perfect summation of rurality, where perception of the self is deluded by the perception of the land.

In the 1980s, rurality as a theme became less in vogue for horror cinema in spite of many slasher films often finding their way into American backwaters and countryside enclaves. But a handful of films did use rurality within the British Isles to achieve a sense of the weird and the macabre. Perhaps the most underrated of these are the short films of Digby Rumsey who is most famous for his string of Lord Dunsany adaptations, especially *The Pledge* (1981).[16] Dunsany's position as a 'weird fiction' writer means that Rumsey's adaptations almost always fit into Folk Horror contexts. Stills from *The Pledge* are even regularly mistaken online for being taken from *Witchfinder General*. When I interviewed Rumsey in 2013, many of his creative ideologies fitted Folk Horror perfectly. Asked about his use of landscape in *The Pledge*, he said that, 'I have always used a lot of landscape in my films and I love to position Man as dominated by it – just to remind us all how insignificant we really are against the forces of Nature' (2013): a quintessential lesson and one often learned violently and surreally when such rural endeavours tip reality sideways.[17]

The obsession with gore that peaked in the 1980s may make some of the films in question seem aesthetically at odds with the more traditionally creepy end of rurality, but their core is still one of rural happenings, communities, and the evil which they unleash, especially in films such as John Landis' *An American Werewolf in London* (1981) and Neil Jordan's *The Company of Wolves* (1984)[18] where literal monsters are set loose. In George Pavlou's admittedly flawed *Rawhead Rex* (1986), a violent demon is accidently unleashed in Ireland by a farmer, though the film fails to capture the essence of Clive Barker's original story and its ruralism. In a similar vein, Ken Russell's *The Lair of the White Worm* (1988) also sees the unleashing of a demon of sorts, brought about in Scotland by an archaeologist's meddling. However, as usual with Russell's films, there is a hyper-eroticism to almost everything that happens which distracts from the Gothic ties of Bram Stoker's original story and the ruralness in which it is framed. It is therefore surprising to find the 1980s ending with one of the strongest examples of rurality in film – only used for more comedic, pulp means – in Bruce Robinson's *Withnail & I* (1987); a film that effectively draws out the dangers and strangeness from rural climes by placing two failed coun-ter-culture creative-types on a farm in the Lake District. This is a film where farmers and country folk are to be feared for their strange behaviour and in-timidating dislike of anyone from towns.[19] In a post-*Straw Dogs* world, the com-edy is almost always tinged with a sense of danger; the farmer with an eel in his pants may be amusing but he is certainly not laughing.[20]

Anomalous Rurality

The character of British rurality extends far beyond films normally considered to be examples of Folk Horror; the sheer scale of the role that the landscape, with its many narrative themes, plays upon British arts means that a number of other areas are addressed. When discussing further examples of British Folk Horror cinema, a number of films crop up whose connection seems to be one specifically of rurality rather than a likeness to Folk Horror itself. They may not conform to the Folk Horror Chain, or any sort of narrative schemata for that matter, but their presence requires explaining and is a good way to begin tying up the looser ends of the Folk Horror canon. It is within this explanation that the grounding ideas of rurality also begin to questioned. Sometimes this rurality can be used as a historical and political tool, connecting disparate in-terests together in film, either for academic ideas or for sheer entertainment value; the British and their fond relationship for period dramas is one often haunted and subtly enhanced by the concepts of rurality. The examples here are, however, far from the typical, now sadly *Downton*-ified, images of what the description of 'period' actually means when applied to a drama.

A connection can be made to the period used in some of the unholy trinity's films in order to account for the occurrence of films set in the same era being put alongside the genre. Though at first it may appear odd, Folk Horror often sits films such as *Witchfinder General* and *The Blood on Satan's Claw* alongside other films that look purely at the drama set in a similar period, albeit without the ultra-violence or erotic occultism. Films such as John Gilling's *The Crimson Blade* (1963),[21] Ken Hughes' *Cromwell* (1970),[22] and Kevin Brownlow and Andrew Mollo's *Winstanley* (1975) sit unusually comfortably within Folk Horror in spite of not being anywhere near answering to a general description of horror cine-ma. This tends to be the linking with history, but a history that is aesthetically realised through the guise of rurality. *Winstanley* most clearly defines this, a film depicting the struggles of Gerrard Winstanley and his Diggers as he fights for the right to work the land owned by the gentry. The film takes great pleas-ure in a Ewart-Evans accuracy, in regards to both its agricultural sociology and its general use of landscape. Both Rob Young and Kim Newman look to *Winstanley* in their own respective mappings of old weird Albion, the former describing the film as one 'whose libertarian impulses chimed well with the underground free-festival movement' (2010: 22), the latter suggesting the film has a 'hyper-real, black-and-white earthiness...' (2013: 48). Connecting the two ideas together leads to the conclusion that the era in which the film was made was ripe for a resurgence in back-to-the-land living, though perhaps it would be a little too far to suggest a link between the film and the BBC comedy series that defined such a resurgence, *The Good Life* (1975–78); Margo Leadbetter and Winstanley would perhaps have not made the best of neighbours.[23] A sense of rurality pervades in such films even when the examples are following members of high-office rather than workers on the land and when surrealist tendencies are seemingly curtailed. An example of this can be found in the ludicrous 1973 version of *Sir Gawain and the Green Knight* directed by Stephen Weeks, where rural mythology mixes with a pre-*Monty Python and the Holy Grail*[24] sense of tongue-in-cheek. Other, stronger examples include Clive Donner's *Alfred the Great* (1969) and Joshua Logan's *Camelot* (1967), though the point is stretched.

These films only briefly touch upon rurality as a concept, meaning that they are on the very precipice of Folk Horror analysis rather than bastions of the genuinely strange worlds of rurality or the genre itself. Other, more ethno-graphic films, however, use the concept to begin journeys towards the more weird and the odd. Both Gladwell and Brownlow owe a huge debt to the doc-umentary and propaganda films of Humphrey Jennings, and a number of his shorts can be seen to represent the very beginnings of rurality in its purest essence, albeit serendipitously. The most obvious example is his short film *The Farm* (1938), which follows the everyday workings of a farm of both arable and pastoral character. Though happy to bask in its day-to-day workings, the film has a sense of the eerie which is difficult to pin down. The shadow of the po-tential war hangs heavy over the whole film, but this only accounts for some of its stranger qualities.[25] The very act of filming such farming practices in detail sees a direct link with Gladwell's film, only *Requiem* highlights its own eeriness deliberately. Jennings' footage of a man scything the land is a natural and un-canny one that is both alien and recognisable, and this is before highlighting the odd inclusion of the voice-over which, when describing a willow tree, eerily states 'Doesn't it make you feel that you'd like to hang your heart to a weeping willow and rest in the shade?'.[26] Its influence extends further, seeing a grub-by, visceral equivalent in Andrew Kötting's *This Filthy Earth* (2001)[27] as well as Gladwell's short films.

Other short films by Jennings also have a sense of the eerie, though, like many examples here, it is far more accidental than later, more pure examples of British Folk Horror. His short film about the travelling of a letter from Manchester to Sussex, *Penny Journey* (1938), at first seems to be idyllic but has something rather subtle underneath its pleasantries. The film charts the postcard's journey from the most urban of centres to the typical English country village of Graffam. The card has to travel some way once in Graffam, over the hill and on foot, thanks to the hardworking postman, and all of the way to yet another farm; the journey itself is solitary and unnerving, a feeling only diluted by the film's over-friendly voice-over. The film makes much of the card being from a young boy to his auntie and perhaps this accounts for its strange quality with the card reading: 'Dear Auntie, Thank you very much for your letter. It must be nice to be in the country...'. There's an abruptness to this moment as the film fades at the reading of this letter, as if there's some undercurrent as to its meaning. Jennings is providing the early raw material for what is now commonly referred to as Hauntology, a concept to be explored in Chapter 5, but, essentially, the forced nature of the film leads to the 'ordinary' playing at such an inconspicuous volume as to invite readings of the 'extraordinary'. Further examples of this include Jennings' short post-war film *The Dim Little Island* (1949), which opens with the logo of the Wessex Film Company, consisting of a white chalk horse akin to those found in Wiltshire and Uffingham, and which then goes on to shoot some unintentionally atmospheric shots of the Minsmere RSPB reserve in Suffolk. Again Gladwell's county finds a naturally sinister character in its marshy reed-beds; 'The Shelducks now rear their brood in peace, under the protectful eye of the watcher...'.

Robert Macfarlane has written extensively about this form of unnerving creativity, naming it the English Eerie, and rurality has some part to play in the conception of this idea. Macfarlane writes that the eerie is 'that form of fear that is felt first as unease, then as dread, and which is incited by glimpses and tremors rather than outright attack. Horror specialises in confrontation and aggression; the eerie in intimation and aggregation' (2015). He further elucidates that the form is one that '...explores the English landscape in terms of its anomalies rather than its continuities, that is sceptical of comfortable notions of "dwelling" and "belonging", and of the packagings of the past as "heritage", and that locates itself within a spectred rather than a sceptred isle' (2015). All of these previous films in a sense do this and the eerie tradition builds heavily on rurality so that it can move away from simply agricultural aesthetics and towards more general, ineffable unearthliness.

Building on Jennings' work, Michael Powell would tap into similar ideas in a handful of his films, namely *The Edge of the World* (1937), *A Canterbury Tale* (1944) and *'I Know Where I'm Going!'* (1945) as well as, to a lesser extent, the colour epic, *Gone To Earth* (1950). The two films from the 1940s have a sense that their happenings, which both deal with disrupted journeys or pilgrimages, are based on a mixture of ancient, unseen magic and fate creating physical anomalies, all of course tied in to the rural landscape (and the people who live and work upon it). This magical aspect of the latter three films may also have something to do with the presence of Emeric Pressburger as dual creator with Powell, who seemed to always add a sense of uncanny esoterica to create a very untypical British cinema.[28] Young describes *A Canterbury Tale* as a film that is 'permeated by the persistence of historical memory' (2010: 19) and it is this historical memory that is in essence the blurred nature of the reality of the film; where rural climes can be so dramatically odd when captured in the cinematic lens as to melt a falconer's hawk into an oncoming spitfire with the sheer ease of realism.

By the time these ideas manifested in *Requiem*, the tone had somewhat changed. From the exuberance of these earlier films, there's a melancholic hubris to Gladwell's film as well as others from subsequent years, including Joseph Losey's *The Go-Between* (1971), Philip Trevelyan's *The Moon and the Sledgehammer* (1971), Peter Hall's *Akenfield* (1974), Clive Donner's *Rogue Male* (1977), Peter Greenaway's *Drowning By Numbers* (1988) and Derek Jarman's short film, *A Journey To Avebury* (1971). In Jarman's film, the presence of people is entirely hinted at rather than shown, with typical country signposts – a quintessential symbol of rurality[29] – being just about the only evidence of civilisation outside of Avebury's famous *menhir*. Donner's adaptation of Geoffrey Household's novel for the BBC also presents the zones of rurality as a brief place of refuge because of their emptiness, but one that, thanks to its own insular idiosyncrasies, can turn from helpfully hidden base to a dangerous hindrance relatively quickly.[30]

To end this brief detour into the landscapism of rurality in British films, we bring the idea full circle to the present day before diving back into the pulpier end of Folk Horror cinema. A cycle of post-millennial films use aspects of rurality for more tranquil than horrific means, and are necessary to mention if only to show how the concept of rurality can be used differently, dependent both upon the director in question and era in which they are working. Amongst these landscape films are Gideon Koppel's *sleep furiously* (2008), Patrick Keiller's *Robinson in Ruins* (2010), Andrea Arnold's *Wuthering Heights* (2011), Pat Collins' *Silence* (2012), Grant Gee's *Patience (After Sebald)* (2012), Andrew Kötting's *By Our Selves* (2015) and, most interestingly, Ben Rivers' *Two Years at Sea* (2011). All of the films have that same awe-inspired relationship with the landscape and its practices, somewhat akin to the transcendentalists of the nineteenth century such as Ralph Waldo Emerson and Henri David Thoreau, but *Two Years at Sea* stands out for its brief detours into the fantastical.

Rivers' practice differs slightly from the other filmmakers and their films in that there is still a sense of the surreal and the odd permeating through, though the style is also perceivable in several films by Kötting as well. *Two Years at Sea* mixes documentary with fantasy as it follows the daily life of a hermit (Jake Williams) who lives off the land in the vast mountains of Scotland. He retains a sense of the mystical and it is not too difficult to imagine him in one of Powell's films; perhaps he would make a perfect magical ploy in stopping Wendy Hiller's doomed journey to her rich husband-to-be. The film's most startling sequence shows a caravan floating to the top of a tree which is the most beautifully subtle example of rurality to be discussed visually; where the rural – and perhaps Jake's relationship with the forest in which he is shown to (in part, fictionally) subsist by – blurs reality to the point where such surreal happenings take on a sense of believability. This is hardly a surprising aspect of Rivers' work as, when interviewing him around the time of film's release, he suggested a wealth of more pulp and fantastical influences on his work:

> I guess my earliest introduction into film and how great it was and how immersive and visceral an experience it could be, was through horror movies. I watched a lot between the age of nine and ten. They were pretty key years of watching horror from Universal, especially the two *Frankenstein* films and *The Old Dark House* by James Whale, which are massively important to me. Through to Jacques Tourneur and then coming through to my childhood around that time when people like John Carpenter and Sam Raimi were about. (2010)

Though the sense of horror is rarely present in Rivers' short or feature-making practice, the trace of its influence, especially when discussing films that are essential to Folk Horror, can be seen to be represented by the crossover of rurality;[31] the uncanny shifting of perception that drags reality along with it through sheer aesthetic weight, thereby creating a subtly haunting work where the magical enters into a pure believability. Though his work often raises questions surrounding the gap between documentary and fiction, Rivers' filmography tends to lean towards rurality more than anything else, accounting for any amount of potential gap or grey area between the states of play.[32] It is fitting that, alongside other documentary filmmakers such as Robert Flaherty, he cites Humphrey Jennings as one of the key examples where 'fiction and documentary become intertwined' (2012: 25), as Andrèa Picard puts it. The spectre of Jennings still haunts the art-house end of rurality even to this day; through idyllic rural vistas concealing an endless array of odd happenings on the very periphery of perception.

Global Ruralities

One common theme has so far been present within all of the examples considered under the banner of Folk Horror; with one or two exceptions, all have been produced in the British Isles. It is common in discussions of the genre for the British iteration to dominate, perhaps because their trends are neater to canonise and appear, at first, to be more linear. If the chapters of this book show one thing, it is that such linearity is a misconception and plenty of film and television have been sprouting on the periphery for quite some time. Aside from the generalisation hinting at a potential tunnel-vision, it also ignores the rich trove of Folk Horror from other cultures. This is a baffling trend in that, arguably, many of the themes and ideas that are now taken for granted as part of Folk Horror's mechanisms first occurred in much earlier cinematic examples made outside of Britain. Paciorek mentions this when discussing the particular flowering of counter-culture Folk Horror in Britain: 'Whilst many of the strongest examples of Folk Horror were created in Britain, both in those decades and now, it does to me still seem too rigid' (2015: 9).

The logic being that, taken from its base assumption in regards to its signifying title, Folk Horror can arguably manifest anywhere and within any culture as long as there are 'folk' to spread it around; every country has *some* relationship with its landscape, with its own folklore, its customs, superstitions and rurality. Even the Folk Horror Chain has the potential to apply to any geographical space on the globe provided that there is a landscape engulfing enough in its isolation to skew the morality of the small communities who inhabit it. It is, therefore, fitting to discuss rurality as a concept on a wider global scale, partly because it widens the field of interest towards how Folk Horror essentially works, but also because so many examples from all around the world tap into their own form of rurality; where folklore, history, agricultural customs and landscape conspire to tip reality sideways. This results in some of the most effective and horrific examples that can fit under the genre's banner.

Folk Horror can be detected in some of the earliest cinematic forms there are, specifically in a wave of largely Scandinavian and German silent cinema in the early 1920s. Films such as Carl T. Dreyer's *Leaves from Satan's Book* (1920), Paul

Wegener's *The Golem* (1920), Victor Sjöström's *The Phantom Carriage* (1921) and F.W. Murnau's *Nosferatu* (1922), all play upon supernatural elements derived from varying folklore in order to build an uncanny sense of horror. The folklore may often slip into the fantastical but this is often juxtaposed with the increased emphasis on other, more grounded elements such as the journey in *The Phantom Carriage* and *Nosferatu*, or the ethnographic window-dressings of *The Golem*. One film, however, stands out from this era's film-making for its sheer macabre audacity, its chilling pushing of the boundaries of the era's moral acceptability, and its retaining of the power to convince of its authenticity even in today's digital landscape, deserving the title of being the first fully-formed example of Folk Horror cinema: the film is Benjamin Christensen's *Häxan: Witchcraft through the Ages* (1922).

Christensen's film manages to predict the sort of aesthetic ploys that post-millennial Hauntology would use for equally horrific and comedic effects, mixing the form of a documentary with fictionalised recreations. *Häxan* charts the evolution of paganism into the witchcraft of the Middle Ages in four episodic parts, taking great delight in drawing the links between rural ways of life and recreations of occult practices while maintaining an unusual level of authenticity. Perhaps the film's age creates this sense of genuine documentation, but it is still far removed from the era in which it is portraying, which can only lead to the conclusion that the director was a pioneering voice. Several scenes of the occult rituals still push the boundaries of horrific content even today, if only because of the malevolent glee with which they are recreated. Kevin Brownlow discusses this horrific content, writing in 1968 that, 'Some scenes are unbearable; fifty years has not dulled their impact. When released, the film shocked and amazed everyone who saw it' (1968: 587). Brownlow was fittingly writing in the same year that the film was re-released in an edit that included a new voice-over by writer William Burroughs, and a jazz score by Daniel Humair; if anything, they make the film feel even more woozy and sickly. Christensen's role in the film, playing The Devil himself, may also have something to do with its joy in the macabre, being an early example of the 'filmmaking as party' atmosphere honed later by the likes of Andy Warhol, Paul Morrissey and Derek Jarman.

Christensen is clearly aware of the power of rurality, and effectively creates horror by harnessing this power to skew the most supposedly truthful of forms, the audio-visual documentary. Perhaps this relationship is in fact reversed in terms of the director's ideology but the starting point in either sense is the effect of rurality. Most interesting is how the film pre-empts the psychologising of more esoteric matters by tying in such practices of witchcraft with mental health. The final segment, which is in itself eerie for its sanatoria melancholy, makes the startling comparison between mentally ill women of the early twentieth century and the persecution of women during the Middle Ages. Though this in some ways simplifies the belief system of the latter, it predicts the more psychological strain that horror would adapt many years hence.[33] The film's final episode is the sort of structural motif that Alfred Hitchcock would use in *Psycho* (1960) or Jonathan Miller would reverse in *Whistle And I'll Come To You*. *Häxan* is, therefore, a fitting starting point for the genre as it touches upon almost all potential strands with which it would later explore; landscape and rurality, occultism and witchcraft, psychology and parapsychology, documentary and fiction. There are few films to be discussed within these pages that manage to cover so many areas and in such overwhelming detail. Christensen's film largely follows rural communities in their recreations of the occult, tying the two together. Films such as Murnau's *Faust* (1926) and Dreyer's *Vampyr* (1932) would also explore similar terrain aesthetically, but would ultimately fail to match Christensen's sense of folkloric authenticity; where the horror of the past is not just occultism, the supernatural or rural furnishings, but our very own lack of understanding. It is fitting then that such a lack can now be perceived today in the film's latter, psychologised section. The past is always a darker, less enlightened place.

Yet the past itself also holds two key aspects for examples of rurality in world cinema; the excuse to look at communities who rely on both the landscape and a strong sense of belief, and the potential to fall into what may be called cinematic Magic Realism. This is perhaps more apt a description for the actual effects of rurality than its overall mechanics. In world cinema examples, the diegesis of the films is not necessarily skewed or surreal but quietly undermined, to the point where something uncanny is detected but not directly perceived until time has been spent within the cinematic vision of the film. This is because the supernatural and magical are treated as ordinary as farming or fishing. Unlike in British cinema, where a fantastical element in the narrative will almost always lead the film down pulpier territory, world cinema treats these elements in most poetically normal of ways; occurring in high end art-house cinema rather than the purely exploitation cinema of the Anglo-American variety.

Occultism plays some part in this but the fantastical of this type never ventures into the enjoyably camp territory of Dennis Wheatley and the like. Ingmar Bergman is a good example of this and, though we may more typically associate the director with art-house cinema, many of his films are imbued with elements of rurality and Folk Horror as a whole. Discounting the very isolation that his later working practice on the Gotland island of Fårö would naturally induce in a wide variety of his films, there are still many examples that fit comfortably into Folk Horror. The medieval paring of *The Seventh Seal* (1957) and *The Virgin Spring* (1960) display varying elements of Folk Horror, though the latter is certainly more relevant when looking at rurality. The former, famous for its scenes of a medieval knight (Max von Sydow) playing a continual game of chess with Death (Bengt Ekerot), is seared into the general nexus of cinematic images, but it is also a quintessential Folk Horror image in its *mise-en-scène* and in its conceptual phantasmagoria (as is the film's final, eerie scenes of the Dance of Death). Writing on its period setting, Peter Cowie suggests it to be a move that attempts to hide the allegoric potential of the film 'so that the figures can become more clearly defined, and so that their symbolic virtues and demerits can be stressed without bathos' (1966: 140). This ignores other facets provided by such a setting; the burgeoning isolation that its lack of swift transport provides, the natural presence of superstition and magic, and the more visceral aesthetics in regard to the rural its inhabitants.

Bergman's only genuine horror film, *Hour of The Wolf* (1968), is also explicitly Folk Horror with its isolated island, its artist tortured by literal demons, and its raw dream sequences. As Maria Bergom-Larsson writes of Bergman's filmmaking, 'Outer violence threatens from the outer world, and from within there is a menace of the "forces," "memories and ghosts," maybe destructive forces from the characters' own past, the forces which seized control completely in *Hour of the Wolf* (1978: 84). Bergom-Larsson could equally be describing any number of plays by Nigel Kneale, especially *The Stone Tape*, or any number of M.R. James stories and adaptations which function largely on the same premise (but instead with the window-dressings of middle-class England as their zone of horror). This link is especially clear as she later writes that the supernatural presences, those which come from inside, effectively triumph, writing that, 'In *Hour of the Wolf* the inner forces win the day' (1978: 116). 'It's in the computer!' is replaced more accurately with 'It's in the ID!' or perhaps vice-versa depending upon one's preference.[34]

The Virgin Spring is, however, a more relevant example to the topic of rurality than *Hour of the Wolf*, and concerns an affluent, land-owning couple (Max von Sydow and Birgitta Valberg) and the fate of their spoiled daughter (Birgitta Pettersson) who, on being sent to deliver candles, is savagely raped and killed by local goat herders. The fourteenth-century setting instantly gives it the traditional aesthetic of Folk Horror, but it is the narrative that conveys most of the genre's usual traits. Apart from the sheer level of violence, arguably again caused by the Folk Horror Chain, there is a sense of paganism as well, due to the murdered girl's servant (Gunnel Lindblom) having supposedly cast a curse on her before she left. With the film's violence being raw and primal, especially that enacted by her parents in their later revenge, the rurality comes from such a hyper-violence being contained within the aesthetics of chiaroscuro, art-house ideals and representations of rural communities. The film can be seen as a precursor to *Straw Dogs*, with its isolation manifesting in a horrifically physical form of misogyny; one that Wes Craven would take up with even more disturbing gusto in his 1972 riff on the film, *The Last House on the Left*. The key difference between the films, however, is that Bergman frames the violence as part of a rural social system – a reaction to a lack of moral education and the sheer absence of consistent sociological contact – whereas Craven 'uses it forcefully to make the point that violence degrades everyone involved, victim and victimiser, just and unjust' (Newman, 1988: 78).

Bergman's differing style and treatment of more esoteric material would find a part-heir in the Russian director, Andrei Tarkovsky. Though Tarkovsky's films are some of most serious and complex pieces of cinema produced in the twentieth century, a number contain elements of a supernatural rurality that are shot with just as much exactitude and poetry as his other thematic interests. This is most overt in his three-hour epic *Andrei Rublev* (1966); a film that follows the life of the fifteenth-century Russian iconographic painter, played by Anatoliy Solonitsyn. The setting already presents the potential for certain forms of rurality to manifest and this potential is fully realised when a pagan ceremony is held by a river, the naked participants brandishing their fire-lit torches before fleeing from the army of the Grand Duke. One pagan women even tries to seduce the devout artist who is watching from a nearby bush; an ancestor of 'The Landlord's Daughter' perhaps. Though the comparison is crass, the spiritual essence of Summerisle's community is effectively rendered again but with the cold, Soviet reality of theology rather than Hardy's counter-culture fun-in-the-sun.

Occultism and sexuality also come into play in Tarkovsky's final film, the heavily Bergman-influenced *The Sacrifice* (1986). In order to prevent a nuclear holocaust from happening (after it has already happened in some form of dream-time), a retired actor (Erland Josephson) must make a sacrifice to a local women (Guðrún Gísladóttir) who is a supposed witch and can prevent the atrocity; the film was even initially scripted under the original title of *The Witch*. With

Tarkovsky's penchant for levitation, and with several occult-tinged scenes involving the witch, the film balances its heavy thematic content with a sense of magical, rural custom. Nairman Skakov writes of the witch's pivotal role in the film: 'The beginning of the end commences while the lone woman is present on the screen: the "witch" is the herald of the nuclear apocalypse, and at the same time its future redeemer. Her ambivalent nature is in keeping with the self-contradictory essence of the film, formed of divergences and digressions' (2012: 206). For a film of such philosophical weight, to put such emphasis on a potentially esoteric power is refreshing, and the rurality that is created has the most extreme of conclusions; the potential for a nuclear holocaust. It is doubly fitting that such scenarios are also filmed on Gotland and Fårö, Bergman's home and the same setting of *Hour of the Wolf* as well as many of his other films.

The Magic Realism of the past that Bergman and Tarkovsky honed, found its way into a wide variety of films from across the globe. Rurality would be pushed to its surreal limits in films such as Erik Blomberg's *The White Reindeer* (1952), Konstantin Ershov and Georgiy Kropachyov's *Viy* (1967), Frantisek Vlácil's *Marketa Lazarová* (1967), Otakar Vávra's *Witchhammer* (1970), Andrzej Zulawski's *The Devil* (1972) and Juraj Herz's *Morgiana* (1972), all of which showcase varied and haphazard relationships with the magical, the rural and the supernatural. These films mix their respective country's historicism with fears of many isolated, magical communities; sometimes playing their drama intensely straight (as in *Marketa Lazarová*) or for more pulp, and even comedic, purposes (as in *Viy*). The fact that three of these films were made in Czechoslovakia, hints at some sort of Magical Realist movement forming in the country's cinema during the counter-culture era. *Morgiana* in particular may seem like an odd inclusion, with its bourgeois household drama being far from the sort of rurality discussed earlier, but its tale of a jealous, murderous sister presents a strange coastal zone that appears to enhance the violent capacity of the main character; another variation of rurality's potential. The most astonishing example of this hyper-floral, Czechoslovakian rurality comes not in *Morgiana*, but in Jaromil Jireš' 1970 film, *Valerie and Her Week Of Wonders*, where a mixture of sexuality and taboo diffuses through a psychotropic flavouring of rural dreamscape.

The film presents the viewer with the sort of florid detail that requires a consistent and in-depth psychoanalysis as it follows the life of thirteen-year-old Valerie (Jaroslava Schallerová) whose reality falls heavily into dark, fairy-tale dreams with the coming of her first period. *Valerie*'s side-ways tipping of reality is perhaps unique in the sense that it is triggered by two particular aspects clashing together; these being a rural isolation (and the strict morality that comes with it) facing up to a sexual awakening precipitated through a biological change. In typical Folk Horror fashion, this conflict can be attributed to an atmosphere of conservatism created by an isolated theology that fights against the forces of such awakenings. Whereas a character like Sgt. Howie is forced to confront such a dilemma and conquers it (though in reality loses his humanity very literally by doing so), Valerie embraces it at all costs and travels through the sexual looking-glass into a world of demons, rituals, ceremonies and eroticism.

Paciorek has suggested that *Valerie* is one of a number of films that 'may not strictly be Folk Horror, perhaps, but which certainly graze in a nearby field' (2015: 12) but its thematic core is strikingly similar to several key themes at the heart of the more popular end of British Folk Horror cinema. By using eroticism in such a casual way, it bypasses the usual negativity that comes as baggage within the British iterations (perhaps almost as a punishment for a confident, anti-patriarchal sexual identity in women) and becomes more optimistic. The lack of nihilism in the film is the most likely reason for it to be discounted as a pure example of the genre, but its sense of erotic rurality becomes refreshing in comparison, even if the symbolism of the film (Valerie having her mother's earrings stolen by a young man) suggests that her own identity is still in the hands of a male character. The film's sense of innocence may be derived from its main character and her openness to the harsh world in which she finds herself in, but this is not to say that it fails to enter darker territory derived from such a power-play of repression. As Peter Hames notes, 'The film is clearly most concerned with Valerie's recognition that her immediate family and friends are sexual beings (and that this sexuality may also be alternative and ambiguous) but also the masking of this sexuality by the repressive structures of religion and authority' (2005: 11).

Valerie's sexual awakening puts her at the mercy of the typical figures of power; for example, the local priest, who attempts and fails to seduce her before trying and failing to burn her as a witch (from which she escapes by the use of magic pearls). If there were ever a character who fitted Lord Summerisle's damning description of the puritanical theologian – 'They do not lie awake in the dark and weep for their sins. They do not make me sick discussing their duty to God' – then the guilty hypocrite of the film, Father Gracián (Jan Klusák) is a perfect embodiment. Though the film attacks patriarchal constructs in their rural guise – through the surreal reoccurrence of the Weasel character, Tchor-konstábl (played by Jirí Prýmek) morphing between sexual predator, vampire, Bergman-esque death figure and daemon – the satirical nature of the Gracián character is the film's most palpable attack due to his strict conformity to a pre-rurality world and its functions. Hames has written of this in regards to its criticism of organised religion, whereby such a force is 'shown as repressive and hypocritical, and is expressly linked to the vampiric manifestations of Valerie's elders' (2005: 9). In terms of rurality, the part-shift from purely rural accoutrements to sexuality (primarily distorting the perception of reality) can account for this difference in tone to the other films mentioned. The ties between *Valerie* and *The Wicker Man* are, therefore, abundantly clear on a number of key thematic levels, notwithstanding liberalism and sexuality triumphing here without the need for violence.[35]

With elements of the fantastical being presented so earnestly in a number of films, it could be suggested that the essence of rurality has been pushed too far from its initial core of ethnographic practices built around a landscape. When the supernatural rears its head in the context of Folk Horror, it almost always distracts from the process that initially lead up to it; the ritual is always forgotten soon after as the end goal is often more aesthetically exciting. In reverse of this and back into the purer realms of world rurality, another cinematic trend can be seen to highlight a harsh and stark reaction to a landscape which results in the tipping of reality but within a symbolically psychological realm. The movement is Australian, though not necessarily uniquely produced by Australian directors, and may be referred to generally as Australian Outback cinema; films that 'frequently display a strong sense of place in which the landscape is crucial to the plot...' (Paciorek, 2015: 10). This also touches upon the recent trend in Ozploitation cinema labelling. These films are an arid variation on the typical rural relationships discerned in the previous section, only the pressure is higher because of the environment's hostility; an eerie meadow or copse is replaced by endless sand, dangerous wildlife and craggy rocks.

Two films from 1971 epitomise Australian Outback cinema, though perhaps their essentially differing takes on the plains suggests that the link between films in the movement is more overtly aesthetic rather than thematic. The two films are Nicolas Roeg's *Walkabout* and Ted Kotcheff's *Wake in Fright*. The defined character of the films perhaps leaves their inclusion open to criticism as their own cinematic history is sufficiently assumed to not need the support of another genre tie. Yet the pair reflect that dual potential character of Folk Horror's happenings; the mystically surreal mixing headily with the grittily social. *Walkabout* represents the former within this argument though does effectively use both elements to create its affective journey. A pair of school children (Jenny Agutter and Luc Roeg) are left to wander the dusty outback only to find another child (David Gulpilil) from a local Aboriginal group who is on 'walkabout'; a ritualistic separation from his family in order to teach him to fend for himself. The mysticism comes from the spiritual potential that this boy's ritual life has to say about the privileged white children who are themselves abandoned after their father commits suicide. *Walkabout* actually turns rurality on its head by highlighting the spiritually skewed character of the inner-city and its inhabitants whilst simultaneously showing such a character to be responsible for the large scale destruction of the world around; where its hypocrisies and fallacies are gradually hidden by the wiping out of all other narratives in the regional topography. This point is argued brilliantly by Gregory Stephens, who writes: 'The visual narrative of *Walkabout* suggests that confinement is a precondition to a sort of delusional acceptance of the illogic of modernized urban societies, which promise freedom but enforce a deforming conformity' (2009).

The opposite is the case in *Wake in Fright*, which arguably shows the hyper-extension of inner-city-type habits, such as gambling and alcoholism, to be heightened to an excruciating degree when in a more isolated realm. Roger Ebert writes of the film that, 'It comes billed as a "horror film" and contains a great deal of horror, but all of the horror is human and brutally realistic' (2012). Kotcheff's film is the other side of Roeg's coin in that the violence, and even the alcohol addiction, is born of human boredom rather than necessity. The film is most famous for its sequence of kangaroo hunting; a wild, disturbing selection of moments where the film's characters, who are heavily intoxicated, reach a level of animism that explicitly links the killing of other forms with a loss of identity. The presence of a post-*Cul-De-Sac* Donald Pleasence, yet again playing a character mixing mania with violence, makes this point hit home even more powerfully. Even though Roeg's film also featured the killing of animals by the characters, the difference between the films is in their context, as the rurality in Roeg's film is diluted by its spirituality. *Wake in Fright*, on the other hand, positively basks in the depravity of rural life until the manic nature of the film blurs into a dusty, hedonistic trip of glaring sun and immeasurable brutality.

The oddness present in these films can be found in a number of other examples of Australian Outback Cinema, including Colin Eggleston's *Long Weekend* (1978), Richard Franklin's *Road Games* (1981), Ann Turner's *Celia* (1989), Greg McLean's *Wolf Creek* (2005) and Jamie Banks' remake of *Long Weekend* (2008). One thing that connects all of these films is their predilection for finding their rurality within the modern day, where it is the butting up of traditional, rural lives with an encroaching modernity (whether in the form of cars and roads, colonials or gambling dens) that sparks the chaos. Newman even likens *Long Weekend* in particular to M.R. James (1988: 90). The colonial aspect is especially poignant in that the concept often haunts these films rather than being something that is directly addressed. The colonial morality is in itself an im-peachment which is again a reversal of Folk Horror's traditional framework of isolated places developing a skewed form of morality. Here, it appears to be imported instead and then brewed (quite literally in some cases) through being cut-off from general society. Yet, with these films all explicitly commenting upon the era in which they are made, it may be surprising to find that the most startling of Australian Outback films is a period drama without violence, mon-sters, or even anything overtly surreal.

Peter Weir's *Picnic at Hanging Rock* (1975) has an intriguing relationship to Folk Horror in that there is a mystery surrounding its very own narrative ambi-guity, according to Newman, 'in which the Australian never-never also takes on a mystic life of its own' (ibid.). Though often purported to be based on a true story, this has neither been confirmed nor denied by the novel's writer, Joan Lindsay, and so an air of secrecy hangs rather aptly over the film and its subsequent interpretations. Unlike the other Australian Outback films, *Picnic* presents an almost prairie-like vision of the landscape because of its period, marking out its narrative as an oneiric parable. A narrative breakdown follows.

Picnic at Hanging Rock – Valentine's Day, 1900. The girls at Appleyard College, Victoria, are planning a local trip with some of their teachers to a site known as Hanging Rock. They organise and venture out on the trip, eating at the rock's shady base. Afterwards, some of the girls begin to climb the rock to make some studies of its formations. Before attempting to leave, several of the party notice that their watches stopped working at midday. After being overcome by the heat at the top of the rock, sever-al of the girls, including Marion (Jane Vallis), Irma (Karen Robson) and Miranda (Anne-Louise Lambert), appear to become entranced and walk into a chasm in the rock. Their friend, Edith (Christine Schuler), sees this and flees in terror back to the camp. The party return to the school hav-ing been unable to find the missing girls. A police search also fails to find either the pupils or their missing teacher, Miss McCraw (Vivean Gray), who was watching the girls on their climb. An Englishman, Michael (Dominic Guard), who saw the girls on the day at the rock, is questioned by police before he himself becomes obsessed and haunted by attempts to find them. Michael's valet, Albert (John Jarratt), eventually finds him col-lapsed as he spent the night on the rock searching. He is clutching a piece of lace dress from one of the girls. Later on, Irma is found but with no recollection as to what happened on the rock. Michael quickly becomes friends with her so as to find out the truth but his pressure scares her away. She is bullied by the other pupils who want to know what happened and is forced to move away. Meanwhile, the school's headmistress, Mrs. Appleyard (Rachael Roberts) is revealed to be in a power-play with one of the girls, Sara (Margaret Nelson), who wanted but failed to go to the rock. She is later found dead in an apparent suicide though it is suggested that Appleyard killed her. It is revealed that Sara was Albert's long lost sister. Appleyard is herself later found dead at the foot of Hanging Rock with the film revealing that the mystery of the girls, their disappearance and the other strangely connected happenings went unresolved.

The film's dreamy aesthetics channel the sense of the unexplained that was in part present in Roeg's film, but it achieves it through a much more subtle editing style. The film's narrative essentially sketches around something unnamed and, through this, creates a great sense of conspiratorial unease. It could be argued that Folk Horror traditions are themselves being subverted, with a small group of urban dwellers being drawn into some otherworldly place whose access point is in the isolated rural terrain. *Picnic* takes pains to never imply that something explicitly bad happened to the girls that disappeared but instead makes them seem lucky compared to the fate of those left behind to live under the strict regime and inquisition of the school. As Megan Abbott writes about the film's various ambiguities:

> At the same time, viewers whose imaginative world veers closer to Gothic terrors, supernatural wonder, divine mysticism, or the imperialist unconscious are all given clues to ultimately support their fantasies that the girls have been, alternately, raped and murdered, abducted by aliens, whisked away by the 'Aboriginal Other' à la colonial melodrama, or been swept up in a holy rapture. But it's a tease. (2014)

Though its narrative journey may appear on its surface to fit Folk Horror perfectly (a strange, potentially supernatural happening befalling urbanites when they venture into the rural), the sense that the characters have escaped a difficult situation through magical forces can't help but make the film seem unusually optimistic in a similar vein to *Valerie*. Whereas the character of Valerie would face negative forces in her exploration of sexuality and eventually conquer them, the girls here are an enigma whose positive essence is achieved by showing how totalitarian the world they left behind is. Perhaps where they went to wasn't better in the end but, in the schema of the film, it is still preferable. It's the same process that Roeg's characters undergo, though this is a fugue on typical Folk Horror narratives and not their norm; journeys usually converge upon enclaves that entrap visiting characters within their twisted morality rather than providing an escape from such situations.

More typical forms of this relationship can be found in the horror cinema of Japan which often employs the supernatural, and specifically ghosts, within such contexts. The natural inclusion of folklore and belief within their cinema, even outside of horror, shows a more open attitude to the paranormal elements that occur in Anglo-American traditions, but are usually reserved for genre films and little else. Japan's real coming-of-age for their esoteric brand of cinema came in the 1960s, and most films relevant to Folk Horror were produced in this period. Themes do arise in earlier examples – such as the ghosts in Kenji Mizoguchi's *Ugetsu Monogatari* (1953) and in Nobou Nakagawa's *Mansion of the Ghost Cat* (1958) – but their treatment is one of surprising realism and not of the character with which later examples would endow their supernatural rurality; that of a primal horror and latent eroticism. In 1964, two films were produced that effectively shifted the sense of horror into both the supernatural and the rural, combining the two elements into fully-formed examples of rurality: Masaki Kobayashi's *Kwaidan* and Kaneto Shindô's *Onibaba*.

Kobayashi's *Kwaidan* is one of the most startlingly realised ghost stories in any supernatural cinematic canon, and follows four separate narratives in the portmanteau style adapted from the writing of Lafcadio Hearn. The tales have some links to M.R. James, with their penchant for haunted objects especially, as well as more typical Jamesian tropes such as hair, musicality, curiosity and a slow release of dread. If proof were needed, Newman's description of the Japanese ghost story as a form could be equally describing James' own practice, though both retain more terror than is suggested: 'The traditional Japanese ghost story is melancholy rather than terrifying, and inherently conservative... Usually, the ghosts' victims are murderers and – worse – restless, dissatisfied with tradition, possessed by a crafty urge to better themselves at the expense of honour' (1988: 415). *Kwaidan*'s narrative also relies on that same sense of rurality, where isolated rural groups and even couples are at the mercy of their own superstition (or, more accurately, their lack of hindrance towards it). Even though Kobayashi's realisation is one of a Corman-like falsity – all hyper-active designs, colourful skies full of eyes reminiscent of Salvador Dali – it still retains the impression that the viewer is witnessing the typical, rural reality of a period Japan being distorted by some supernatural calamity.

Onibaba takes a different pathway and opts for a high-contrast sense of stark and brutal drama, as it follows a pair of a women (Nobuko Otowa and Jitsuko

Yoshimura) living in the reed-beds who secretly kill stray samurai warriors in order to sell their equipment to a local dealer. Though the film does have some sense of the supernatural – in the presence of a mysterious warrior wearing what turns out to be a cursed and immovable mask – the film is a more traditional example of rurality in that the rural environment is shown explicitly to bring out the most malevolent of aspects in the characters (who use it for their livelihood). As Doug Cummings argues, 'Its widescreen vision of pampas grass endlessly waving in the breeze seductively coveys natural undulating motions and whispering sounds, but beneath its beauty lies savagery, supernatural terror, and death' (2007: 4). Cummings is articulating a very basic Folk Horror premise, one touched upon when analysing *Witchfinder General*; that the rural can create a subtle but eventually disturbing contrast to violent narratives. Shindô emphasises the reed-bed of the film's setting, visually and aurally, highlighting how his characters interact with it as it becomes a more sentient force. When the young daughter begins to have a secret, sexual relationship with a recently returned warrior friend of her missing husband, each rendezvous necessitates an unnerving night-time journey through the reeds. When her mother-in-law realises, she dons the strange mask and pretends to be a demon. Even when this presence is obviously not supernatural to the viewer, the moments still have a horrific quality about them because of the rural setting and the subverting of the reality aesthetically that Shindô indulges in.

Shindô would make another horror film four years later in the form of *Kuroneko* (1968). The film has a similar structure in that it follows two isolated women again before they are raped and killed by a rampaging group of fighters. The building of narratives on *yurei* mythology, which often involves wronged women coming back to enact revenge, is, in many ways, crucial to Japanese horror and has obvious Folk Horror potential as well. This time, Shindô opts to go all out for a supernatural tone that sees the women reincarnated as powerful cat-demons who prey upon wandering samurai. The film plays like a Magic Realist take on the narrative of *The Virgin Spring*, but with the added eeriness of a ghostly rural vista. *Kuroneko* combines two separate elements of Folk Horror rurality to create its horror; the initial gritty violence that sparks the narrative (of a similar vein to the likes of *Straw Dogs* and other violently rural films) and the uncanny consequences of that violence (that the film spends most of its time dealing with) through the prism of a folk tale. Cummings notes that the former aspect is heightened largely to concentrate the rest of the film on the secondary paranormal revenge saga, where the director 'intensifies the violence with a stoic representation and selective ellipses that highlights need for response and establishes the desire for revenge that simmers throughout the picture' (2009: 5). Morality may be skewed in the film, but so is reality itself, as seen in the ghost-house in which the demons reside and take their lone samurais in order to seduce and later kill them. Some parallel elements can be perceived in Japanese horror films such as Hiroshi Teshigahara's *Woman in the Dunes* (1964), Nobuhiko Ôbayashi's *House* (1977), Hideo Nakata's *Ringu* (1999) and Takashi Shimizu's *Ju-on* (2002), but there's a modernity to these films that perhaps undermines their occasional foray into the workings of Folk Horror (if having any such element at all).

Unlike Japanese rurality, which verges on spiritual levity, American rurality is often as pure as its Anglo-Saxon cousin when in the cinematic form. Rurality has played such a huge role in the country's horror cinema that separating the examples relevant to Folk Horror from its general horror cinema is a difficult task. This is a horror cinema that is already fragmented by endless sub-genre identification, and many films have used elements of rurality to induce a heady and sometimes extreme form of the horrific while not being even vaguely related to Folk Horror. In any number of films from the slasher sub-genre, for example, an essence of rurality can be traced. Mikel J. Koven even goes so far as to connect the genre with the mechanisms of urban folk-lore production:

> The slasher film, like the urban legends that these films so closely resemble, may be seen to share one final similarity, that of *effect*... These may seem banal, but for folklorists specifically and cultural scholars more generally, these narratives can be seen as moral templates to be used as behavioural surveys of contemporary adolescent mores, that is, social scripts. (2008: 131)

Whether a film such as Sean S. Cunningham's *Friday the 13th* (1980), or even a proto-slasher like Mario Bava's *A Bay of Blood* (1971), actually fit within the Folk Horror genre – films which both conform in some way to the causations of the Folk Horror Chain as well – is a murky, debatable area, as is the place of many films in this section. But a number of key films from the previously mentioned Backwoods Horror trend, as well as several from what is commonly called the Southern Gothic genre, can be seen to use aspects of rurality to create a paral-lel vision to Folk Horror that is at the least a play on its narrative ploys.

A strong starting point is Charles Laughton's adaptation of Davis Grubb's novel *The Night of the Hunter* (1955). The film follows a recently released convict who goes downriver in search of a jailed (and later executed) bank robber's mon-ey, which he has secretly bestowed upon his two children. The convict, known as Preacher (Robert Mitchum), is a highly religious but sadistic misogynist responsible for a string of inheritance murders. He is most famous for having the words 'Love' and 'Hate' tattooed upon the fingers of each hand, but he is also the perfect example of a character whose isolation has twisted his own beliefs and morality into something violent. The film heightens this further by including fairytale elements and aesthetics, most obviously in its riverboat sequence, which features an array of animals and dream-images as the children escape from the close clutches of Preacher. Terrence Rafferty calls the scene the film's 'centrepiece' where 'you feel as if you were inside their heads, dreaming a child's dreams, part blind terror and part sweet hope' (2010: 7). For what is a *noir* film, to have a folkloric dreamscape as its centrepiece is daring but also shows how fundamentally different the film is from its peers. The fact that the community presented is also highly religious (critiqued heavily in the film by Laughton, who ties their beliefs with their easy delusion in regards to Preacher's manipulations), connects overt, perhaps even dangerous, belief systems with rural communities.

This branch of Southern Gothic is short lived in that most examples of the genre tend to lack the fantastical elements of *The Night of the Hunter*. Robert Mulligan's *The Other* (1972) is a rare similar example as it sees a young boy on a farm in rural Connecticut haunted by his dead twin. Instead, however, it is better to turn to an equally visceral example of the proto-slasher sub-genre, in order to find an extreme form of twisted rurality. Tobe Hooper's *The Texas Chainsaw Massacre* (1974) is, in many ways, *sui generis*. Its main ploy is the sort of monster building nightmare that Universal used to kick-start the horror genre in the 1930s, but it also mixes documentary realist techniques and political comment into a vital, if queasy, mix. *Texas* is, by any standards of the criteria set out in this book, a fully formed example of Folk Horror. Hooper based the narrative on the second-hand tellings he had encountered surrounding the notorious serial killer Ed Gein; an oft-repeated facet of the film in its analysis but one that is quintessentially folkloric. The overall narrative, of a group of teenagers stumbling upon a rural enclave occupied by violent (albeit business savvy) cannibals, follows the Folk Horror Chain note for note. The rural Texas isolation has allowed a potentially inbred clan to evolve, whereby the idea of brutally killing people (and selling them at roadside diners as food) is perfectly acceptable. *Texas* is Southern Gothic without hope, nihilistic in the same way that *Witchfinder General* was. Newman points out an ironic element that adds to this macabre character: 'In Texas, a householder is legally entitled to shoot anyone who trespasses on his property, so Leatherface's murder spree barely breaks the law' (1988: 75). In fact, the film's antagonist, Leatherface (Gunnar Hansen), is himself a naive equivalent of the John Stearne character from *Witchfinder*, with the family's father figure comparable to Hopkins himself in their shared enjoyment of small-scale sadistic power, all arguably committed within lawful boundaries.

These sorts of relationships can be found in a number of American Backwoods horror including Wes Craven's *The Last House on the Left* and *The Hills Have Eyes* (1977), and, most effectively, in John Boorman's *Deliverance* (1972), an intensely powerful watch that mimics Gladwell's reactionary attacks on encroaching modernity and rural retaliation (albeit before Gladwell had made his film). Whereas the viewer in *Requiem for a Village* is generally unsure as to what perspective the film is from (aside from the director's), Boorman situates the viewer very much *as* the townie interloper, on the side of the four country weekenders as they go deep into the forestland surrounding the Cahulawassee River. Just like in Gladwell's film, the collision induces violence (and, infamously, sexual violence), which builds a tension typical of films using rurality as a concept. Stephen Farber wrote on the film's release for the New York Times that it was a simultaneous deflation of both rural mythmaking and machismo:

> Along with deflating myths about nature and primitive life, the film is a devastating critique of machismo. Like Sam Peckinpah's *Straw Dogs*, *Deliverance* focuses on a ritualized battle for survival, a primal masculine adventure. The heroes of both movies are decent, rather fastidious men forced to confront the violence in nature and in themselves. (1972)

Though the dangers of the film range from psychopathic hillbillies to that of a raging river, the reality becomes increasingly perturbing, especially as it's clear that the area is full of people over the ridge, currently turning the river into a commercial lake. Are they simply ignoring the violence going on in the woods below or are they, in fact, causing it? Rurality induces a reading of the violence being a strangely defensive act and symbolic of what the urban dwellers are potentially doing to the land that they are 'developing'. It's an uncomfortable reading but a powerful one, whereby the land literally manifests defenders to mimic what is being done to its own soil (in a not-too-dissimilar way to the television show *Sky*, as seen in the previous chapter). Gladwell's vision comes off as somewhat poetic in comparison to the rawness of *Deliverance*.

This violence can sometimes have a supernatural edge as well, though often it turns the films into more overt, pulp enterprises. Films such as John Llewellyn Moxey's *The City of the Dead* (1960), William Huyuk's *Messiah of Evil* (1973), Jack Starrett's *Race with the Devil* (1975), Robert Fuest's *The Devil's Rain* (1975), Peter

Carter's *Rituals* (1977),[36] Sam Raimi's *The Evil Dead* (1981) and Fritz Keirsch's *Children of the Corn* (1984), are only a small number of examples that add the elements of violence to isolated rural groups. The reality flips even further when these elements are brought to the fore, overtaking any emphasis on farming or rural practices, and replacing them solely with pulp Satanic tendencies. One interesting example of this, and one that falls short of rurality itself, is the H.P. Lovecraft adaptation *The Shuttered Room* (1967) by David Greene. The film takes on a strange tone if only because of its clearly East Anglian location filming, which adds a British hue to a very American film; the Anglo-American backwaters mixing into a uniquely surreal pool.[37] American rurality brings world cinema examples around full circle in the unusual case of Daniel Myrick's and Eduardo Sánchez's *The Blair Witch Project* (1999).

The film is most famous for heightening the craze for found-footage horror in the early 2000s, but the narrative is quintessential Folk Horror through its use of rurality. A narrative breakdown follows.

The Blair Witch Project – Heather (Heather Donahue), Josh (Joshua Leonard) and Mike (Michael C. Williams) are three film students who are engaged on a film project in Maryland. Their project is to uncover the mystery of the local folklore surrounding the infamous Blair Witch who is purported to be responsible for a spate of missing children in the area since the 1940s. The film is composed of footage shot by the trio in the woods, apparently later found after their subsequent disappearance. Filming initially goes well when on the outer fringes of the woods and when interviewing local people, but things begin to unravel as they make their way into the woodland itself. They are met upon waking from their tents by piles of stones and (later on) occult wooden paraphernalia hanging outside as a macabre form of greeting or warning. At night they hear noises and screeches which further unnerve the group as it gradually becomes apparent that they are lost in the woods. One night, Josh disappears completely and Heather and Mike venture out to find him in spite of knowing they are now being stalked. They find an abandoned building at night with Josh inside. The footage cuts out before it can reveal why Josh is standing unresponsively in the corner of an empty room.

The Blair Witch Project basks in its rural/urban divide, where the naive students have completely underestimated both the landscape and the power of its folklore. This is, again, not rurality in the sense of using farming practice aesthetics, but instead of Enlightenment figures arrogantly underestimating older ways and their narrative legitimacy. The film is Jamesian, showing the horror of those curious and arrogant enough to step into the rural unknown and to be blasé about its dangers. The film is perhaps most successful because it is working through a form of faux-documentary, its believability befitting to the internet age and its various conspiracy and urban folklore theories. Yet if this chapter has shown anything, it is that such a trend in rurality is not new but something as old as horror cinema itself. Newman likened *Blair*'s back-to-basics directorial style to Tobe Hooper's style of filmmaking, suggesting that the film 'is a successor to the independent 1970s horrors which depict an insane universe by implying that the director is a madman with no internal (or external) censor who will do *anything* to terrorise his characters and audience' (2011: 442). *Blair* is, however, harking back to an even older tradition, and it is its rurality that ultimately skews the lives of its characters. Think back to Christensen's *Häxan* and the technique is effectively the same; the rurality of documentary creating a psychologised and deeply effective horror through the potential of an unseen and underground alternative rural sociology. It is fitting then that Myrick and Sánchez named their production company Haxan Films, so named not simply after the invisible witch that made their breakthrough such a success, but after the film that arguably started off the trend of rurality-infused Folk Horror all around the globe. This is the rural breaking reality down, tipping it to the point of extreme tension and horror. It has come full circle, from witches to witches and country to country, from *Häxan* to *Blair*.

Endnotes

1 The cinema in question is the Small Cinema project in Liverpool.

2 See Chapters 5 and 6.

3 See, for example, his short untitled film commonly referred to as *The Killing* (1964). Made with support from the British Film Institute's Experimental Film Fund, the film uses rurality to create a feeling of dread and unease as farming practices are portrayed in hypnotic slow-motion, like a Humphrey Jennings short on Ketamin.

4 This final image is especially indebted to Stanley Spencer's painting, *Resurrection* (1927).

5 For other examples of this type of orientalist Folk Horror, see the voodoo segments from both *Dr Terror's House of Horrors* (1965) and *The Vault of Horror* (1973).

6 Written by Jakub Goldberg and Jerzy Skolimowski.

7 Written by Gérard Brach and David Stone.

8 Sometimes known as *The Exorcism of Hugh*.

9 Written by Clive Exton but based on ideas by Gerry Davis and Kit Pedler.

10 Sometimes known as *These are the Damned*.

11 The film's controversy in part derives from this ambiguity, which blurs seduction and

sexual assault. In parts of the scene she is portrayed as wanting him, in other parts she is clearly the victim of assault. The context is also skewed by what happens after Charlie has had sex with her. The whole segment is deeply misogynistic in tone.

12 The film also acquires its experimental character from having a soundtrack by Genesis members Mike Rutherford and Tony Banks.

13 Sometimes known under the name *The Death Wheelers*.

14 Directed by Alfred Hitchcock, the film is fitting in the thematic sense as the German spies can only hope to siphon off their captured spy by diverting the train into more rural areas of the Alps. The film is, of course, not Folk Horror.

15 A theme brilliantly used in Robert Mulligan's *The Other* (1972) as well.

16 The film is perhaps most famous for having an early score by Michael Nyman, and Peter Greenaway was also its editor.

17 For further elucidation, when asked about his interest in Dunsany, he suggested that, 'In the 70s and 80s, I was attracted by his anti-industrial and environmental stance and he also had a very interesting take on Death, which was a major preoccupation in many of my films of that time' (2013). This also ties to the anomalous examples of rurality where environmental concerns often filter through in some guise.

18 Based on stories by Angela Carter, who also helped with screenplay duties.

19 This may also have something to do with the main characters being largely drunk or stoned during the film's happenings. It is worth noting that Uncle Monty (Richard Griffiths) deliberately takes the pair to the countryside in order to seduce 'I' (Paul McGann); something he seems to dare not do whilst in the comfy confines of his London pad.

20 Played by Michael Elphick who earlier in his career played Thomas Venables in *Red Shift*.

21 The film is sometimes known also as *The Scarlet Blade*.

22 The character of Oliver Cromwell has strong links to Folk Horror thanks to his appearance in *Witchfinder General*.

23 The theme is also prominent in Mike Leigh's *Play For Today* episode, *Nuts In May* (1976).

24 A film that arguably sends up all that is recognisable as Folk Horror as much as *Carry On Screaming* (1966) sends up Gothic Horror.

25 To see the difference the war would make, its re-edit under the title of *Spring Harvest* is essential viewing.

26 The film's commentary remains somewhat of a mystery as to both who is speaking and who wrote the voice-over, though, in the re-edited propaganda version, *Spring Harvest* (1940), the script is written by Hugh Gray and spoken by A.G. Street.

27 A film adapted by Kötting and Sean Lock from Émile Zola's novel, *La Terre (The Earth)*.

28 Other excellent examples include *The Red Shoes* (1948) and *Black Narcissus* (1947), the latter being a perfect, if surprising, example of the Folk Horror Chain in full flow.

29 See also the wonderful segment from *sleep furiously* (2008), where a local Welshman reads a poem about the changing of his local sign from a wooden one to steel.

30 The film follows a man called Robert (Peter O'Toole) on the run from the Gestapo after a sporting attempt at assassinating Hitler (Michael Sheard) before the outbreak of

WW2. Robert escapes back to England but is chased down to the Dorset coast by SS officers, where he hides out, living off (and under) the land in the sandstone holloways. The story was also adapted by Fritz Lang as *Man Hunt* in 1941 though it pales in comparison to Donner's visceral interpretation.

31   Rivers mentioned Jacques Tourneur in the interview and went on to discuss the director's work at length afterwards, with particular emphasis on *Night of the Demon* (see Chapter 3). This may have been to do with my wearing a T-shirt for the interview with the film's poster emblazoned upon it, but the conversation naturally veered into more Folk Horror related directions.

32   This extends to other cultures outside of the UK with Rivers having made a large number of ethnographic shorts set all around the world.

33   Many cases of witchcraft in Britain especially are now considered to be both misogynistic (in their working and punishments) but also examples of people genuinely believing themselves to have occult powers.

34   This line being the most famous quote from Nigel Kneale's *The Stone Tape*. See Chapter 5 for further detail.

35   This is summarised perfectly in contrasting Valerie's escape from being burnt at the stake for being a witch with Howie's death in the wicker man.

36   Sometimes known under the lesser title of *The Creeper*.

37   The film was, in fact, shot in Norfolk and on the Essex and Kent coastlines.

Occultism, Hauntology and the Urban 'Wyrd'

Introduction

In April 2014 I was working on an essay on the music used in Folk Horror films when I was confronted with a rather intriguing photograph. At first, I believed it to be merely another film still with the potential to illustrate a thematic point in the essay for when it was eventually to be put online. There was, however, something unnerving about it. The image showed a beautiful summer's day in a rural backdrop, depicting a group of medieval characters dragging a woman up a hillside. This was supervised by some sort of religious figure in a black cloak while onlookers watched from afar further down the hill. The still was from Michael Reeves' *Witchfinder General*, specifically from the film's opening scene which was analysed in an earlier chapter. The image is disturbing, capturing the essence and casual brutality of Reeves' film, but something was still not quite right overall. On closer inspection, the uncanny element, one that was sparking several ideas thematically, was that there was a surprisingly modern house just down the hill in full view.

Further into the photograph's vista, several more modern houses could be seen in a variety of Suffolk pinks and pastels. The events depicted in the photo were not taking place in darker times long since past, but in 1968, in the days of the popularisation of the counter-culture. What was shocking about the photo was that this aspect did not at first present itself as anachronistic to the action that was taking place but, fundamentally, was actually a part of it. Of course, barbaric violence, skewed belief and moral systems, and implicit, direct misogyny could be perceived as normalised in this era; this was the late 1960s and, in taking into account Folk Horror's most popular examples, the early 1970s were naturally a hyper-extension. Throughout this book, the overriding feeling of being haunted by an era should have been building, suggesting that something odd was in the water during the late 1960s, sowing the seeds towards the wealth of horror to come in the 1970s; diegetically within such fictional examples but, quintessentially, also non-diegetically in 1970s Britain itself.

This chapter is exploring two separate strands that both deal with this post-war period through the context of Hauntology; a word that has cropped up on several occasions already but has yet to be properly qualified. Hauntology was specifically referring to the 'Spectre of Marx' as Jacques Derrida called it in his 1993 book of the same title. It is now commonly used to account for our own cultural, and sometimes moral, relationships with British artefacts from the 1970s as well as artwork that deals with the concept of lost futures. In this context, it is largely a word denoting relationships in and towards 1970s British culture, especially on film and television, and how this reflects social elements in both the period and in our need to look back towards it. Mark Fisher has split the term into two distinct types, which is appropriate as it will be used to discuss two interconnected but still relatively separate areas. Fisher writes of Hauntology's two potential areas that:

> The first refers to that which is (in actuality is) *no longer*, but which *remains* effective as a virtuality (the traumatic 'compulsion to repeat', a fatal pattern). The second sense of hauntology refers to that which (in actuality) has *not yet* happened, but which is *already* effective in the virtual (an attractor, an anticipation shaping current behaviour). (2014: 19)

Through these areas, two separate problems regarding Folk Horror can be discussed, namely:

- The resurgence, with hindsight, of interest in occultism and other forms of 'occulture' in counter-culture film and television.
- The presence of an urban setting and a concept in a genre which has been shown to rely on both rural settings and sociological isolation; two things which, in traditional cinematic practices, are difficult and relatively uncommon in urban-set dramas.

These are not, however, the only questions that framing certain issues of Folk Horror within Hauntology can ask. The other element suggested by the uncanny relationships in the photograph of *Witchfinder General* was one specifically to do with the moral climate and paranoia of 1970s Britain as a whole – one depressingly mimicked in modern day British politics – and how this created some of the odder examples that come under the banner of Folk Horror. Though many examples from the previous chapters, from the unholy trinity to television examples such as *Robin Redbreast*, all conform in some way to the arguments of their relative chapters, they also have a relationship specifically with the era in which they are made. This is often raised by writers on Folk Horror but the quality of the cultural product often overrides questioning of the reality of the era which produced it. Take Vic Pratt's argument on *The Wicker Man*, for example, where 'It's hard to imagine anything visually like it happening in this "born digital" age. When you switch on that hard drive, it either works, or it doesn't; you get it all, or none of it' (2013: 31). Underneath this is a form of nostalgia, but one that is essentially hauntological in character; a film like this couldn't be made exactly again today because the era is removed, the trauma being a perceived lack in today's cultural potential. The same sort of realisation can be found in Darius Drew Shimon's analysis of *The Blood on Satan's Claw*, though there is at least some recognition as to the difficulties presented in the film's era, even if only at an industrial level:

> Today's self-appointed moral guardians would balk at the very thought, but such a film probably wouldn't get made in the current climate anyway – not that 1970, supposedly horror's 'golden age' but actually a time of precarious uncertainty, was any kinder. (2010: 1)

This is important when dealing with many of the moral problems presented in the work so far, problems which have been largely put to one side until now. This sort of questioning also asks why paraphernalia of the period seems to evoke the same folkloric/Folk Horror responses as work set much further back within Britain's past. There is a great sense that the critics of Folk Horror so far share a 'Sam Tyler mentality'. Tyler is the main character played by John Simm in the television programme *Life on Mars* (2006–2007), where a police detective travels back in time after a car accident (or does he?) to the 1970s, where he is then trapped. At the end of the series, in spite of the huge range of unattractive facets of the period presented in the programme (casual racism and sexism, for example), he opts, after briefly returning to the 2000s, to commit suicide and head back to the period, warts and all; politically incorrect in every way with no 'self-appointed moral guardians'. There is indeed a strange form of nostalgia manifesting in some corners of cultural analysis here. Hauntology, however, combats this and realigns the arguments so that the positive elements of the period can be mourned while acknowledging its problematic areas (of which there are clearly many).

Whether or not it was genuinely as paranoid as it is now perceived, the culture surrounding the 1970s in Britain has in itself become a form of Folk Horror through the mechanisms of Hauntology, whereby the traumas seen and unseen within the period are now repeating through our constant rediscovery of such culture, thanks largely to the internet. Artefacts such as Public Information Films now sit comfortably under the banner of Folk Horror just as much as *The Wicker Man* because they portray a vision of the 1970s not unlike the paranoid, skewed visions of many cinematic examples. These examples specifically play their horror for real, if only because their desired effect was often behavioural augmentation through fear and worry. This can open up many questions regarding the treatment of children, misogyny, racism and other generally ubiquitous forms of trauma present or represented through narratives of 1970s film and television, and it requires Hauntology's melancholic inflection to perceive and analyse these things.

Considering the treatment of women especially, it is worth noting the lack of female directors detailed so far. Though a number have been noted generally, especially in the writing and adaptation of work, if we were to consider this book to be concerned primarily with British cinema from the 1970s (which does make up the bulk of the analysis), then it would have to be stated that, incredibly, only one theatrically distributed film was solely directed by a woman during this decade in Britain; Jane Arden's powerful *The Other Side of the Underneath* (1972). This may partly explain the almost consistent treatment of female characters as victims, sometimes even in a fetishist sense, in Folk Horror from this period; the lack of voice for women leading to their often one-dimensional treatment in many more pulp films. This is an aspect addressed within this chapter diegetically but one that comments explicitly on the non-diegetic reality of the decade.

What is essential though, whether dealing with questions of occultism, urbanity, analogue technology, or other odds and ends that have become attached to the banner of Folk Horror, is to tie these aspects into the sociological character of the period. This provides new ways of dealing with work such as the collected output of Nigel Kneale, the prolific collection of occult films made during the era, or even just our own relationship with the era today through other forms of media, manifesting in such strange memoranda such as Ghost Box Records, Scarfolk designs and the vast array of nostalgia-driven television programmes that emerged in the late 1990s and early 2000s.[1]

The photo from *Witchfinder General* opened up all of these areas to some degree, not because of its content but more specifically because of my own reaction to such content; that its happening was just as believable in the period in which the film was made as in the period in which the film was set. This isn't a literal exaggeration; I, of course, do not believe groups of religious fundamentalists went on killing sprees, targeting women who they thought to be witches in the interval between *Crackerjack* and *Match of the Day*. But the openness of the violence, of the treatment of woman, and the sheer popularity of pagan, magic(k) and occult practices, means that it at least felt more real and more genuine than it probably ought to have.[2] Hauntology can help explain this relationship by psychologising it and contextualising specifically our own relationships with what is essentially a clash; a conflict between our nostalgic visions of a period and its artwork, and the reality behind such visions. This reality often can be seen as attempting to break through the white-washing of the period, portrayed as being as warm and cosy as a *Morecambe & Wise* Christmas special. Folk Horror, in hindsight, often presents this release of reality with gusto.

We begin this exploration, then, by looking in detail at the occult cinema that was produced in Britain and America, before and during the period in question. By highlighting several reoccurring themes and by analysing their popularity, a general analysis of the period in question can begin the final grounding of Folk Horror; not as a pulp slice of escapism, but as a subtle and unnerving vision of the then-modern day. Fisher writes of the decade that it was 'a time before the switch, a time at once kinder and harsher than now. Forms of (social) security then taken for granted have long since been destroyed, but vicious prejudices that were then freely aired have become unacceptable' (2014: 50). This chapter deals more in these harsher aspects, if only because Folk Horror is so often a visceral and unforgiving genre, whether dealing with the skewed beliefs leading to violent occultist sacrifices, the barbaric actions found in Ballardian suburban estates, or our very own fascist race-memories being rekindled through crashed Martian spaceships unearthed from tube station redevelopments.

Occultism and Hauntology

In 1968, the British psychedelic singer Julie Driscoll released a cover version of Donovan's 1966 hit single 'Season of the Witch'; a song that lyrically linked the era of the counter-culture with an interest in pagan and, more specifically, occult themes. The Donovan original has had a resurgence in recent years, being used in a 2010 advert for Microsoft, in part hinting at Folk Horror's general post-millennial resurgence, but the Driscoll version of the song is more poignant when looking at the links between psychedelia, occultism and, ultimately, Hauntology. This is because her version, perhaps more so than many of its other cover variations, emphasises the link between the sheer popularity of the swinging King's Road atmosphere of late 1960s Britain and an interest in occult practices. Only the year before, Aleister Crowley appeared on Peter Blake's album artwork for The Beatles' *Sgt. Pepper's Lonely Hearts Club Band* (1967), whilst a year later, The Rolling Stones were singing about Satan in 'Sympathy for the Devil'. This was, of course, when Mick Jagger was also making avant-garde music for occultist filmmaker Kenneth Anger.[3] Yardbirds and Led Zeppelin guitarist Jimmy Page would even open an occult bookshop in Holland Street some years after. Named The Equinox and designed more as a printing house for Crowley's work, it was the least of Page's occult obsessions; he went so far as to buy the occultist's Loch Ness Manor, Boleskine House in 1970. Occultism of various forms seems to be ubiquitous in the period's pop culture and this extends heavily to cinema and TV. This requires a certain questioning in regards to what this sociologically says about both British and American popular culture from the period. As Matthew Sweet points out in his Radio 4 documentary on the subject, *Black Aquarius* (2015):

> Was the post-war British love affair with the occult just an index on our boredom, frustration, our hunger for a bit of psychedelic colour, the spiritual equivalent of buying a lava lamp? Or does it reveal something darker about the people we once were, the people we became? (2015)

With hauntological hindsight, this can also be seen as a vision of another lost future, one that was prevalent long enough to become an incredibly popular theme in various media, as well as within the general iconography of the coun-ter-culture's aesthetics. This emphasis is one that, in terms of Hauntology, comes to act as a signifier for the era in a very particular but peculiar light; where Satanic rites were deemed to be as common in the rural, urban *and* suburban environments as Polaroid cameras, Space Hoppers and *Play for Today*. This was a time where Sainsbury's could advertise their Cornflakes with log-os straight out of The Hermetic Order of the Golden Dawn and where *Play School* presenters could be devout, erotic occultists who released pagan folk al-bums.[4] Yet occultism went on to represent more than just a casual dabbling in Tarot or séances as series such as *Zodiac* (1974) suggested.[5] The divergence can be split into two separate entities or two separate thematic pathways, both in part inspired by the music of 'Season of the Witch'.

The song was used for George A. Romero's film of the same title in 1972 (this time using the original performed by Donovan), though the film is sometimes known as *Hungry Wives*. The film's narrative, one of an innocent woman be-coming involved with a murderous and witchcraft-practicing neighbour, can represent the first form of occultism; one that seeps into the middle-class socie-ty of suburbanites, often for the most pulp means of entertainment. There has long been a link between such occultist interests and ideas of class, especially in British cinema, but also, as is evident in Romero's film, in America as well. The second form of occultism can be seen in the BBC *Wednesday Play* also titled *Season of the Witch*, broadcast in 1970. The play, directed by Desmond McCarthy and written by Johnny Byrne, charts the rebellious nature of a young woman who quits her job, much to the dismay of the establishment figures around her. The young woman is notably played by Julie Driscoll; the evolution from her singing the song to playing the part suggesting the normali-sation of the occult in this period. There appears to be an unconscious linking between the growing rebellion of young people in the period and the concept of possession, noted succinctly by Mark Gatiss when exploring American hor-ror from the period. Gatiss suggests that the popularisation of occultism, and other forms of belief-based paranormality in cinema, was down to the genuine likeness found in the possessed actions of young people in protests and riots, suggesting that:

> Looking back, it's clear why this theme may have resonated with American
> audiences. At the time, a generation gap appeared to be opening up between the
> establishment and young people. The model, clean-cut youth of America seems
> increasingly to have been replaced by shouting, swearing young men and women.
> It was like they had become... possessed. (2010)

Gatiss is correct, though this also applies back over the Atlantic where occult-ism, witchcraft and other forms of esoteric mischief became the norm for young people as a pastime in British cinema, meaning an increased presence of its paraphernalia in horror and elsewhere.

Yet occultism in film appears long before this sprouting of heathen heritage, starting earlier in the years after the Second World War. In Mark Robson's 1943 film *The Seventh Victim*, a hapless young woman in search of her missing sister in New York accidently uncovers a sinister Satanic cult group in Greenwich Village. With the film being produced by Val Lewton, it has more of an in-flection of *film noir* aesthetics typical of his RKO productions, but it opens up questions regarding the formation of belief systems in more populated and central urban spaces. Other films from the period that dabble in such popular Gothic occultism are Jacques Tourneur's *Night of the Demon*, Roger Corman's *The Undead* (1957) and John Llewellyn Moxey's *The City of the Dead* (1960); all three films feature the stumbling upon of occult power-plays hiding in base-ments, flats or country manors. The lack of connection with counter-culture ideals means that there is more to occultism as a theme in the cinema than the buying into of a passing fancy. What is quintessential about these films and their influence is the domestication of witchcraft and occultism into the upper-class and upper-middle-class urban zones; where there is definitive class connotation in regards to the ability to gain access to such information and the necessary accoutrements of occult rituals and practices.

This is far removed from other Folk Horror mechanisms, which have, up to this point, been shown to evolve largely within rural labouring settings and communities. Though there is still a potential isolation within the urban locales, something else is happening for such a visceral belief system to pass from dark-age secrets, which carried the penalty of death if studied, to its treatment as a literal hobby alongside interests in antiques and Reader's Digest subscriptions. There is no better film that deals with this evolution and the casual, domestic application of such magic than Sidney Hayers' *Night of the Eagle* (1962), some-times known as *Burn, Witch, Burn*.[6] Hayers already had one flawed horror pic-ture under his belt in the form of *Circus of Horrors* (1960) before he attempted another in the genre. *Eagle* is an altogether more mature and complex film, whose influence on how occultism was normalised into the domestic environ-ment cannot be overstated. A narrative breakdown follows.

> ***Night of the Eagle*** – Norman Taylor (Peter Wyngarde) is a college pro-fessor at a semi-rural institution. He lives in a large house with his wife

Tansy (Janet Blair), who appears to be a typical 1960s house wife. Norman is sceptical of the paranormal and the film shows him questioning the belief in such ideas in his lectures. Norman's success at the college is un-paralleled, both financially and socially. Even some of his female students fancy him, and the other wives in Tansy's social scene are jealous of their success. On finding a spider strangely positioned in a jar at home, Norman discovers that Tansy has been practising witchcraft in order to better their lives. Insulted by her belief, both in witchcraft itself and that their suc-cess is due to this, Norman forces his wife to throw away all of her spells, enchantments and witchcraft paraphernalia. His life immediately begins to go wrong. He is falsely accused of assault by a female student (Judith Stott) who has a crush on him, and is later confronted by her angry boy-friend (Bill Mitchell) with a gun. His job is consequently put on the line. A fellow witch is now operating against the pair since Tansy's protections have been destroyed. A force is sent to kill Norman but Tansy switches places with him. She wanders down to a nearby beach and attempts to drown herself but Norman saves her. She then becomes possessed and tries to kill him before he locks her in her room. It becomes clear that her opponent in witchcraft is Flora (Margaret Johnston), who is secretary at the college and whose husband Lindsay (Colin Gordon) has been sidelined career-wise by Norman's success. Flora uses magic to set fire to their house in an attempt to kill Tansy, whilst using the loud-speaker system at the col-lege to convince Norman that the school's eagle mascot has come to life to attack him. Both attempts at murder fail. The pair are reunited and safely make their escape. Flora and Lindsay are still in the school. Lindsay heads back to close the doors of the college's chapel, briefly leaving Flora, who is then killed by the falling of the school's stone eagle monument.

Eagle is a key film because it moves the occult into the domestic environment, where disputes with neighbours are not resolved over the garden fence but through spells and enchantments. There's rich potential within the thematic fall-out of the film because of this; virtually every inane detail, from orna-ments in the house to Norman's job, become a potential cipher for something occult. The filmmaker Patrick Keiller uses the film to discuss why he finds the countryside more unnerving than the built-up spaces that preoccupies his own cinematic practice.[7] He suggests in an interview with Patrick Wright that:

> The countryside seems more scary. I don't know how real this is because I don't
> live in the countryside... There's a film called *Night of the Eagle* made in 1961,
> with Peter Wyngarde as a lecturer at an educational institution in a country

house with large eagles on its gateposts. His colleagues are practising witchcraft, which (I think) leads to some chilling effect involving eagles. I remember it whenever I drive past a pair of monumental gateposts. There's a new Gothic genre in the present day English countryside... (1998: 21)

Though the film is far more suburban than Keiller's description, films like *Eagle* normalise the paranormal, to the point where its ubiquity is suspected in just about any type of middle-class enclave. Pratt highlights this point succinctly, writing that, '*Night of the Eagle* inaugurated a film era where witchcraft could be carried out casually by whole communities in kitchen or classroom' (2013: 29). This is the key point when considering why the film is important; it was the first British film to properly domesticate the occult, an idea that became un-nervingly common in the early 1970s. Though it could be argued that *Night of the Demon* also went some way in achieving this, the main villain, Karswell, had too much of a boyish, childish motivation to properly signpost such normalisa-tion; like a wronged schoolboy, he uses his occult power to get revenge on those bad-mouthing and questioning him. In *Eagle*, the magic is used to solve the very basic and typical problems of everyday middle-class life such as promotions at work and social climbing on the dinner party circuit. This, of course, is an as-pect that cannot be discussed further without reference to the many novels and film adaptations of British writer and occult expert, Dennis Wheatley.

Wheatley's writing output was prodigious, and went in and out of fashion. Yet the writer seemed to consistently channel and highlight the post-war era's in-terest in occultism, emphasising a flourishing link between the idle upper ech-elons of society and how they overcame their boredom; adding weight to the dictum, 'the Devil makes work for idle hands'. As Sweet suggests, 'Cinema is not the source of the 1960s occult revival. That's to be found in a series of older texts; texts possessed of a monstrous power despite the cheap, acidic paper that bore their words. Works by Dennis Wheatley, who, between the age of Stanley Baldwin and the age of Sid Vicious, wrote night-black paper-backs...' (2015). In many ways, Wheatley made a career of exploring such a potential, epitomised by perhaps the most famous occult film of the decade, Hammer's *The Devil Rides Out* (1968). Adapted from Wheatley's 1934 novel, Terence Fisher's film firmly plants occultism within the lavish aesthetics and glamour typically associated with the more Gothic pictures of the studio. It fol-lows aristocratic friends Rex (Leon Greene) and Duc de Richleau (Christopher Lee), who are trying to save the souls of their friends Simon (Patrick Mower) and Tanith (Nike Arrighi) from the clutches of the local Satanist group, led by the campy Mocata (Charles Gray). The film acts as an excuse for an array of occult imagery and devilish demons, whilst simultaneously critiquing what is, in essence, a social dispute between dinner-party socialites. Mocata, whether in sharp suits or purple ceremony gowns, seems somewhat envied by Rex and Richleau, if only because his parties are clearly more lively and Simon is keener to stay and indulge his Devilish desires. This may seem a blasé approach to a film that literally relies on the *deus ex machina* to solve its problems of devilry and the Goat of Mendes, but Fisher's film is perhaps most responsible for making X-rated material (at least at the time) seductively alluring and even fun.

Marcus Hearn and Alan Barnes suggest that the film was dated even at the time of its release but survives with continued popularity today because, unlike other Hammer films of the period, it failed to be creatively affected by the censorship concessions required by the BBFC:

> As a finely crafted Hammer horror, redolent of Terence Fisher's Gothics from the late fifties, *The Devil Rides Out* seems little compromised by concessions made to appease the BBFC. While perhaps too dated to appeal to American audiences of the time, the film is now regarded as a milestone in the careers of Terence Fisher and Christopher Lee. (2007: 121)

The film actually captures the shift in taste regarding the occult in both British and American cinema during this period, where occult decor and window-dressings would find their way into a variety of cinematic households, whether it be the New York apartment of Rosemary and Guy[8] or the quaint English village squired by that other learned Fisher who collects 'sherds'.[9] Another relevant connection, which Hammer admittedly could not fully explore until later films thanks to the 1970s relaxation in censorship, was between sexuality and occultism. Kim Newman writes of *Devil*'s refreshing nature in this sense, recognising the gender hypocrisy of the film in what is still a highly conservative and patriarchal take on Devil worship: 'In a variant, *Devil* has the secondary male lead (Patrick Mower) lured into the evil cult: noticeably, his punishment for surrendering to his sensual impulses is far less extreme than that meted out to women' (2011: 28). But *The Devil Rides Out* was not the first occult-tinged film on Hammer's books and much of what is taken for granted in Folk Horror can be found in its predecessor by two years, Cyril Frankel's *The Witches* (1966).

Based on the novel by Norah Lofts, *The Witches* distinctly follows the Folk Horror Chain and, as occultism and its subsequent happenings easily fit the chain theory in regards to the skewing of beliefs and morality, it can be said to epitomise the causational nature of the genre with perfect pitch. The belief system within the film is again subject to an Orientalist hue which gives it a flavour far away from the English upper-class mischief of Wheatley's world, and marks it out as wholly different. Whereas there is a genuine supernatural malignancy in *The Devil Rides Out*, *The Witches* captures that casual village interest in the occult and its potential power over small communities, where the evil and danger is distinctly human. Joan Fontaine, who initially obtained the rights to Loft's novel, plays an outsider schoolteacher to a small country village who soon suspects that something wicked is afoot. Coming across yet another local occultist group, she seeks to stop what the film builds up to; a sacrificial ceremony involving a young, gradually sexualised girl (Ingrid Boulting).[10] The paranoid character of the film can be seen to derive from the script having been written by Nigel Kneale, who invokes a conspiratorial tone akin to later examples such as *The Wicker Man* and *Robin Redbreast*. Occultism is again in the realms of the middle-classes though is imported rather than dug up from old libraries of the Golden Dawn movement and the like. Hearn and Barnes write of the film: 'Unsettling, though compromised by an hysterical climax, *The Witches'* effective exploitation of its picturesque location predates both *The Prisoner* and *The Wicker Man*' (2007: 109). This highlights how enclosed (and important) the social space of the film is, one that is permeable at first but one which can also lock down when necessary upon an individual, as is typical in many Folk Horror examples.

Hammer would later dabble with occult material again in another Wheatley adaptation, *To the Devil a Daughter* (1976). It lacks the thematic and aesthetic detail of the earlier film and doesn't quite pull off the nuances of class because of its move from country mansions to London high-rises; the characters are still stiflingly wealthy but lack the *joie de vivre* that a younger, hip set of counter-culture characters often typically brings with such a topographical shift. Even Dracula, that seemingly indestructible franchise, would turn to occultism for new entertainments, whether in *The Satanic Rites of Dracula* (1973) – where the Count (Christopher Lee) is masquerading as a successful, 1970s property developer in a modern high-rise building[11] – or, more entertainingly, in *Dracula A.D. 1972* – where a bored group of hip Chelsea-ites accidently, through dabbling in occultism, raise Dracula in the modern day to do battle with Van Helsing's descendants around the King's Road. The latter film marks a key point in the difference within the four years between the Wheatley type of occultism and the full British counter-occultism; the devilry in this film is enacted by young, beautiful types in Chelsea coffee shops rather than camp aristocrats in country houses.[12] The point being that, as Sweet suggests, 'At the end of the 1960s, you didn't need to be dropping acid with Timothy Leary to believe that western culture was on the edge of something...' (2015). It did, however, help to be part of a well-to-do counter-culture social group with access to abandoned churches and sacred, erotic texts.

This is where Hauntology can begin to fit into the occult equation, as the aesthetics of this younger, sexier occultism still lingers within the aesthetics and themes which come under the Hauntology label today. How this works in terms of its cultural mechanisms is another matter, though the mid-1960s saw a wealth of occult cinema burgeoning with the sort of casual pulp aesthetics that instantly recall the period's slow but enjoyable shift into sleazier territory; a lost vision of a pagan free-love utopia. This was yet to be the purely exploitation flavour that occultism would take in the grimier corner of counter-culture film (which would produce the most hauntological of forms; the domesticated erotic occultism that mixed the worlds of rituals with wife-swapping) but of the older form of Corman-type drive-in picture. The 1960s arguably already opened with the connection between the embracement of the sexual revolution of later years (far before such a revolution had actually occurred) with the darker, macabre aspects of occult practice found in Mario Bava's lavish horror, *Black Sunday* (1960).[13] The influence of this lurid, Gothic tale, surrounding the resurrection of an executed witch (Barbara Steele), can be found in many other, albeit lesser, films from the 1960s. In the likes of *The Devil's Hand* (1961), *Witchcraft* (1964), *Devils of Darkness* (1965), *The Curse of the Crimson Altar* (1968) and *The Witchmaker* (1969), occultism gradually established itself as a cheap B-movie trope, making a financially viable film with little means. Such pulpy trends would find their way into other European films in the following decade, with such films as *Don't Deliver Us from Evil* (1971), *Satanic Pandemonium* (1975) and *Satan's Blood* (1978).

In the days before Michael Reeves had found creative success with *Witchfinder General*, his earlier dabbling in this type of B-picture heathenism helped pave the way for his career before it was sadly and untimely cut short. In *The She Beast* (1966), Barbara Steele plays a woman who, after a car accident, morphs into the possessed spirit of a witch executed in the 1700s. The film is flawed, but the director essentially again captures all of the period's interest in occultism and possession right on the tip of it becoming the more ubiquitous, accessible type that Hauntology thrives off. Even more intriguing is Reeves' second feature, *The Sorcerers* (1967), where happenings that were becoming traditionally monopolised by occult cinema (psychic possession, perception thieving, etc.), are churned through a pulp pseudoscience. The film concerns an elderly couple (Boris Karloff and Catherine Lacey) who hypnotise a younger man (Ian Ogilvy) and share/control his experiences, gradually leading him to commit more violent acts for their own pleasure. The voyeuristic delight at violence solidifies in the film, clearly in preparation for *Witchfinder*, but it also captures and hones the era's increased interest in the 'wyrd' sciences, of which occultism could also be deemed as being part.

Also of interest, at least in terms of class and ritual, is J. Lee Thompson's 1967 film *Eye of the Devil*, though the film is far less pulpier than the examples around it. Apart from an A-list cast (David Niven, Deborah Kerr, David Hemmings, Sharon Tate, etc.), the film deliberately situates occult practices at the high end of the class spectrum again. Niven plays the Marquis Philippe de Montfaucon who is called back to his castle in the country under the false premise of seeing to his business in the local vineyards. His wife (Kerr) follows and finds that he has returned to take part in an ancient local ritual in aid of the grapevine crops flourishing again. From the premise alone, it is a clear forerunner to *The Wicker Man* and *Robin Redbreast*, even managing to just pre-date *The Wicker Man's* source novel, *Ritual*. Essentially, the occult practices are linked with both class and pastoral farming, framing it differently to *The Devil Rides Out* in its open discussion of class boundaries and the totemic ritual that comes with such a class status. A trip to the country and to the vineyards may seem like an idyllic concept in comparison to other films' gritty, urban occultism (similar in tone to a visit to sunny Summerisle) but, as Mark Fisher suggests, 'Far from being some refuge from political strife, the English landscape is the site of numerous struggles between the forces of power and privilege and those who sought to resist them' (2014: 225). *Eye of the Devil* situates these struggles within an occult framework, albeit in the landscapes of France. The difference is clear; that such occultism became household by the time of the later films, being sung about in pubs and discussed at the local Post Office rather than being monopolised by the land-owning upper-class.

The shift, or at least the amalgamation of other factors into occultism in film, arguably occurred during the years in which the unholy trinity shifted the fashions of British horror toward more typical forms of belief systems; that, like *Häxan* – the first film to show occult practice on a large scale – the beliefs would be moved gradually out of the hands of the ultra rich alone and back into the lives of people who worked the land in older times. Whilst the power structures and links with the upper-class is still present (often as a guiding force for both good and evil), the narrative shift from mansions to furrows brewed a number of copycat films that also elide occultism into exploitation cinema. The most famous of these is Gordon Hessler's *Cry of the Banshee* (1970); a film that arguably (in terms of its themes) could sit easily within the unholy trinity to make it an unholy quartet, if not for several weaker aspects. A narrative breakdown follows.

Cry of the Banshee – In the 1700s, Lord Edward Whitman (Vincent Price) rules over his local town as a magistrate with an iron fist. He has a Hopkins-like thirst for the blood of 'witches' and holds several sham trials against local women. There *are* devilish things afoot in the town, however, and Whitman leads a raid on a local coven, killing many of those present and warning the rest to flee. The coven's leader Oona (Elisabeth Bergener) vows revenge and calls upon a demon that takes possession of the Whitman's family servant Roderick (Patrick Mower), who then begins to kill off members of the family. To add complexity to the scenario, Lord Whitman's daughter Maureen (Hilary Dwyer) has been in love with Roderick for some time, and this is before considering that Whitman's son Sean (Stephan Chase) has been shown to be effectively forcing himself upon his own step-mother Lady Patricia (Essy Persson). Whitman's bastard son Harry (Carl Rigg) tracks down a further meeting of the coven with the help of Maureen and a local priest who is keen to find Roderick. They kill Oona and break up the final coven with Maureen forced to shoot the demonic version of Roderick. Satisfied with the proceedings, Lord Whitman plans to leave. He stops at the local cemetery to check on Roderick's grave, only to find it empty. Returning to his carriage in panic, he finds his son and daughter killed: Roderick has killed the coach driver and taken his place. The film ends with Lord Whitman screaming as he is driven away to his fate at the hands of the demonic creature.

Cry of the Banshee can be seen in some ways as an amalgamation of the ideals of *Witchfinder General* with the supernatural occultism of *The Blood on Satan's Claw*, though feels more of a misfire in many other regards. Whilst it aesthetically captures the pure essence of British Folk Horror from this period, there is a lack of balance between the horrors on display and the strange presence of a camp strain of comedy, making the violence against women in particular even more uncomfortable than it already is. Ian Cooper notes this in his analysis of the film which, though a definite product of the success of the original Tigon Folk Horror pairing, fails on too many levels to be considered part of the unholy trinity:

> It manages to be remarkably sleazy and lurid with very little actual sex but lots
> of exposed breasts as witches are manhandled, tavern wenches mauled and Lady
> Edward raped by her step-son. This, and the rickety sets, make the film look like
> nothing so much as 'Carry on Witchfinder'. (2011: 88)

It is an apt summation of the film, but also explains its links with a potential hauntological ideal; that, no matter how detailed the period trapping are within the diegesis of the film, *Cry* is arguably a summation of its production era's attitudes towards women, albeit unconsciously; where such violence is treated as potentially titillating. This is, of course, in the context of a pulp piece of cinema, one whose chief catchphrase is 'H is for heretic!' The film also demonstrates the excesses that Reeves could have potentially let into his film if he had not been strict with Vincent Price's performance. Gone is the cold directness of Reeves' Hopkins, replaced instead by a camp, sleazy caricature. Aptly, Fisher writes of our distanced, perhaps somewhat rose-tinted relationship with the 1970s, whereby 'Hearing T-Rex now doesn't remind you of 73, it reminds you of nostalgia programmes about 1973' (2014: 77). Films like *Cry of the Banshee* storm through this process of rewriting and actually act as an uncomfortable time-capsule of the era as a whole; the cosy, lava-lamp veneer ripped away by sweaty skin, small scale atrocities, and a ubiquitous abuse against women of all classes.

Cry was, perhaps surprisingly, designed *as* some form of social comment, being born of both genuine historical happening and commenting on several political aspects of the period. This is, as Cooper suggests, diluted through its blasé approach to the violence, framed more for its potential exploitation than as a Reevesian comment on nihilism and violence by the hands of those in power:

> In much the same way, although the cavorting coven are very 1960s, with their hippyish dancing and incantations such as 'Oona is peace, Oona is love', they are, it turns out, in league with Satan and as such, it's hard to regard them as hapless victims of state violence, which dilutes any pretensions the film has to social comment. (2011: 89)

The optimistic end of the counter-culture is still in surprising flow here, though it takes on a strange, demented character, unsure whether to laugh or shudder at the many acts of extreme sexual and physical violence on display; the era's sexual politics are on full, horrific show in all of their ugliness. This relates in part to Julia Kristeva's theory of 'abjection' in horror, where the female body itself goes through a representative process towards becoming a component recognised and debased through its relationship with the self: 'The clean and proper (in the sense of incorporated and incorporable) becomes filthy, the sought-after turns into banished, fascination into shame' (1982: 6).[14] This is present within much horror cinema to the extent that, where a film is aging, gaining a patina of discomfort, it arguably makes it more effective, with socio-political progress highlighting the 'abjection' of the female body more with every passing year; the horror being one of recent (as well as ancient) history, leading back to my reaction to the behind-the-scenes picture of *Witchfinder*. Another example of this is another *Witchfinder* copycat, Michael Armstrong's *Mark of the Devil* (1970); another film that follows the sadistic exploits of a witch-finder against various innocent women housed in an isolated rural landscape. Interestingly, the notion of such actions being a sadistic sham are not negated largely to pathos as in Reeves' film, but instead becomes part of the narrative as the equivalent John Stearne character of the film realises quickly that the chief witchfinder (played with mixed results by Herbert Lom) is out for his own ends of pleasurable violence. Cooper again dismisses this film as another failed attempt to capture the Reeves/Haggard brilliance, though he does highlight an intriguing point about the violence:

> *Mark of the Devil* is a strange film, an unusual blend of the atmospheric and the silly... Armstrong's film manages to be far more graphic than *Witchfinder General* without being anywhere near as harrowing. (2011: 93)

Even though Armstrong's film is more graphically violent in its detail,[15] it fails to live up to the depressive nihilism of Reeves' pastoral dystopia.[16] These films highlight further how astonishing Reeves' film really is, where a genuine mental depression is channelled into as stark a territory as horror cinema of the period would dare venture into. Reeves didn't need to show tongues hanging out to display to the audience the full course of misogynistic violence and its repercussions (and, as importantly, its local sources). He relies more on the re-action to violence and the disturbing voyeurism of violence, both aspects which Hessler's and Armstrong's films fail to properly comprehend. These films pale in comparison to the Tigon equivalents of the period but also to other cinematic peers such as Daniel Haller's H.P. Lovecraft adaptation *The Dunwich Horror* (1970) and Ken Russell's *The Devils* (1971) – an astonishing, big-budget production based on Aldous Huxley's *The Devils Of Loudun* (1952)[17] that mixes eroticism and false occult accusations typical of this period, to disturbing, similarly dystopian, effect. The power-play in Russell's film channels the injustice of this grit-under-the-nails occult cinema, showing the twisted power of theological institutions a little too earnestly for the era's censorship board. *The Devils* is one of *the* films that epitomises the 1970s in that the dark psychedelia of the era decays and becomes part of the narrative, even if only through style and lifestyle; free-love finding punishment within the white, wipe-clean (Derek Jarman-designed) walls of Loudun.

The extremity of these films did not go unnoticed at the cheaper end of British film and a parallel strain building on the similar elements of sex, nudity and violence is consistent in British exploitation cinema like a dark, grimy mirror; already reflecting on a muddy, violent and uncomfortable realm of British cinematic topography. Of course, the sexuality within occult media had been brewing for some time. With the rise in interest during the period in the work, life and writing of English occultist Aleister Crowley, this was to be expected. As Sweet suggests, 'So, Crowley is the person who is responsible for importing that kind of sexualised atmosphere to ritual practise. He in a way is packaging this stuff and his perfect audience then turns up in the sixties' (2015). The sexual revolution that came with the counter-culture found its perfect, emblematic figure, but his form of sexualised occult ritual can also be linked to the rise at the exploitation end of occult cinema; not including the fact that many of the films so far already mentioned had an atmosphere of heady, dangerous sexuality anyway.

The most effective of this strain of British exploitation occult cinema is in the surprisingly effective *Virgin Witch* (1972), directed by Ray Austin. His film links the objectifying visions of the modelling world with a secret, middle-class enclave of erotic occultism, whereby a model and her sister are lured away to a Home Counties mansion under the semi-false premise of a photo-shoot, only to find themselves embroiled in a nudity-embellished set of occult rituals. The film's opulent, heady reality is again channelling the period; in fact, the film's narrative can be symbolically summarised in its totality by the behind-the-scenes *Witchfinder* photo, only replacing the Suffolk cottages with a low budget, faux-opulence of the swinging, sexualised bourgeoisie of Surrey. The same atmosphere is also present in Roddy McDowall's only directorial feature film, *The Devil's Widow* or *The Ballad of Tam-Lin* (1970) as it's also known. Apart from being one of the few films to actually recreate a full, folkloric tale, McDowall's film also represents that dual vision of early 1970s British topography, mixing motorways and pylons with hills and mountains. Though its swinging Chelsea set are decamped to a Scottish landscape as opposed to the Home Counties, under the seductive power of an older witch (Ava Gardner), the hauntological impact is explicit; 1970s Britain in the diegetic realm seems overwhelmingly occult-worshipping rather than Church of England. This is before mentioning the soundtrack, written and recorded by the group Pentangle; equally symbolic of the period's interest in folklore and the older ways.

Yet this sort of film was arguably pioneered more in American trash and pulp cinema than in the British Isles, with films like *Something Weird* (1967), *Mark of the Witch* (1970), *The Brotherhood of Satan* (1971), *Daughters of Satan* (1972), *Blood Orgy of the She-Devils* (1973) and *Warlock Moon* (1973) all being trashy examples of a US equivalent. When this breed of seedy occultism does rear its head in British cinema, it takes on a rather different tone that certainly speaks more of do-mesticity and class than when in the realm of American trash cinema, a good example being the England-set *Satan's Slave* (1976). These would often take the form of documentaries, though the documentary aesthetic (as an excuse for exploitation tropes such as nudity and violence) has been somewhat blurred since the nudist exploits of British cinema in the 1960s in films such as *London in the Raw* (1965). One of the most interesting examples of this documentary approach is Malcolm Leigh's *Legend of the Witches* (1970). Leigh's film exem-plifies a unique facet of British occultism; one defined by it being explored by presenters and producers who were sufficiently straight-edged to make the gen-uine occult practices of the British public seem positively eccentric, perhaps more so than they actually were. The faux-documentary format of films such as *Legend of the Witches* also helps tie in to more hauntological aspects, where the sense of the real within the social realm adds horror and discomfort. There's also a patina of age within these films aesthetically, as if buried under the earth for a number of years like the book in Sam Raimi's *The Evil Dead* (1981). The links to Hauntology come from such artefacts as Leigh's film going through the very process of *becoming* artefacts, largely discovered in shady uploads into the digital realm on YouTube and the like. Fisher recognises this aspect to be a key propagator of Hauntology as a force in the twenty-first century. He writes:

> But here we have a first reason why the concept of hauntology should have
> become attached to popular culture in the first decade of the 21st century. For
> it was at this moment when cyberspace enjoyed unprecedented dominion over
> the reception, distribution and consumption of culture – especially music culture.
> (2014: 20)

These artefacts would rise through such 'cyberspace', perhaps because of their obvious aesthetic distinctiveness; their grainy, patchy and morally dubious po-sition standing out naturally in the clean-cut digital world of new visual culture. Though films like the unholy trinity work within Folk Horror by mixing the por-trayal of a darker age with an actual rejuvenation of that age through their nar-ratives (both within and outside the diegesis), occult examples such as *Legend of the Witches* work purely by showing an underside to their production era; an un-derside that now appears more and more prescient given what we have learned of this period in recent years.[18] Leigh's film isn't the only example of this. It aptly has an Italian doppelgänger in the form of *Witchcraft '70* (1970) by Luigi Scattini, and a televisual twin in the BBC documentary *Power of the Witch*: *Real or Imaginary*, presented by Michael Bakewell in 1971. With the entry into the home, both for the occult practices in the documentary and in how the documentary could be solely viewed, this presents some transition in regards to hauntological occultism, where there was a literal invasion into the domestic household and not just in the questionable Soho cinemas where it undoubtedly proliferated.

Several examples from previous chapters have already shown the interest in such practices in all forms of television from this period. Bowen's *Robin Redbreast* is an obvious example, one that fits Sweet's assessment that, 'The country is a place where you can escape the stress of urban life but it's also an alien environment, where city dwellers don't know how to conduct themselves; a place where no one can hear you scream' (2015). This theme seemed to infect and find its way into all sorts of drama strands, even children's television with programs like *The Owl Service*, *Children of the Stones* and *Doctor Who* stories such as *The Daemons* and *The Stones of Blood*. The decade even saw the dramatisation of the Pendle witch trials in *The Witches of Pendle* (1977) for the BBC. Perhaps the narrative of British occult television would be re-written if the BBC adaptation of John Buchan's *Witch Wood* from 1964 had not been wiped from the archives, moving the interest earlier into the 1960s. Yet occultism confidently prevails into the very heart of 1970s cathode-ray tube culture as well as in cinema. As Betty exclaims to Frank in *Some Mother's Do 'Ave 'Em* (1973–1978) (a moment enhanced by Betty being played by Michele Dotrice – second in command to Angel Blake in the Devil's gang of *The Blood on Satan's Claw*), 'The Satanic frightens me, Frank!'; such was its common, even domestic, currency during this period.

This wouldn't be a theme wholly contained within 1970s television, though there is undoubtedly a strong connection between the sociology of the era and the wide-spread scale of the theme in its pop culture. Occult window dressings can be found in 1980s oddities such as the first two-part serial of the *Campion* series, where a mystery of inheritance is doused with strange demonic and occult presences on a local patch of English village green. Even more baffling is the failed *Doctor Who* spin-off *K-9 And Company: A Girl's Best Friend* (1981),[19] which produces the daring mixture of local village occultism and the dramatic dynamics of market gardening. It's surprisingly effective in hindsight, though perhaps more so because of its own acknowledged awfulness; the occult clearly has little hold in the dark, early days of Thatcherism and neo-liberal England, looking more to gardening than erotic ceremonies. Back in the early days of counter-culture, however, even Danny Wilde (Tony Curtis) and Lord Brett Sinclair (Roger Moore) had to deal with a gang using occultism as a scare tactic to keep the locals away in the episode of *The Persuaders!*, *A Home Of One's Own* (1971). Perhaps in anticipation of this, occultism found more and more favour with American pictures as a whole as the 1970s went on. Robert Fuest's underrated

The Devil's Rain (1975) sees an occult group stalking typically isolated American plains, as does Jack Starrett's *Race with the Devil*, made during the same year.[20]

It could be argued that occultism of the hauntological kind gave way to a different type of occultism altogether, though one that developed alongside these films.[21] When films like *The Devil Rides Out* and *The Satanic Rites of Dracula* introduced occultism and Devil worship via pulpy, Wheatley-indebted narratives, they were often in constant dialogue with the themes of power; whether financial, political or otherwise. This strand developed into the most popular branch of occult film, the 'demonic child' picture, starting off with Roman Polanski's *Rosemary's Baby* (1968). Polanski's film not only links such theological practices to financial necessity – after all, the ritual and happenings of the film occur because of Guy's (John Cassavetes) desire to further his acting career by offering his wife Rosemary (Mia Farrow) up to the OAP occultists that live on the floor above – but directly disassociates it from the rural into the very heart of the most urban of environments. The same ideas can be seen in William Friedkin's *The Exorcist* (1973) and Richard Donner's *The Omen* (1976) as well as their numerous sequels. Newman highlights a theme that connects *Rosemary* with *The Exorcist*, in that there is a definite link of required bodies, so to speak, recalling Kristeva's abjection theories again. He writes that, '*Rosemary's Baby* and *The Exorcist* use one of the oldest Big Scary Ideas in the *Necronomicon*: the Monster wants your body' (1988: 58), further writing in regards to *Rosemary* that its trick was 'to give the "Mysterious They" a decidedly Satanic cast' (1988: 59).

These big-budget films represent a significant improvement in cinematic quality, at least in comparison to their previous occult peers, but this in a sense removes the more interesting hauntological quality of the subject matter. Though they indeed go some way to expanding on the causations surrounding the theory of the Folk Horror Chain – whereby urban environments can isolate and, in other ways, enhance the stimulation and potential of occult activity – their sense of smoothness against the grimy grain of the exploitation films make them less receptive to hauntological analysis. For, in spite of these American films making the useful connection between affluence and Satanism yet again, Hauntology functions in the British iteration by being counter in virtually every aesthetic option to the typical British film. Films like *Virgin Witch* and *Legend of the Witches* say more about the era and our relationship to that era by being thoroughly earnest about the vices and pleasures of period audiences and even period society as a whole. As discussed during our analysis of the unholy trinity, films of this ilk are of such interest *because* they are so of their time; their aged form revealing the picture of society like Dorian Gray's stabbed portrait, aging into an unsettling vision with a morally battered body. These big-budget films feel perhaps less 'of their time', even with their various scenes of projectile vomiting, bloody masturbation with a metal cross, violence, rape and dismemberment.

This raises questions regarding nostalgia, a notion that undoubtedly manifests repeatedly when analysing hauntological relationships. Is the resurgence in interest around the predominance of kitsch occultism in British pop culture of this period formed around a desire to go back to what seems a more open era? Fisher questioned this earlier, acknowledging that the freedom was de-pendent explicitly on being a white, middle-class male. But these ideas are the sort of thematic starting point for, as an example, when critics side with the Summerisle-anders in their burning of another human. Is such a phe-nomenon simply blasé hyperbole?[22] Jamie Sexton has critiqued the thematic framework of Hauntology as a movement in his paper on Ghost Box records, writing in detail of the problematic nature that nostalgia plays in these types of media:

> Mark Fisher, meanwhile, has argued that because many hauntological artists openly address nostalgia in their work, they do not belong to the 'nostalgia mode' that he considers indicative of postmodernism. I think Fisher's contention can be accepted up to a point: certainly, self-conscious references to the process of nostalgia should not be conflated with nostalgia per se. However, there is for me too neat a distinction being drawn between hauntology and postmodernist nostalgia here. Fisher uses postmodernism as an example of negative nostalgia—of a crash-and-grab retro mindset which actually conceals its nostalgic operations and instead posits a kind of 'end of history' timelessness (where all temporal moments collapse into the present). (2012: 20)

The relationship with such artefacts of film and television is most definitely not simply a case of nostalgic postmodernism; such an argument is in itself reductive of Fisher's overall framework and choice of case-studies. Fisher even addresses this notion, asking 'is hauntology, as many of its critics have main-tained, simply a name for nostalgia?' (2014: 25). But nostalgia does play its part in the recognition of the era's occultism, even if it is a nostalgia purely for a different, perhaps more daring, kind of popular culture; when the dam-ming of film censorship broke down, allowing a flood of provocation to gush forth. There are more reasons for this than simply the sheer aesthetic abun-dance of the work presented here. It has mapped the sociology and the very aesthetics of the era itself as well. This is where Hauntology must move away from the purely occult as a theme and account for the final body of work to be assessed from this period; where Britain in the 1970s becomes folkloric in itself, where the diegesis of the themes of Folk Horror becomes disturbingly permeable, and where the era's paranoia can be seen to have come full circle in our current decade. The horror of the 1970s may have been doused in occultism, sacrifices, naked witches and the Devil – it may have even been what Sweet calls 'a time when darkness fell on the hippy dreams of love and peace' (2015) – but it is a darkness that breaks the surface into the very reality of the 1970s, and not one that is simply defined by pervy witch flicks and buying Alex Sanders' *A Witch if Born* album (1970) for a naughty, late-night party. It is a darkness that arguably still haunts, with its past calamities and twisted visions of urban zones, Public Information Films that failed to protect, and haunted analogue tape players forever doomed to torture with their repeated, never-ending traumas.

The 'Urban Wyrd' and Hauntology

> There was much public concern about a new brand of bureaucracy,
> which manifested itself in the form of secret establishments: giant radars
> reputed to endanger human life and concealed huge plastic pods; germ-
> warfare establishments behind barbed wire; atom-proof shelters for chosen
> administrators. – Nigel Kneale (1979: 6)

The television and film writer Nigel Kneale produced a large body of work, the impact of which is great though often invisible and subtle. He is a figure, rather like his forebear M.R. James, who haunts this book, but I have resisted the temptation to dive deep into the dark recesses of his work until this point. This is because, although the range of Kneale's work thematically has a number of ties to the theoretical frameworks of previous chapters (a number of his plays deal explicitly with the causational working of the Folk Horror Chain, while others deal with themes of rurality, television topography and occultism), his work acts as a suitable introduction to the starkest and most complex of theories surrounding both Hauntology and Folk Horror. The above quote from Kneale gives some context as to his inspiration: he is discussing what it was like in Britain in the 1950s rather than the time in which he wrote it, at the tail-end of the 1970s. In other words, Kneale's work seemed to portray fantastical ideas that were then often on the cusp of becoming a reality within only a few years of writing. Because of this, he can be considered a predictor of the modern era in the same vein as J.G. Ballard. This section brings together a number of Knealian ideas to discuss several key themes in Folk Horror. They are:

- The presence of urban topographies and zones in film and television in a genre that has been shown to be traditionally rural based.
- The overflow of public paranoia and how it manifests in the fictional worlds of film and television, especially in the 1970s.
- The treatment of 1970s Britain as a Folkloric realm in itself, now, with Hauntology as a contextualising influence.

Peter Hutchings suggests in relation to Kneale's work – specifically in regards to *Quatermass II* – that the nationalistic interpretations of rural and urban concepts bring to their drama a certain otherness within their subversion, writing that, 'Definitions of Englishness and Britishness often deploy particular notions of rural and urban landscape' (2004: 38). Bringing such Jamesian elements as cursed artefacts and objects into purely urban realms is one of Kneale's key traits in this sense, whereby supernatural tendencies spark both a mirroring of the genuine social paranoia of post-war Britain and a subversion of these traditional delineations of the urban and the rural. It is this quality that must be first assessed when dealing with the hauntological questions surrounding Britain in the 1970s, especially as the key example of Kneale's writing in this regard – *Quatermass and the Pit* – is written and produced well before such sociological intrigues occur.[23] *Quatermass and the Pit*, more so than the previous two *Quatermass* instalments in their various incarnations, questions both a post-war relationship with the most urban of landscapes (inner-city London) and raises further questions about the workings of the Folk Horror Chain, as well as urban reactions to folklore in the face of enlightenment knowledge. As Rob Young writes, the film differs from many of Hammer's other fantastical horrors because of its modern, urban setting: '*Quatermass and the Pit* was unusual in the Hammer oeuvre in being set squarely in the present, as the majority of horror scripts were set in the past...' (2011: 417). A narrative breakdown of the cinematic version by Roy Ward Baker rather than the BBC original follows.

> ***Quatermass and the Pit*** – Renovation is in progress at the Hobbs Lane Underground station in London when builders uncover remains of skeletons that look like earlier forms of man. Alongside this, a strange object is gradually uncovered and the military bomb-disposal team are called in, thinking that it may be an unexploded device from the war. Professor Quatermass (Andrew Keir) is brought to the site with Colonel Breen (Julian Glover), the pair forced to work together following the miltary's takeover of the Professor's moon colonisation project. With research and help from Barbara Judd (Barbara Shelley), Quatermass begins to believe that the object is not a bomb or a failed piece of enemy

propaganda from the war but an alien ship that landed on the Earth some five million years ago. His research reveals that Hobbs Lane has folkloric connections with the Devil, and that the site has been one perpetually haunted throughout history. The army break into the ship and find the carcasses of insect-like aliens, which instantly begin to rot. It is established that they are from Mars. The man who drilled into the vessel, Sladden (Duncan Lamont), becomes possessed by telekinetic energy which acts as some sort of race memory, his body being spun around the area and into a local church. Something powerful has been unleashed from the vessel and Sladden's mind-print is played back to a disbelieving group of officials, showing images of the Martian' purges on their own planet, which, it is claimed, explains humanity's unconscious leaning towards fascism. Breen insists the whole thing is fake and organises a press viewing to televise his explanation of the object. The power from all of the broadcasting equipment unleashes a huge, psychokinetic presence over London in the form of one of the aliens, inciting people towards a primitive violence by activating the population's race memories. Even Quatermass becomes susceptible. His palaeontologist friend Roney (James Donald) concludes that the energy could be grounded by earthing it. He climbs and controls a nearby crane into the image of the alien which destroys it, killing himself in the process.

Quatermass has a subtle relationship to Folk Horror and to Hauntology. In the former it presents an urban vision of the Folk Horror Chain, where the belief system has already been founded, enacted and subsequently buried; physically under the tube station in the artefact and psychically in the minds of the human race. Kneale's masterstroke is to link our own fascist leanings to an alien causation, whereby he addresses the stark questions left hanging after the atrocities of the Second World War by intelligently recontextualising them. There's an obvious hauntological element here as well, where the first of Fisher's definitions of the term is given dramatic corporeality. It could be argued that the evolution, from the station and the area being haunted by the power of the vessel (and its subsequent influence on the area's very name and folklore) to the final alien manifestation, is a transition from Hauntology to Folk Horror in formal terms. When its forgotten presence is enacting its will and power through what is perceived to be ghosts in the past, this is hauntological. When this power is unleashed, eventually through the energy of the analogue broadcast equipment, this is Folk Horror. *Quatermass*, therefore, shows Hauntology to be yet another part of the causation towards Folk Horror narratives, but one that can also be self-contained within its psychological causations and relations.

Hutchings suggests that Professor Quatermass' optimistic need to explain away the darker side of human nature as being derived from aliens is 'reactionary', writing further that, 'As was the case with *Quatermass and the Pit*, the tendency in *Quatermass* to blame social rebellion on an alien influence does have distinctly reactionary qualities' (2004: 37). Yet such a reading ignores the obvious, pessimistic reality of that realisation; that, even if it's not the fault of humanity itself, the violent tendencies will always be there, always with the potential to manifest again in the physical world, whether that be in the form of giant, Martian ghost-prints on the London skyline, or in the concentration camps erected mere decades before the film was made. This is hauntological again but in the second form, the potential 'already in the virtual...' as Fisher writes. Andy Murray recognises this strain in Kneale's writing more overtly, arguing that, 'In much of his work, humankind's darker urges – destruction, repression, the hate of the unlike, the march of hazardous science – are represented for dramatic purposes by alien threats, terrifying, uncontrollable ghosts, or simply the spectre of all-out Armageddon' (2006: 13). The key difference with *Quatermass* is that it posits potential Folk Horror themes in an entirely different setting. The danger Kneale presents is one not caused purely by the skewing isolation of rural enclaves – the enlightenment knowledge of the city effectively antagonises the situation in this case in spite of eventually solving it – but one that is inherent outside of location as an instigating factor. Because of this, its setting fills this eventual gap, linking usefully the cramped claustrophobia of urban environments with esoteric happenings. Considering the many films made after this, such as the unholy trinity, that would argue for the reverse in regards to rural locations being the supreme backdrop for esoteric summonings and violence, *Quatermass* sticks out for its own hauntological breed of nihilism.

Kneale can be seen as a writer who channels a number of these hauntological concerns, often aesthetically (in hindsight) as well as thematically. The Jamesian object at the centre of *Quatermass* seems to crop up again and again in his work, though the theme becomes more and more hauntological as time goes by. Straight after Hammer's final version of *Quatermass*, Kneale would predict communication technology's distancing effect and even the popularity of reality television in the BBC play *The Year of the Sex Olympics* (1968) for *Theatre 625*.[24] Our history of Kneale's Folk Horror relationship would perhaps continue into the 1960s if his episode of *First Night*, *The Road* (1963), still existed in the archives. The play's script tells of a pair of seventeenth-century academics investigating a haunted pathway in a wood, only for it to be revealed that the ghosts of a future nuclear holocaust are somehow haunting the past; an intriguing take on Fisher's second theory of Hauntology, with its haunting being of a future rather than past calamity (or more accurately, a present concern in the period of Kneale's writing). But it was not until 1972 when the themes at the core in *Quatermass and the Pit* would align with a technological emphasis to create the sort of aesthetic outcome now ubiquitous in our own relationship to popular culture of the 1970s.

Nineteen seventy-two was itself a bumper Christmas in regards to ghost stories, and Kneale added to this astonishing run of programs in the form of the television film *The Stone Tape*. This was the same Christmas where viewers were treated to Paxton's demise at the hands of meddling with cursed objects in Clark's adaptation of *A Warning to the Curious*, as well as the November–December run of the haunted series *Dead of Night*. The year's winter is probably the most haunted within the whole of British popular culture. Of course, Kneale and James have strong likenesses within their narrative structures, even down to the humour which Murray picks up on, postulating that, 'This blending of horror and arch mockery – as Kneale had observed of M.R. James, dry humour heightening the frightful – was effective indeed' (2006: 9). Ghosts were already becoming a common theme in Kneale's work, of course, through recontextualisaion in *Quatermass and the Pit*, in *The Road*, and in the (yet again, missing) episode of *Out of the Unknown*, *The Chopper* (1971).[25] But it was to be a theme honed in *The Stone Tape*, where technology breaks open a wound in the history of a semi-built-up space to unleash horrific and disturbing consequences. Being yet another key example of Folk Horror, it requires detailed analysis, in its context as a ghost story from the period, in its role in the portrayal of analogue technology, and in its portrayal of 1970s sociology. A narrative breakdown follows.

> ***The Stone Tape*** – Ryan Electrics, a sound technology company, are relocating their research teams to an old Victorian mansion known as Taskerlands. Peter Brock (Michael Bryant) is the lead researcher developing sound recording and playback technology. On bringing his team to the newly refurbished castle, its manager, Roy (Iain Cuthbertson), informs them that not all of the work has been completed by the builders on their specific computer space as they have refused to work in one room in particular as it is supposedly haunted. He and his team explore the room and his lead computer programmer Jill (Jane Asher) hears a terrifying scream and sees the figure of a women running up a derelict flight of stairs. After research in the local village, Brock concludes that the very stone of the Saxon room has somehow recorded an event that happened in the past, calling it the 'stone tape' and instantly breaks off all of his team's other research to study the phenomena in the hope of commercialising it to get ahead of their Japanese competitors. The team begins an aurally

harrowing series of tests upon the room, bombarding it with analogue (radiophonic heavy) sound, hoping that the secrets of the supposed technology will be revealed. It instead becomes clear that Brock has, in a sense, wiped the tape. Jill continues her research and argues that there is, in fact, a much older recording in the room, but Brock dismisses her theories in the wake of rival researchers taking his space in the establishment. She is forced to take time off, Brock claiming that she is mentally unstable. She visits the room one last time and is killed by a malevolent force contained within the stone, hidden underneath the recording of the girl. Brock lies to an inquiry about her death, claiming she was unbalanced. On returning to the establishment, he enters the room again but finds, to his horror, that the room has recorded Jill's final moments, screaming his name before she died in torment.

The Stone Tape has genuine applications in regards to cultural and technological theories, but this is not to distract from its sheer success as a piece of drama.[26] In the trend to fetishise analogue technology over the last decade especially (arguably a link built by Kneale and the play in the first place), its legend looms large over Folk Horror and the genre's growth in recent years. *The Stone Tape* opens up a whole variety of areas even outside of these many avenues, including (appropriately) the portrayal, attitudes and treatment of race and gender in early 1970s Britain. Essentially, Brock is a patriarchal figure but one whose assumptions of academic superiority over his supposed inferior (both in status and gender apropos Jill's treatment) comes back to literally haunt him. Hutchings acknowledges this, writing:

> However, this confident assertion of rational (and implicitly masculine) knowledge is overturned when a female scientist inadvertently 'plays' the stone tape and becomes the latest in a long line of sacrifices at what is revealed to be an ancient stone construction described by the writer Nigel Kneale as 'a proto-Stonehenge'. (2004: 37)

The female here is sacrificed for the preservation of the masculine academic status; an almost Enlightenment inversion of the occult tendencies of many films from the previous section, though women were largely punished for their sexual confidence in those examples rather than intellectual equality and superiority. *The Stone Tape*, in spite of its casual period sexism and racism, actually ends up commenting on such issues rather than partaking of them. It perhaps explains why the play has aged so well as it is equally a narrative about the failings of 1970s society as it is a play about Jamesian intellectual carelessness and haunted analogue equipment. Fisher aligns these problems within modern hauntological arguments in regards to neo-liberal capitalism, writing (in a similar strain to that of *The Stone Tape*'s dramatic relationships) that, 'Haunting, then, can be construed as a failed mourning. It is about refusing to give up the ghost or – and this can sometimes amount for the same thing – the refusal of the ghost to give up on us' (2014: 22). Brock's mourning is motivated by guilt more than anything (further indebted to Fisher's argument by the fact that he was driven by commercial rather than academic forces) but *The Stone Tape* activates this phenomenon by literally and hysterically replaying past traumas. Earlier in the play, these are simply the traumas of a more violent society (the victim is, of course, still a woman, almost certainly at the hands of a man) but, by the end of the play, they are very earnestly replaying modern traumas; playing the 1970s back to itself and showing it to be utterly horrified by what it sees. One character's infamous realisation of 'It's in the computer!' is slightly inaccurate. If any object in the play houses such ineffable forces, it is the ancient parts of its main building, but he should really have screamed, 'It's in the 1970s!'.

Analogue equipment of the recording kind would often play on this relationship outside of Kneale, especially in work after the broadcast of *The Stone Tape* but also before. When *Out of the Unknown* moved from hard science-fiction to strange tales of 1970s suburbia in its third and fourth series, the shift opened up even starker areas of questioning. The second episode of series four highlights this disturbingly in the story *To Lay a Ghost* (1971). The narrative follows the lives of a newly-wed couple who have moved into a new house. Diana (Lesley-Anne Down)[27] has a seeming aversion to sexual intercourse due to being raped when she was younger (an event which opens the play). Her photographer husband Eric (Iain Gregory) begins to notice her strange behaviour in the new house, almost as if she's becoming possessed. A figure appears in several of his photographs of her and a parapsychologist (Peter Barkworth) is brought in with a variety of analogue equipment, to track down the ghostly figure. It transpires that Diana has developed a fetish regarding assault and can only become sexually aroused through force (explaining why Eric has failed to have sex with her). This is being taken advantage of by the ghost of a seventeenth-century rapist who is shown to fulfil her desires at the end of the play. Again, it is the analogue technology that seems to link the palimpsest of past events from buildings and landscape, though it also again shows a disturbing contemporary attitude against women; pairing *The Stone Tape* and *To Lay a Ghost* together makes for a shocking but intriguing double bill of technology-enabling ghosts of the past to manifest, but also demonstrates the manifestation of a very literal patriarchy evident in the period of production.

The same technological paraphernalia can be found in examples such as the one-off ghost story *A Child's Voice* (1978), the fantastical BBC series *The Omega Factor* (1979),[28] the second assignment for *Sapphire and Steel* (1979), the *Dramarama*: *Spooky* episode, *The Danny Roberts Show* (1983) and, even more overtly knowing, in the *Doctor Who* episodes *Image of the Fendahl* (1977) and *Hide* (2013). All of these are slightly one removed from the initial linkages with a counter-culture paranormal, however, even those made during the 1970s, and none of them quite achieve the same sort of effects as in *To Lay a Ghost* or in Kneale's use of analogue equipment. Kneale put his stamp onto the hauntological potential in analogue equipment and its ability to draw up the past into literal permutations of physical horror. This was not to be Kneale's only contribution to Folk Horror narrative tendencies but it is without a doubt his most prescient in regards to how such cultural material is remembered and revived today. Three years after *The Stone Tape*, Kneale would move into even starker, if more traditional, Folk Horror territory, coinciding with his move away from the BBC to ITV. The writer now focused on channelling ideas still reverberating from *Quatermass and the Pit* into more domestic environments; the sheer fact of this move's success raises further questions about the era.

In 1975 Kneale wrote an episode for the ITV series *Against The Crowd*, entitled *Murrain*. The play follows a vet, Alan (David Simeon), who stumbles across the rural bullying of an eccentric women (Una Brandon-Jones)[29] by local farmers who believe she has put a curse on their cattle after one farmer cut off her water supply. The farmers are led by Beeley (Bernard Lee), who is heading the campaign against her by killing her cat and being generally antisocial; almost starving her out of her ramshackle barn. With help from Alan, the authorities are alerted to her situation, but there is little that he can do when the mob attacks. However, his Enlightenment beliefs are called into question by the surprising results of such an attack (the 1970s seeming to often downgrade Enlightenment knowledge in the face of old ways). The play has the added period frisson of being shot entirely on video, making it feel very much like a documentary or a news reel from the period. Murray highlights the play's shift to a domesticated form of horror and how such a shift chimed with Kneale's own writing:

> Filmed entirely on video, with a generous helping of location work, *Murrain* is an intriguing twist on a perennial Kneale preoccupation – the clash of the old and superstitious with the new and rational. Kneale himself is dismissive of the supernatural, and yet fascinated by it, and specifically, by the idea of everyday life suffused with extraordinary happenings. (2006: 4)

Murrain is both an example of this suffusing of the extraordinary into the ordinary but also a brilliant, if ambiguous, example of the Folk Horror Chain.
Because the focus of the play is from the perspective of the Enlightenment
figure yet again (the vet with his science), the play's drama begins almost as
a social realist account of bullying. It's only as the vet becomes aware of
why the bullying is happening that *Murrain*'s perspective begins to change.
His scientific outlook, in spite of being useless in the face of an unknown
illness plaguing the farmer's herd of cattle, aids his arrogant assumptions
and good-Samaritan nature which disintegrates when, after defending the
old woman from a final raid by the group of men, she appears to strike one
dead with some sort of supernatural power. Hutchings argues this trait to
be typical of Kneale and brought over from *Quatermass II*, writing that, 'The
verdant countryside becomes a residuum of old beliefs that have survived the
modernization and urbanization of British society and which in various ways
challenge modern social norms' (2004: 36). It's played as a straight drama,
with the suggestion that the lead farmer's heart attack is naturally occurring,
if unlikely. Alan's reaction to this moment, which finishes the play, is that typical Knealian and Jamesian twist of horror being derived from a secular belief system crumbling in the face of the terrifying unknown. Like *Quatermass
and the Pit*, the scientist is left dumbfounded and in shock at the realisation of
an almost inevitable void in his knowledge.

In a similar vein, though perhaps not so consistently successful, is the series that
Kneale would write after *Murrain*; the short-lived anthology horror serial *Beasts*
(1976). The central premise of the series is slightly unusual for Kneale in that it
looks towards a continuous battle between Man vs. Beast, though is deliberately blurring the line between such a delineation anyway. From the hordes of rats
in *During Barty's Party* to lycanthropy in *What Big Eyes*, the series channels contact with strange, even ghostly forms of mammalia into claustrophobic forms
of horror. The most successful of these is the fourth episode, *Baby*, which has
a narrative of disturbing resonances, again from an intriguingly female perspective, which also manages to channel themes present in *Quatermass* and *The
Stone Tape*. Another newly married couple, Jo (Jane Wymark) and Peter (Simon
MacCorkindale), are having their rural cottage renovated when the workers
find a strange jar embedded into the wall. Jo is heavily pregnant and disturbed
by the contents of the jar which appear to be foetus-like remains. It becomes
clear that the jar has been put in the house as some sort of curse, meaning that
animals of all forms (including people) on the land around cannot successfully
give birth, perhaps put there by rival farmers at an earlier period in the house's
history.

Baby feels very much like a Jamesian fable, though one that also channels *The Blood on Satan's Claw*, where a cursed object is used to summon up something far more horrendous. In the case of *Baby*, the manifestation is an indistinct form found suckling the foetus in the living room one night when Jo investigates some noises downstairs. *Baby* highlights the present-day 1970s setting deliberately, where ancient evil and menace hide comfortably within the most garishly decorated of fashionable homes. In fact, *Baby* edges away from its inorganic demon forefathers by such a time-shift; into the colder climate of the 1970s where Enlightenment thinking has apparently 'won' but with few genuine social benefits, especially for women. Putting *Baby*, *Murrain* and *The Stone Tape* together, Kneale's writing can be seen as something of a reaction to the 1970s; with hysteria manifesting through intriguing mechanisms hidden within rooms, jars and animals. The latter may seem the oddest of these, but, as Murray argues:

> It's pretty easy to assess the ways in which *Beasts* fits into the larger warp and weft of Kneale's work. The series' umbrella theme of Man in conflict with assorted creatures – for which read Man's own bestial nature – is a favourite Kneale preoccupation. (2006: 13)

This can appropriately return to *Quatermass* and Hauntology, as man's own nature and its role in horror is the key theme in *Quatermass and the Pit*; the evil is not only within us but has *always* been within us. Though the jar in *Baby* hasn't always been there, it has in the sense of the play's timeline. Perhaps this makes its horror slightly differing from *Quatermass* as the jar itself is a diegetic concoction within potential living memory, perhaps even belonging to the cottage's previous owners. Again, there is a hauntological difference between the two narratives that speaks of the era in question. In *Quatermass*, the period in which the film or series is really set matters very little (in spite of it invoking Cold War paranoia) as the evil will always have the potential to manifest. In *Baby*, and *The Stone Tape* for that matter, the horror refuses to give up on the protagonists, be it through the sentience of the esoteric forms and the rabid curiosity which they inspire à la James. At this point, the modern setting seems to distance them dangerously from such harmful 'olde ways'. It is fitting that Kneale would conclude Professor Quatermass' narrative in particular with a well-made four-part dystopian serial in 1979 that removes such questioning almost entirely.

In *Quatermass* (or *The Quatermass Conclusion*),[30] the world has become a Ballardian dystopia full of *High-Rise*-style gangs of youths[31] roaming the derelict streets and violent hippy groups of Planet People, wandering and wishing to be taken somewhere else. An unidentified alien force is using marker points on the planet to feed on the gathering groups of people, usually (but not exclusively) Planet People meeting at *menhir* formations. The series has several obvious Folk Horror motifs – stone circles being the marker points built by ancestors to show where the alien force previously used its harvester beam, the inclusion of the nursery rhyme *Ringstone Round*, and contrasting man-made oblique objects such as radio telescopes – but overall, it feels more akin to the earlier, more science-fiction infused entries for the Professor.[32] The series' date of broadcast is also outside the peak of the hauntological visions of the 1970s; its inclusion of counter-culture flower-power vibes seeming a period feature by 1979. Urban spaces were no longer the sites of occult rituals or manifesting ancient evils at this point, but there were other examples alongside Kneale's staggering body of ghosts in the machine that channelled hauntological themes or the 'Urban Wyrd', some within the fictional pulp of cinema but others, more disturbingly, in the potential reality of the decade itself.

The 'Urban Wyrd' of Quatermass' encounter with Hobbs Lane resonates with a number of intriguing films treading along similar lines but for differing reasons. The portrayal of inner-city London and its outer reaches in the 1970s has a strange feeling to it that is perhaps one built more through the angle of perception than anything truly inherent in the films. The shift in emphasis can be seen in Derek Jarman's surreal punk film *Jubilee* (1978), where a character is tied to a lamppost and forced to partake in a May Day celebration of sorts. This is, however, late in the decade and the flowery sexuality of similar scenes found in *The Wicker Man*, and even more darkly in *The Daemons*, is replaced with a punk pessimism.[33] For the punks are not tying the girl up with ribbons but instead with barbed wire; such is the difference that later films of the decade and even the following decade showcases. This is somewhat removed from the actual strangeness that urban environments displayed in the post-counter-culture climate, but it at least summarises the teleology of such a movement's progression.

Urban environments became more than places to unearth forgotten horrors but were instead sleazy, grimy zones where horror took on a surprisingly urban-folkloric character. This can be seen at the start of decade in a number of British films, especially in Alfred Hitchcock's *Frenzy* (1972).[34] *Frenzy* highlights how greasy and sweaty the urban environment had become after the free love upheaval, and British cinema relished in showing its darker potential. The urban zone was no longer the place of enlightenment TV script editors safely away from older rural practices, but a place of equal torment and ritual; whether it be the occult practices indulged in by the upper-class or the primitive, erotic violence enacted by a man with a neck-tie murder fetish. Hitchcock taps into the era's openness to the sleazy reality of such urban spaces; places that simultaneously hide past *and* present traumas. If there was a hauntological measuring device (a Spectre-meter?), it would be going as haywire as a Knealian oscillator possessed by an older spirit. In films such as Gordon Hessler's *Scream and Scream Again* (1970),[35] Michael Tuchner's *Villain* (1971),[36] Douglas Hickox's *Sitting Target* (1972)[37] and *Theatre of Blood* (1973),[38] Lindsay Anderson's *O' Lucky Man!* (1973),[39] Stanley Kubrick's *A Clockwork Orange*[40] and Sidney Lumet's *The Offence* (1973)[41] there's a mixed sense of grease on the era's cutlery; where a grimy underground of varying forms is up to all sorts of horrendous, almost ritualistic, acts of violence. These acts aren't only enabled by the literal caverns of derelict 1970s London but by the very era itself. Kubrick's film especially may be set in the future to begin with but, after its halfway mark, it gives up the game and quietly admits that it's 1970s London through and through; a place of victimised homeless people, police violence, political paranoia and the apparent tolerance of sadistic acts of sexual violence, both within the diegesis and, even more disturbingly, amongst contemporary audiences.

These elements may seem disparate but, in spite of the obvious genre differences of many of these films, something does tangibly connect them: a permissiveness with which their settings allow such events to unfold. As Paciorek notes when discussing the potential for Folk Horror to travel to more urban locations:

> The tradition of the horror may indeed have rustic roots and pastoral locations may provide the setting for many stronger examples, but people carry their lore and fears with them on their travels and sometimes into a built-up environment. (2015: 10)

The best of these 'Urban Wyrd' films (and certainly the most relevant to Folk Horror) is an underrated horror picture that actually exaggerates elements of the Folk Horror Chain but within an urban setting. The film is Gary Sherman's *Death Line* (1972), sometimes referred to even more disturbingly and grittily as *Raw Meat*. Newman describes it as 'a uniquely British modern massacre...' (2011: 86) and this highlights its reputation as the UK equivalent to Hooper's *The Texas Chainsaw Massacre*. Its mixture of isolation, ambiguous morality and cannibalism all takes place on the London Underground, again another link with *Quatermass*. *Death Line* portrays the last remnants of a party of builders who were left for dead after the part of the tube they were building collapsed in upon them. They survived, but degenerated into cannibalism and inbreeding, with one lone male survivor still haunting tube stations for food/people (the film opens with the genuinely touching death of his 'wife'). The film mixes horror with a police procedural drama, the two being inseparable at this point in British cinema. Linking this horror to the sort of 'sleazy Soho'-type sex murder that had dominated pop culture since the mid-1960s, Sherman brings in Donald Pleasence as quite possibly the most useless police detective in British cinema, who seems to do little else except drink cups of tea for some light relief and fend off an even odder cameo role from Christopher Lee.

The Folk Horror Chain is cataclysmic in *Death Line* with genuine sympathy felt for the cannibal man who loses his partner but is unable to communicate his trauma except through grunts and phrases picked up from the tube; the man's final, disturbing screams being 'Mind the doors!'. *Death Line* isn't so much hauntological as its trauma continues through the will to survive rather than in a Freudian sense of compulsion to repeat, but its aesthetics place it firmly in that group of grimy, violent films that characterise the country's cinema of the decade. Of similar ilk is the even more nihilistic cannibal film *Frightmare* (1974) by Pete Walker.[42] Like many of Walker's films, it mixes extreme violence with a skin-flick mentality. The violence, and the psychology, surprisingly, is detailed enough to be incredibly disturbing and realistic. The cannibals in this case are in a Home Counties cottage rather than the city, enacting *Texas Chainsaw*-type massacres again, only with drills and a backdrop of a doyley-covered domesticity. The film even boasts an ending far bleaker than Hooper's film, where the cannibals win against yet another Enlightenment figure in the form of a psychologist; the 1970s is the era of violent primitivism triumphing over Enlightenment society as a whole, urban *or* rural based.[43]

Most intriguing is how these urban environments channel the reality of interest in Folk Horror material while also becoming a part of it; where hindsight allows these films to feel themselves folklorically produced from a darker period. Peter Collinson's film *Fright* (1971), for example, features Susan George watching John Gilling's *The Plague Of The Zombies* whilst babysitting. It is perhaps the most accidentally meta-diegetic of Folk Horror imagery from this period, where the 'real' of Collinson's film mixes with the images of Gilling's and even Peckinpah's by association through the casting of Susan George. Diegesis blurs in the 1970s to create the most unusual and disturbing of effects. Hauntology reflects this by aesthetically summoning certain types of images from the period that reflect this potential for reality; Brutalist architecture and urban learning environments such as polytechnic colleges, as well as the learning material used in such spaces, find a new oddness in the twenty-first century. With writers like J.G. Ballard, urban spaces and suburban spaces were opened out far beyond the clichés of wife-swapping parties and cheese and pineapple hedgehogs.

Television was where this type Folk Horror – the horror of the now as opposed to the purely past-tense iteration – found another strong foothold; the urban, rather than the rural, was the veil hiding much rawer tendencies.

To Lay a Ghost, discussed earlier, sets the tone in this sense, as suburbia became the place that was far more conducive to the weird than the outer space, jet-pack visions of the future.[44] Other *Out of the Unknown* episodes such as *This Body is Mine*, *Deathday* and *Welcome Home* present new visions of strange horror that have the feel of gossip shared over garden fences. Again, misogyny is rife, often manifesting either in the murder of a woman or betrayal by a woman, with the drama often following men breaking down under social constraints and lashing out with primitive barbarism. In *Deathday*, a perfectly sane suburban man reverts to raw violence upon learning that his wife is having an affair because of their boring sex life. The play becomes more surreal as he is haunted by the man whom he invented as an alibi, taunting him into psychological crevasses from which he can't escape. He brings another woman back home after the police have left. She purrs to him 'Rape me'; sexual assault becomes a fantasy in these suburban worlds, even when it genuinely happens, as in *To Lay a Ghost*. Many of these episodes actually reverse the reasoning that Sexton expounds when discussing the resurgence and subsequent envisioning of analogue media and the era it signifies. He writes that:

> The warmth and human associations that various analogue media have accrued may also relate to their ghostly nature: if digital media are marked by absence of humanity, for example, then they are perhaps capable not so much of producing ghosts as they are of producing a form of 'soulless' interference. (2012: 18)

The 'human associations' with analogue media are considered attractive today, though it's easy to forget that the ghosts summoned by it in the 1970s were rarely pleasant; if they did have the human associations that digital media is apparently incapable of ultimately possessing, it relied on the very worst of humanity's impulses being retained. *Out of the Unknown*'s later serials are engrossing in their portrayal of this stark realisation, though it also balanced this with a sense of human geography in suburbia. Even in the missing episode, *The Sons and Daughters of Tomorrow*,[45] a journalist finds his arrogance leading him into danger in the suburban zone where 'the community, the idyllic retreat for the chattering classes, is actually a witches' coven, managed on local council terms, who then kill him as part of their business agenda' (Ward, 2014: 14). Though reminiscent of *The Witches*, suburbia here would undoubtedly present a differing view to the picture-postcard vista that Joan Fontaine found herself trapped within, even if that suburbia is still appropriately East Anglian. *Deathday*, in particular, seems to portray violent murder and casual sex with the sort of relish unthinkable a mere four years previously; the social distancing of the new suburbia was quietly unleashing the Martian instincts for violence and preservation, even if that preservation was only of the patriarchy or simply a flawed vision of male dignity.

This type of urbanism, arguably pioneered by Ballard in novels like *Crash* (1973) and later solidified in *The Unlimited Dream Company* (1979), makes for an intriguing hauntological critique, where a fantasy program deems the modern day sufficiently horrific enough to set the most abstract and complex of dramas within. The same logical application happened to *Doctor Who* in Jon Pertwee's era; one full of 70s shop window dummies smashing out of Ealing Broadway department stores,[46] plastic chairs and toy dolls killing people,[47] parasitic aliens high-jacking nuclear power stations,[48] and hippy communes confronting Welsh oil refineries.[49] Even odder is the later HTV series *King of the Castle* (1977), which presides over the gradually dystopian outlook of late 70s Britain through the mind of a boy bullied and left unconscious in a lift in his new council block. It would arguably make for an excellent social realist drama about urban bullying if the *Adventure Game*-style episodes of fantasy were removed, but it is again far removed from the sort of greasy, nasty urbanism that opened the decade. Similar tower block ideas occur much more effectively in *Sapphire and Steel*'s third assignment (1980) and much less effectively in the *Doctor Who* story *Paradise Towers* (1987),[50] though neither compare to Ballard's novel, which pioneered the setting and its social themes. With the fictional realm desperately clawing at the real world, it's of no surprise that early 1970s culture was fertile ground for strange artefacts to arise such as Public Information Films; short, macabre information snippets, shown on television and in schools, gleefully warning of various real-life dangers. The hauntological potential of these oddities of audio-visual culture has been well and truly tapped by modern Hauntology, using the musical tropes especially of these short films to both highlight and comment upon the era's hypocrisies in regards to the safety of children.

Folk Horror's general relationship with these Public Information Films is an interesting one in that they often deploy the same aesthetic tactics that many genuine examples of the genre use, only their intention is to warn against all-too-real dangers (drowning, electrocution, etc.) and, of course, their primary audience was far younger than that for X-rated films. Perhaps they can be regarded as short horror films for children but that doesn't quite articulate just how genuinely horrific they actually were. They reveal the unnerving reality of what was deemed suitable to show a younger audience of the period; far from the strangeness of the fictional television drama aimed at children, the PIFs (as they became known) used horror conventions to generate a genuine, behaviour-changing fear. Young writes of these films (and is clearly having to hold back on the sheer nostalgic pleasure they evoke):

> Viewed in retrospect, they offer a surreally exaggerated warning of potential domestic dangers or road hazards. A hooded, Bergman-esque Death stalks a group of children playing around a riverbank strewn with rusting junk; pylons loom over happy kite-flyers, threatening high-voltage electrocution; vintage Austins cheat tractor death on improbably empty country lanes. (2011: 596)

In spite of this questionable ruse, there is considerable interest in these films from a certain generation of viewers. Paciorek notes the relationship between these films and a general nostalgia in the Folk Horror Revival Group he runs online: 'A noticeable factor that has often recurred upon the Folk Horror Revival Facebook group page is a keen sense of nostalgia. Another aspect of nostalgia linking Hauntology to horror are memories of the Public Information Films (PIFs) that seemed omnipresent in childhoods past' (2015: 13). Whether this is nostalgia of the hauntological variety (i.e. a questioning of the past through its lost futures rather than a reductive form of looking back) or is simply the memory of being terrified by something placed so uncomfortably outside of fantasy and into the real world, is heavily debatable. Perhaps these films cover both areas. The latter point is emphasised by the main crux of these strange artefacts having elements more commonly found in adult horror. The implicit threat of these films is essentially real and they can be seen as the final blurring of horror in a decade that was not short of real world diegesis, some of it only now being unearthed in retrospect. Sexton has written of one of the most popular of these films and its ability to very literally smuggle in elements of horror that are still unnerving even today:

> Certain films, such as *Lonely Water* (Grant, 1973), became noted for their eerie, unsettling atmosphere: narrated by Donald Pleasence (as the 'spirit of dark and lonely water') and featuring foggy, gothic shots of swampy territory, it demonstrated how public information films could unsettle through smuggling horror-influenced material into programming aimed at children. (2012: 16)

The 'spirit of dark and lonely water', as the villain calls himself, haunts the derelict edge-lands of London as a group of young children play near spots of potentially hazardous water. The idea being that, as Donald Pleasence's eerie voice conveys, there are many dangers under the water that can cause death. This being the 1970s, the best way conceived to warn children of these dangers was to mythologise these tragedies with a potential figure, the spirit, who is in fact causing these deaths rather than the inherent dangers themselves. In hindsight, it's a baffling but enjoyable ruse, whereby the same aesthetics present in Lawrence Gordon Clark's Christmas ghost stories are used to create a short fragment of prime-time horror. Even more alarming is how well filmed the short is, especially considering how limited the career of its director (Jeff Grant) was, with only a handful of other PIFs to his name, including *Excuse Me, But That's My Car* (1987) narrated by Dennis Waterman.

These PIFs remain visceral because of their joint attack of (sur)realist nightmare alongside a virtuoso cinematic quality to their narratives, even when only a minute or two long. Consider, for example, many of the short 'electrocution films' put out about pylons and substations such as *Climbing Pylons Can Kill*, *Play Safe* (1978),[51] *Substation Dangers* (1979), *Powerful Stuff* (1988) and many others. Though the theme stretches into the 1980s and beyond as a paranoid idea, they are films built around the edge-lands that came to the fore visually in 1970s popular culture. The same sort of landscapes can be found in Martin Rosen's adaptation of Richard Adams' *Watership Down* (1978); another film that found horror in surprising spaces, again aiming visceral content at a younger audience. These were everyday spaces in the real *and* in the fictional sense, and so these PIFs, with their ektachrome vibrancy and sheer audacity, feel like the sort of everyday horror that would become the norm in more adult horror films and television around the same time; if William Ager or Azal weren't going to get you, the spirit of dark and lonely water or the nearest pylon were. The use of pylons especially evokes the odd children's series *The Changes* (1975), where reactions to such objects and their power was a key narrative device. Oblique objects were not, however, the only aspect of everyday life that 1970s Britain wanted to warn its young about.

Many PIFs have a Jamesian flavour of curiosity being punished, which may explain why so many adaptations of his work did well during the same period. In a film like *Apaches* (1977), where a group of children playing in a farmyard encounter all sorts of horrific, *Final Destination*-style ways to die, this becomes palpable. The visceral nature of the film can in part be explained by its director being John Mackenzie, director of *Red Shift* (1978) and *The Long Good Friday* (1980), one of the most violent British gangster films of the period. Grey Malkin has written that the PIFs reflect the fears of the era, but *Apaches* feels distinctly odd even in this remit. Malkin suggests that:

> PIFs are now for the most part a curious and of-its-age anomaly; the idea of mini-films demonstrating the dangers of flying kites near power lines being shown today between children's TV shows seems almost fanciful. Instead, they have become historical documents, a means by which to chart the preoccupations and fears of society throughout the post-war era. (2015: 29)

If anything, Mackenzie's film shows how overly paranoid the era was about protecting children from dangerous places. *Apaches* highlights the sort of Whitehouse-isms that dominated pop culture discussions in the decade by turning a perfectly normal area into a psychotic place of sentience with multiple ways to be killed. As Malkin suggests earlier in his essay, the PIFs remit was 'to help Britain recover, retain and maintain resolve following the devastation of the previous years and to do so in a curiously and uniquely British manner, the celluloid equivalent of a polite but firm, well-spoken chap shouting "You there, stop doing that!"' (2015: 26). PIFs such as *Apaches* can, therefore, be seen almost as a conservative force (paranoid danger warnings) using liberal means (horror films tropes) for its own ends.[52] This, of course, applies to more violent entries rather than the tamer examples; Jon Pertwee effusing 'SPLINK!' and *Dad's Army*'s Captain Mainwaring and his platoon helping children learn how to use a Pelican crossing were not going to cause any nightmares. It is, however, interesting to consider how generally morbid these films really could be. The most startling of these comes in the work of documentary filmmaker John Krish, who is responsible for a number of state-funded documentaries for the military such as *Captured* (1959) and a variety of features including the pulp sci-fi film *Unearthly Stranger* (1963) and the Children's Film Foundation horror short *Out of the Darkness* (1985). But he is more interesting here as the director of such disturbing PIFs as *Sewing Machine* (1973) – a one-minute long film showing how a mother's distraction leads to the death of her daughter on the road, shot horrifically in a real-time count-down to the girl's death – and *Searching* (1974), a surreal fragment tracking, Alan Clarke-like, around a burnt house but with audible fragments of the family in it burning to death (the fire is, typically for a PIF, caused by a child playing with matches). Patrick Russell suggests of *Searching* that, 'A generation later, it still hits hard and still hurts' (2013: 11). He is correct; it is still truly horrifying.

Krish's real master-stroke comes in the most surreal of the PIF's, *The Finishing Line* (1977). The film is a warning for children not to mess about around open railway lines but, instead of going about this in a straightforward, *Apaches*-like way, he films it instead like a (more) surreal Lindsay Anderson film, looking into the mind of a boy who imagines what a sports day built around a railway line would look like. As the film progresses, the tone darkens as each 'event' – from throwing rocks at a passing train to running in front of one – kills off more and more of the participants. Their parents look on, more disappointed at their children's display than agonised by the fact that they've been mangled to death by a high speed vehicle. Stephen Thrower writes of the film, 'Shocking though it is, one feels sure that the valuable message of [Krish's] film will have resonated long in the minds of the kids to whom it was shown' (2013: 17). It's hard to disagree, but there's a lingering point to PIFs such as this; that the decade in which they are made, with hauntological insight, can be considered both simultaneously alarmingly paranoid about the protection of the vulnerable at the same time, we now know, as their systematic, wide-spread abuse was being enabled and covered up.

Richard Littler, designer of the fictional Hauntology town of Scarfolk (to be examined in the next chapter), suggests as much in an interview with *The Honest Ulsterman*, where the decade 'may have had good intentions ("we want kids to be safe"), but was misguided and made errors ("we'll terrify them into submission")' (2014). The 'Urban Wyrd' plays its part in this as the era, just as its topography now plays as its own horror film of sorts, not just out of the paranoia of material like PIFs, but through a genuine horror at the realisation of the society that we once were. This was not the rosy Glam Rock vision of the 1970s as recycled by nostalgia-driven TV programming, but a hazardous realm stalked by predators such as Jimmy Savile. Today, Savile himself represents the Dorian Gray picture that popular media especially had been trying its best to look away from. On writing about Savile, Fisher draws links to the same era that could produce (and later ironically ban) work such as Dennis Potter's *Brimstone And Treacle* (1976),[53] with the dark reality of the decade's hypocrisy: 'By the end of 2012, the 70s was returning, no longer as some bittersweet nostalgia trip, but as a trauma' (2014: 89). With the context of this section opening with the urban work of Nigel Kneale – where various narratives recapitulate horrific drama of the present by digging up past traumas – this idea should be uncomfortably familiar.

It is horrifically fitting that Savile himself starred in his very own PIF, about the necessary safety precaution of the car seatbelt and that most Ballardian of dangers, the car-crash. He intones that the potential accident 'is going to happen to a lot of you ladies, doing shopping, collecting the kids, going to the laundrette...' over graphic shots of women drivers flying through windscreens. The film is a literal snapshot of the horrifying under-layer of the era, trying desperately to claw through, away from nostalgia and towards something else entirely. Hauntology allows the decade as a whole to be viewed in this way, often highlighting more interesting and sometimes even jovial elements, such as the interest in occultism of the previous section and the modern placing of Jamesian ideas finding their equivalents in the modern realm. More importantly, Hauntology presents Britain in the 1970s as a place of skewed morality, of isolated Brutalist zones, of the 'Urban Wyrd' and of paranoid, dystopian delusions surrounding the treatment of women and children. In other words, Hauntology shows the decade in its true guise; not just the place where Folk Horror was produced most abundantly but itself the most terrifying form of Folk Horror conceivable.

Endnotes

1   These latter forms are to be dealt with in the final chapter.

2   Especially in the context of today's Brexit Britain, which seems determined to depressingly recapitulate the more extreme end of all of these ideas.

3   Apt for the point being raised as the film was the ritualistic, occult short *Invocation of My Demon Brother* (1969).

4   This is a reference to the presenter Toni Arthur, whose simultaneous role as a children's television presenter and occultist is best described by Rob Young: 'Anyone of a certain age exposed to BBC children's television during the 1970s will recall Toni Arthur: the enthusiastic, female, polo-necked co-presenter of toddler show *Play School* and its all-singing, all-dancing big brother *Playaway*, plus the folksy round-Britain travelogue series *Take a Ticket to...* But would parents have been so keen on exposing their little ones to the acoustic guitar-wielding wrangler of Big Ted, Humpty and their stuffed chums had they known that Toni had recently attended naked pagan ceremonies conducted by Britain's self-styled "King of the Witches"?' (2011: 438).

5   A series about a police detective teaming up with an astrologer to solve crimes.

6   Based on the novel by Fritz Lieber Jr., who also wrote the original story behind the aptly 1944 film *Weird Woman*.

7   Even if the film is notably and largely suburban in its setting.

8   *Rosemary's Baby* (1968).

9   *Robin Redbreast* (1970).

10 Also of note is the presence of Michele Dotrice, again; a familiar Folk Horror face.

11 Of even more poignancy, Van Helsing (Peter Cushing) needs the help of a heritage blue plaque to find Dracula's lair at the top of the high-rise as the original church has been demolished.

12 Though they are undoubtedly still affluent and potentially even the offspring of the previous generation. This shift is a generational one rather than purely one of class.

13 For further Italian occult links, see Camillo Mastrocinque's *An Angel For Satan* (1966) and Antonio Margheriti's *The Long Hair of Death* (1964); both of which look to similar themes and both with Barbara Steele in the lead role. Also, Bava's portmanteau *Black*

Sabbath (1963) has notable Folk Horror relevance, largely through the story *The Wurdulak*, based on genuine Balkan folklore, and a story by Aleksey Tolstoy.

14 She further suggests that, 'Abjection appears as a rite of defilement and pollution in the paganism that accompanies societies with a dominant or surviving matrilinear character' (1982: 17).

15 Especially in its infamous tongue-pulling scene which was rather strangely used as the defining image of the film when promoting it.

16 The same can be said for the film's appalling sequel, directed by Adrian Hoven (the first film's joint screenwriter) in 1973.

17 And based on the subsequent play by John Whiting.

18 Young writes of this film in relation again to Toni Arthur, where the film 'shows the [Alex] Sanders coven as Dave and Toni Arthur would have found it on their frequent visits to the basement flat in Notting Hill Gate. Intriguingly, the coven can be seen to have adopted some of the technology of modern psychedelia, using stroboscopic lights and flickering Op Art circles reminiscent of the hypnotic "dreamachines" invented by William Burroughs and Brion Gysin' (2011: 443).

19 For hauntological reference, the series' occult chant of 'Hacate' is sampled by Ghost Box artist Belbury Poly (Jim Jupp) in the song 'Hither and Yon' from the very first EP on the label, *Farmer's Angle* (2004).

20 See the previous chapter for *Race with the Devil*'s relationship with rurality.

21 One that couldn't be referenced by later material as being defining of the era, which is in essence how Hauntology functions when dealing with occult.

22 A good example of this is director Ben Wheatley, whose perhaps light-hearted embracing of this opinion is on record.

23 Filmed for the BBC in late 1958 and early 1959, but also famously remade by Hammer studios into a feature film in 1967.

24 Directed by Michael Elliot.

25 An episode which sees Patrick Troughton in the story of a journalist who comes across a motorbike still haunted by its dead owner. The episode was directed by Peter Cregeen.

26 T.C. Lethbridge's noted 'theory of residual hauntings' is now commonly known as the 'Stone Tape Theory'.

27 The actor would play a remarkably similar role in the film *Assault* (dir. Sidney Hayers, 1971), sometimes known as *In the Devil's Garden*. The links between her role as an object for the audience *and* for the diegetic characters in both this film and *To Lay a Ghost* are deeply disturbing in hindsight, especially with her being famously voted as the county's 'Most Beautiful Teenager' at the age of 15; the same year she made her debut film role.

28 Especially in the episode *Visitations*, directed by Norman Stewart and written by Eric MacDonald. The series is noted for drawing the ire of Mary Whitehouse, which is arguably to its credit creatively.

29 A role she would effectively repeat some years later in *Withnail & I*.

30 Directed in 1979 by Piers Haggard, who brings his usual visual flair for Folk Horror narratives to the series.

31 Ballard's 1975 novel which has unparalleled influence over alternative pop culture of the mid-1970s, especially in music.

32 Here, Quatermass is played brilliantly and doggedly by John Mills.

33 In spite of being a film framed around a visit to the decade by Queen Elizabeth I and John Dee.

34 Screenplay by Anthony Shaffer, written the year before his work on *The Wicker Man*. The narrative is taken from a novel by Arthur La Bern, *Goodbye Piccadilly, Farewell Leicester Square* from 1966.

35 Screenplay by Christopher Wicking from a novel by Peter Saxon.

36 Adapted from the James Barlow novel by Dick Clement and Ian La Frenais.

37 Screenplay by Alexander Jacobs from a novel by Laurence Henderson.

38 Screenplay by Anthony Greville-Bell.

39 Screenplay by David Shirwin, most famous for writing *If.... (1968)* by Lindsay Anderson.

40 Based on Anthony Burgess' novel.

41 Based on the play by John Hopkins who was also on screenplay duty.

42 The film is sometimes referred to as *Cover Up*, again hinting at links towards more crime-based drama.

43 Something equally reflected with growing despair in the current Brexit Britain climate.

44 As did other series such as *Ace of Wands* (1970–1972), *Thriller* (1973–1976), *Zodiac* (1974) and *Shadows* (1975–1978).

45 Directed by Gerald Blake and written by Edward Boyd.

46 *Spearhead From Space* (1970) – written by Robert Holmes and directed by Derek Martinus.

47 *Terror Of The Autons* (1971) – written by Robert Holmes and directed by Barry Letts.

48 *The Claws Of Axos* (1971) – written by Bob Baker and Dave Martin and directed by Michael Ferguson.

49 *The Green Death* – see Chapter 4 for more detail.

50 Directed by Nicholas Mallett, written by Stephen Wyatt.

51 Written and directed by David Eady. Eady is perhaps more famous for directing a segment of the portmanteau drama *Three Cases of Murder* (1955), though he also directed the cycling safety film *Betcher!* (1971).

52 This is, of course, a generalisation, with many horror writers being far from any definition of liberal.

53 Directed by Barry Davis.

Chapter 6

'Sumer-Is-Icumen-In': Modern Folk Horror

Introduction

'I conjure thee to speak to me!' – Thomasin (Anya Taylor-Joy) in *The Witch* (2015)

In March 2016, the weather had yet to turn into anything vaguely resembling spring; the skies and evenings were constantly moody with their overhanging clouds and drizzle. It seemed almost omen-like in its foreshadowing of what was then occurring both cinematically and politically in the UK. Appropriately, one film was dominating horror discussions, especially those concerning Folk Horror. From its warm reception at festivals in 2015, and a few teasingly esoteric trailers trickled out over the following months, Robert Eggers' paranoid horror film *The Witch* was bound to take precedence in discussions of the genre.[1] Though an American film set in seventeenth-century New England, there's something recognisably 'Olde English' about its character as a form; the actors have British accents,[2] the visuals are muted palettes of dark greens, browns and greys, and the superstition and toil is recognisably of the same breed found in films as diverse as *Witchfinder General*, *Winstanley* and *Cry of the Banshee*. The film even plays with that most typical of Folk Horror ideals, the initial ambiguity surrounding its supernatural elements: is this a film about the cruelty and susceptibility of humans and their cloaking of it around a belief system, or something more ineffable that is beyond mere reason? It is quintessential Folk Horror, chiming with the same themes that brought the genre to the fore almost forty years previously.

Unlike its forebears, especially many of those made during the last decade, *The Witch* has had a positive critical response from the off, not requiring time to be rediscovered by a cult audience for it to gain its artistic and critical acclaim. In Benjamin Lee's review for The Guardian, he writes, 'Like any outstanding horror film, its true impact only reveals itself once the credits have rolled and it stays buried under your skin, breaking through every now and then to remind you of its insidious power' (2016). The film clearly has that Knealian quality of lingering in the mind long after viewing; but, more than this, the very production of the film has recalled many of the ideas that went into the cinema discussed throughout this book: that of mining history and its horrors to speak of more modern, psychological traumas such as misogyny, violence and religion. In another article for The Guardian, Alex Godfrey makes an interesting observation that, 'With its olde Englishe lingo, broad hats and bonnets, and the odd demonic goat, *The Witch* is certainly unlike any of those other horror films doing such big business in the multiplexes' (2016). In one sense he is right and a key theme of many reviews of Eggers' film is its reluctance to conform to such modern horror tropes as jump-scares, instead relying on the building of a slow, inescapable dread. Though it may not be a common occurrence today, the film's many themes are drawing on ideas heavily examined throughout the Folk Horror genre, even if the term rarely (if at all) crops up when reviewers or the director himself discusses the film; there's almost a reluctance to assign anything horror-like to it, for fear of burdening the film with the assumptions that modern examples of the genre often bring.

The reason for highlighting *The Witch* here, however, is not simply because the film has managed to put folklorically psychological material back into the cinematic mainstream (and to do it with creative flair and acclaim), but because it can actually be seen as the high point of a period of new films, television and music re-exploring Folk Horror as a form that started at the beginning of the new millennium. In the tagline for Godfrey's article, he states of *The Witch* that 'Set in 1630s New-England, Robert Eggers's film is redefining the horror genre with its period detail and scares' (ibid.). This is somewhat of a misnomer when, in actuality, Eggers' film and its success (in spite of repeatedly stating to not be particularly influenced by horror films outside of Stanley Kubrick's *The Shining* (1980)),[3] can be seen as the culmination of over a decade's worth of films exploring that same type of Folk Horror territory, albeit with varying degrees of success. To use a Folk Horror metaphor, many artists since the early 2000s have been merely watching the girl scream and run on the Knealian stone tape, whereas Eggers has come to it with that memory wiped, revealing the greater evils underneath, and with accessibility to the darker aspects of history, humanity and morality all within easy grasp.

This resurgence in all things Folk Horror, from delving into familiar thematic territory, remaking older examples, or even just generally rediscovering long lost relics from its more dominant period, has a number of contributing factors but arguably two chief specific outcomes to chart:

- Work that reflects nostalgia, whether effectively subverting it (hauntologically) or succumbing to the past visions of Folk Horror's primary era, to produce referential work.
- Using certain thematic traces within the inner workings of Folk Horror to assess current political issues and even reflect on the parallels of the political climate from the period of 1970s Britain in particular.

With the ubiquity of technology and the internet, Folk Horror has entered a new realm but it is one that at first seems contrary to its potential causational factors. If the genre requires some sort of narrative mechanism such as the Folk Horror Chain to function – a chain that explicitly involves the isolation of its communities and characters – then how can/does it function in an era of hyper-connectivity? Something as simple as a mobile phone or a decent internet connection could well put pay to the modern-set narratives of, for example, *The Wicker Man, Murrain* or *The Devil Rides Out*; Mocata foiled by a quick text to the authorities from the Duc de Richleau's iPhone, or an email forwarded from Howie to the mainland asking for back-up. The narrative factors of digital life logically play against the potential for Folk Horror to build, but the reality of the work is actually enjoyably illogical; on the contrary, digital life enables Folk Horror to thrive in both a diegetic and a nondiegetic way. In regards to the latter, Western society's increasing reliance on digital technology, and specifically connectivity ports such as social media, means that a fear of being isolated and removed from such technology is itself actually a far more unnerving prospect than it probably was forty years ago. Even to confront communities and characters removed from this social architecture has great Folk Horror potential, whether that community ignores the moral codes and etiquette that comes with such technology or is actually using such technology for its own ends.[4]

The internet plays an even greater role in regards to activating our nostalgia modes (or at least those of a certain generation of British citizens) and so functions as a summoning device for artefacts long since passed, rather like the house in *Sapphire and Steel*'s first assignment. This functions heavily within the workings of the first group of post-millennial examples of Folk Horror, especially the record label Ghost Box (see below). When discussing the label, Mark Fisher suggests its rise, influences and core texts are directly linked with the internet's facility for accessing cult material, writing that, 'it's perhaps no accident that the rise of Ghost Box has coincided with the emergence of YouTube, which has made public information films and other street furniture of 1970s audio-visual experience widely available again' (2014: 139). This does not, however, simply apply to Ghost Box, but to many of the examples already discussed. To contextualise this further, consider the backdrop against which *The Witch* is now playing; an audience that has free and easy access to virtually all of the films and television mentioned in this book for free, even the rarer, more obscure examples that were left gathering dust soon after their initial broadcasts or releases. To convey the point further, after seeing *The Witch* on the big screen, it can now be easily doubled up with a home screening of *Power of the Witch* followed by a listening session of a restored cut of Alex Sanders' *A Witch Is Born* LP.

Perhaps most striking is how Folk Horror reflects its narrative workings within its very own resurgence. Any number of metaphors built from Folk Horror narratives could be applied to the subsequent rediscovery of its many works. The repopularisation of the BBC Ghost Stories mimics the finding of Parkins' whistle or Paxton's cursed crown; the capturing of the girl on *The Stone Tape* reflects the relooping trauma of many of Nigel Kneale's television programs and a recent, popular surge of interest in his work and writing; the continued cult success of Hardy's *The Wicker Man* ironically apes the parthenogenesis cycle that its own characters believe in but bears fruit that is appropriately inedible and rotten in its poor sequel and remake. This is an era where, like the Devil itself in *The Blood on Satan's Claw*, obscure and weird pop culture can rise again from the furrows thanks to technological advancement. 'Rise now from the forests, from the furrows, from the fields and live...' indeed.

'Mind How You Go!' – Modern Folk Horror and Nostalgia

'I'll be back (back, back, back)!' – The Spirit of Dark and Lonely Water

As discussed in the preceding chapter, there's little doubt that nostalgia plays *some* role in Folk Horror's various guises. The post-millennium period serves as a dividing line of sorts in regards to Hauntology, but also within the very narratives of modern Folk Horror itself. Even if realigning nostalgia to a more critical position regarding 1970s Britain, Hauntology itself cannot alone provide all of the answers to Folk Horror's nostalgic functioning: are modern-day fans really aching for a fear once felt in their childhood or is interest in the genre more multivalent? Nostalgia in Folk Horror can function both *within* and *about* a nostalgic piece of artwork itself. The longing for an apparently simpler, more communal period often envisioned in Folk Horror narratives has already been somewhat dissected in earlier examples; where an older, even pagan, vision of England dominates the moral ambiguity of cinematic and televisual narratives. In the last decade or so, however, nostalgia has functioned predominantly in relation to the era of Folk Horror's non-diegetic production and this mechanism has arguably kick-started the resurgence in all things esoteric in film, television and music.[5]

This manifests most effectively in the Ghost Box record label and its various musical and visual outputs, perhaps more so than any examples in film or television. The label's work highlights many of the current trends surrounding Folk Horror and Hauntology. It was set up in 2004 by Julian House (signed to the label itself as The Focus Group, and responsible for much of the label's visual artwork) and Jim Jupp (likewise, signed as Belbury Poly). The music produced on the label is an odd mixture of elements; 1970s paraphernalia and culture melding with the paranoia and hindsight towards the era's darker hues and reality. They mine many of the examples discussed in this book for inspiration, especially those of Chapter 3 and British cult television as a whole; the name 'Ghost Box' hints at the haunted nature of the cathode-ray tube and the spirits that proliferated on it in the 1970s.[6] Rob Young suggests that the turn of the millennium was indeed a time where these stranger visions of the country's past pop culture influenced a new form of nostalgic music, writing:

> In the opening decade of the twenty-first century, there are a surprisingly large
> number of musicians, working underground, churning out similarly haunting
> and disquieting sonic fictions that chime with the notion of an alternative
> Albion... (2011: 596)

Many of the musicians Young is discussing are in some way affiliated with Ghost Box and their output. This mining of the past consists of a huge variety of influences, from artwork influenced by *The Owl Service* and *Children of the Stones*, samples used from *The Blood on Satan's Claw* and *K9 & Company*, or simply aural textures evoking the many Radiophonic Workshop soundtracks and effects that dominated the period's television soundscapes. With this rich tapestry, music by the likes of The Advisory Circle,[7] Pye Corner Audio[8] and Mount Vernon Arts Lab,[9] provide what some have deemed to be new soundtracks for films and television programs that never quite happened:

> The spectres in Ghost Box's hauntology are the lost contexts which, we imagine, must have prompted the sounds we are hearing: forgotten programmes, uncommissioned series, pilots that were never followed up. (Fisher, 2014: 134)

Drew Mulholland's Mount Vernon Arts Lab, with its conceptual reworking of Nigel Kneale's *Quatermass and the Pit* in the 2006 reissue of the *Séance at Hobbs Lane*, emphasises the point where nostalgia is acting very much to blur diegetic boundaries and again mimic the narrative happenings; the album itself foreshadows a rising of interest in Kneale's work that is as virulent as the film's Martian insects and their psychic capacity. Ghost Box albums can be seen to work as lodestone symbols, balancing that sense of recognisability within something also seemingly unknown, again in the Knealian sense but also in the sense of the Freudian uncanny; the ambiguity surrounding why we disowned these memories makes many of these albums as haunting as they are enjoyable. This form of creativity may seem almost reactionary to the augmentation effectively enforced upon popular creativity by digital technology, though there is a sense of irony and even humour involved in Ghost Box's self-conscious, esoteric channelling.

Perhaps, then, Ghost Box are 'reghosting' popular culture via references to examples clearly produced through analogue means redolent of the Dickensian ideal of the 'ghost in the machine', as exemplified wonderfully in Lawrence Gordon Clark's *The Signalman*. By doing this, they supply an alternative vision of pop culture heritage, built on a mixture of obscurities and false memories; where the esoteric visions of 1970s television rewrites the map of cultural lay-lines. As Jamie Sexton suggests: 'Thus, similar to the way in which Ghost Box can be seen as engaging in alternative forms of heritage, it can also be considered to be practicing alternative forms of nostalgia and pastiche' (2012: 20). It recalls the work of the musician English Heretic,[10] aptly named in this sense as he similarly channels such ideas into music and visual culture, as well as a number of other musicians including the more landscape-infused work of Laura Cannell, J. Harvey and Sharron Kraus, who engage with various permutations of this alternative heritage.[11] Fisher describes this relationship as one of an 'unhomesickness' which rather aptly surmises the nostalgia-driven instigators of Folk Horror's revival in the 2000s: 'If nostalgia famously means "homesickness", then Ghost Box's sound is about unhomesickness, about the uncanny spectres entering the domestic environment through the cathode ray tube' (2014: 133). Of similar ilk is Richard Littler's visual project, Scarfolk – a website (and spin-off book) that produces unsettling public information material for a fictional town that is stuck in the 1970s. It has that same character of 'unhomesickness', whereby the nostalgia circuits are activated by classic designs, emulating Pelican and Penguin design work by the likes of Germano Facetti, but smuggling in dark undertones for comedic effect; e.g. a harmless-looking book that at first glance seems to be about some aspect of childcare will actually be about how to eat children or wash their brains.

Littler's work seems so aesthetically convincing that it has on several occasions been mistaken for actual public information material, which arguably again reflects the arguments surrounding the era of the previous chapter; that of a stark and unnerving brutality contrasted with aesthetic esoterica. Littler takes the reality of the 1970s and applies it, Folk Horror Chain-like, to one isolated dystopian town, implicitly questioning the paranoia and the strangeness of popular culture from the period. Both Ghost Box and Scarfolk channel that already-suffused strangeness found in the Public Information Films and 1970s children's television, creating subversive effects that are uncommon in the purely rose-tinted, nostalgia-built relationships with popular culture. Sexton argues this to be a key component of Hauntology as a whole: 'The past and present commonly intertwine within the sphere of human memory, so it is no surprise that memory constitutes an important trope within hauntology (the term "memoradelia" has occasionally been employed to refer to the work of some of these artists)' (2012: 3). The link to television is, however, especially poignant when considering post-millennial Folk Horror, as it was in this medium where it found its next rebirth, very often through mining the type of pop culture which was ubiquitous in the 1970s; recreating and remaking this very particular type of 'memoradelia'.

In comparison to the original programs that have at least inspired them, if not being remade entirely, there is arguably a slight drop in quality in modern televisual equivalents by and large, but this does not negate their role in the genre's revival. The 2000s was a decade where a live broadcast of the original *The Quatermass Experiment*, the BBC Christmas Ghost Story, and *Doctor Who* would all be revived and broadcast along with numerous others in a similar vein. *Doctor Who* is especially fitting as Russell T. Davies' own series opened with the Doctor (played by Christopher Eccleston) fighting the same alien foes as Jon Pertwee's Doctor did in his first adventure in *Spearhead from Space* in 1970; almost kick-starting a very literal ghosting of that decade. Chapter 3 has already gone into some detail regarding the recent developments in such television but it is worth considering the sheer volume produced today that uses Folk Horror themes to evoke memories of such programmes. Although efforts at bringing back the BBC Christmas Ghost Story slot have been mixed, there have been a variety of attempts at the same type of programme by the BBC and rival broadcasters.

One series that maintains a consistent effect is Mark Gatiss' three-part tale, *Crooked House* (2008), which earnestly mixes a passion for Folk Horror films and television series with a knowingness for what can work in the format. *Crooked House* is the most unnerving of these new supernatural serials and even betters some of the more modern M.R. James efforts by the BBC. Gatiss and his 'League of Gentleman' colleagues can take some credit for Folk Horror's subsequent revival, the 'local shop for local people' being a sinister, comedic twist on the belief system propagated through the Folk Horror Chain and depressingly normalised in the politics of Brexit Britain. In 2014, the BBC made another three-part ghost serial, *Remember Me*; an original series starring Michael Palin as an almost Hordern-like character in a mixture of *Whistle And I'll Come To You* coastal terror and police procedural drama. It is burdened with attempting to combine too many elements, sometimes fulfilling the Folk Horror Chain in its isolated Yorkshire setting, but rarely attaining to the high quality thematically that it achieves visually. The form labours it and, with the obvious influence of M.R. James again, it's unsurprising; very few ghost stories, whether of James' quality or otherwise, should need three hours to tell.

Of similar flavour is the James Herbert adaptation *The Secret of Crickley Hall* (2012), the five-part ITV serials *Marchlands* (2011)[12] and *Lightfields* (2013),[13] the Channel 5-debuting, Kickstarter-funded TV film *The Haunting Of Radcliffe House* (2014),[14] and, most interestingly, Sky's dramatisation of *The Enfield Haunting* (2015). The latter series, again a three-part drama, takes great, hauntological pleasure in recreating its 1970s period detail and links it with the haunting's moral ambiguity. Though it may be accused of falling into the trap of recreation, leading to a rewriting of history (where the 1970s loses its edges and becomes the rewritten vision of talking-heads documentaries, as Fisher suggested in an earlier quote), it is the most effective of these soapy spook dramas. If anything, the majority are a response to the rise in interest in the original BBC Ghost Stories, following their restored DVD re-release courtesy of the British Film Institute in 2012; the subsequent equivalent gap being filled only once to-date by the BBC with Gatiss' take on *The Tractate Middoth* (2013).[15] Even American television has been trying its hand at more Folk Horror-esque themes, most famously with the first series of *True Detective* (2014).[16]

In film, nostalgia follows similar lines, either involving remakes or allusions towards older themes addressed in past work. This can be seen in remakes of *The Wicker Man* (2006) and *The Woman In Black* (2012), or variations on a theme in films such as the domesticated oddness of Nicolas Roeg's *Puffball* (2007), the heavily *Sapphire and Steel*-influenced *Blackwood* (2014), the medieval Folk Horror visions of *Black Death* (2010) and *Macbeth* (2015), the Peter Weir-esque, 1960s-in-fused *The Falling* (2014) or the paranormal Americana of *The Sixth Sense* (1999), *The Others* (2001) and *The Exorcism Of Emily Rose* (2005). *The Woman in Black* is interesting in that it signifies the revival of Hammer Studios and their penchant for horror; another revival to come about in the 2000s. Appropriately, its first real attempt at a comeback was in 2009's *Wake Wood*;[17] a proto Folk Horror film in the vein of a traumatic repetition, with supernatural flavours and ritualistic happenings. Hammer went on to adapt Susan Hill's novella into a relatively effective horror film, though one built largely on the techniques harnessed in jump-scare ghost films such as *Paranormal Activity* (2007) (and, in more Folk Horror-themed territory, *The Borderlands* (2013)[18] and *The Hallow* (2015)). This, however, also led to the frustrating suppression of the original 1989 ITV adaptation. The earlier is superior in terms of its representation of the landscape and the capture of the grain of Folk Horror.

Going further into retrospective Folk Horror territory, Hammer produced another ghost film in *The Quiet Ones* (2014); a film that deliberately harnesses the post-Knealian fetishisms surrounding haunted analogue technology, though in actuality comes out looking more akin to David Rudkin's *The Living Grave* (only not quite as effective). The same ideas can also be seen in *The Conjuring* (2013), another mixed film about paranormal investigators coming across something nasty from the past (the 2016 sequel revisited the territory of the Enfield haunting). Modern Folk Horror cinema looks to older examples with acute obsession, whether channelling *Death Line*'s urban terror of tube stations in *Creep* (2004), the strange goings on of village life in *The Village* (2004), or even in Robin Hardy himself writing and directing a poor sequel to *The Wicker Man* in the form of *The Wicker Tree* (2011). The director even attempted to crowd-fund a third instalment, *The Wrath of the Gods*, in 2015. The attempt failed, however, with the campaign only raising just over $8000 of its required $210,000 target;

such was the creative and thematic failings of Hardy's attempt at a previous sequel. Even the more exploitative side of occult and esoteric cinema from this period finds some nostalgic blossoming, especially in what looks to be the most overt (but yet to be released at the time of writing) film, Anna Biller's *The Love Witch* (2016); a deliberate play on the American sexploitation occult genre which, from its trailer alone, wouldn't look out of place alongside Malcolm Leigh's *Legend of the Witches*.

It would be tempting to label some of these films and television series as regressive; after all, in Hauntology arguments, modern popular culture has been stuck in a rut for some time, in part due to political stasis inducing a lack of daring and even uncertainty over a potential, envisioned future. In other words, creative artists in all media are almost forced to look back if only to avoid the very lack of an ahead, so to speak, in their respective forms. But this underestimates the many interesting and creative relationships produced in many of these works, across media forms. More importantly, this has also arguably laid the groundwork for more political examples of Folk Horror in the twenty-first century, where the genre is delivering some uncomfortable truths about power, greed, corruption, xenophobia and class. The sacrifice to the land did eventually bring forth new crops, but of a far more sour and rotten variety.

A Field in England – Modern Folk Horror and Politics

'Sooner I get back to fucking London, the fucking better. A new fucking coat. Fucking doors that fucking shut. And citizens that pay small fucking reckoning to astrology. I would rather die of the fucking plague in the fucking fleet than spend another fucking minute in the countryside.' – Whitehead in *A Field in England* (2013)

Politics and Folk Horror have an unusual relationship, sometimes one that is openly embracing of ideas critical of the state, whilst at other times deliberate in its ambiguity surrounding political issues. The best examples of cinematic, post-millennial Folk Horror often do two things in regards to the genre's relationship with politics:

- Link modern political issues with certain Folk Horror narratives in order to add elements of modern grounding to their fantastical nature.
- Reflect on past political moments that provide a temporal link between the era of the counter-culture and the present day (showing both the differences and the horrific likenesses between the periods).

With this as a framework, modern Folk Horror films can be extremely visceral because of their questioning of complex political conundrums involving class, the treatment of women and other issues.[19] In some ways, these films channel older texts in a similar way to those discussed in the previous section, but do so in order to bring their political parallels between narrative and era into light rather than as simply *homage*. This parallel is best perceived in an essay by Aaron Jolly about the most socially conscious (and arguably the best) practitioner of modern Folk Horror, Ben Wheatley. In Jolly's essay, he is the first to suggest a political and social parallel between Folk Horror's two most prolific periods, arguing that:

> The 2010s have been a time of global economic crisis and, similarly to the 1970s, a Conservative government has been elected into power. This means we are seeing higher taxes and cuts in spending on the arts, social welfare and education. This in turn has created a period of social unrest and dissatisfaction with the government. (2015: 278)

This perhaps also veers into Hauntology territory, whereby the parallels of the politics equal some fantastical link between the two temporal positions, allowing similar cultural material to rise up. However, it is worth pointing out that there is a feeling of repetition again in these newer films more than of strictly original storytelling; the responses are similar either because they are reflecting similar political climates or because they have looked to how the older examples responded *to* the same type of issues. Either way, it has resulted in many powerful and sometimes even controversial examples of the genre. Though by no means the first director to resummon the genre's various demons, Wheatley is its most prolific and knowing exponent in the twenty-first century, channelling earlier Folk Horror ideas through modern digital filmmaking techniques which deserves some in-depth analysis. The director has gone repeatedly on record citing his own relationship with the genre, including this interview with Uncut Magazine in 2013:

> Things like *Children of the Stones* and *The Owl Service* I came to as an adult more being interested in getting into folk horror. When I was a kid, I grew up in Essex next to some woods, and I always had nightmares about the woods and things that would happen to you in the woods. There was something going on there definitely. I remember finding all these strange bottles and stuff there. It was real *Blood on Satan's Claw* stuff. (2013)

Wheatley is better considered as one part of a film-making duo, with his partner and scriptwriter (and sometimes co-editor) Amy Jump. Working as a director on a number of TV programmes and web films before finishing his debut feature *Down Terrace* (2009),[20] Wheatley's relationship with Folk Horror arguably didn't properly begin until working with Jump on *Kill List* in 2011. This is especially relevant, not only because Jump seems to kick-start Wheatley's Folk Horror inclinations, but also because it is a film made during the first years of the UK coalition government, and the first Conservative-led government since the 1990s. As Andy Paciorek suggests in his essay on the film, 'The social realism aspect of *Kill List* is not simply another genre mashed into the film. As well as being an integral part of the individual style of the film, it extends into an underlying symbolism in the movie' (2015: 435). That symbolism is political and *Kill List*, therefore, resonates to political issues that were already beginning to brew with regards to class. Though seeming to start as a straightforward film about two hitmen, it turns into a nihilistic, Reevesian journey into a very English (albeit disturbing) form of class-conscious horror. A narrative breakdown follows.

Kill List – Jay (Neil Maskell) and Gal (Michael Smiley) are hired hitmen living in suburbia. Jay is suffering from PTSD after a military trip to Kiev which manifests when Gal and his new girlfriend Fiona (Emma Fryer) come around for a meal cooked by Jay's wife Shel (MyAnna Buring). During the evening, Fiona scratches a strange symbol onto the back of a picture in Jay's bathroom. Gal convinces Jay to join him on a new contract killing job and they go to meet their rich, mysterious client (Struan Rodger) in a hotel. They agree to the killing of three people but, before they leave, the client cuts Jay's hand with a knife, laced with something unknown, akin to a ritual pact. They kill their first victim, a vicar (Gareth Tunley), which goes smoothly, though the priest recognises Jay and oddly thanks him for the killing before he is disposed of. Their second victim, known only as the librarian (Mark Kempner), is shown to be involved in some sort of violent pornography racket involving children. Unable to contain himself, Jay breaks into his house and tortures him with instruments from a toolbox before killing him. In spite of this, the librarian still thanks him, further raising the hitmen's suspicion regarding the contract. They decide to terminate it but the client threatens to kill their families if they do not go through with the final killing. Jay moves Shel and his son to a safe-house in the country whilst the pair go off to a mansion to kill the final victim, a politician. They hide in the grounds and witness what looks to be a pagan ritual – the participants being mostly naked, wearing straw masks and chanting – that culminates in a sacrifice. Jay, armed with an assault rifle, fires upon the ceremony, with its leader offering himself up to the bullets. The other members chase the pair into the tunnels underneath the mansion, killing Gal and capturing Jay. When he awakens he is in the middle of a ceremony. He is stripped and forced to a fight a handicapped 'hunchback' with knives. He stabs and kills the hunchback only for it to be revealed that it was in fact Shel with their son strapped to her back. He is crowned king by the group who reveal themselves to be familiar faces from earlier in the film, including Fiona. The symbol that she scratched onto the picture flashes up briefly on the screen before the film ends.

Kill List is a tough watch, not simply because of its level of violence (the torture scene is especially gruelling) but because of the reality upon which it reflects; one where politicians, priests and other representatives of powerful interests are able to get away with ritualised murder. Jolly writes of this being a question of class, whereby 'Jay is only brought to this conclusion by being led through this ritual by cult leaders who symbolise the bourgeois conservative government forcing the working classes, in this case Jay, into an economic recession' (2015: 279). It seems more of a moral recession within the film, as well as an economic one implied by Jay having to accept contract killing for work. This may reflect the nature found even on Summerisle, where the working-class are used for the ends of the upper elites, though *Kill List* firmly showcases upper-class interests to be devoted to a sadistic belief system rather than simply trying to grow apples through cheap labour. Paciorek argues the same point, where 'Reading *Kill List* in a political context, it is difficult to ascertain what the social intentions of the cult are, but it is clear that they want to invoke change' (2015: 437). What this change is, however, is unnervingly ambiguous.

More so than its grittiness, in *Kill List* Wheatley is clearly interested in isolating characters through physical and social parameters; a fitting ploy considering how essential isolation in its many forms is to many Folk Horror narratives. *Kill List* isn't quite as literally isolated as other Folk Horror films, but it is so in terms of morality and emotion; this is a world where power has been taken away from working-class people who, even when armed with weapons, are still ultimately mere tools in an upper elite's social game.[21] Jolly summarises the arguments using an idea of Robin Wood's to show a temporal link between economics, class, and horror: 'We see the nihilism of the horror genre to be symbolic of what [Robin] Wood describes as the "cultural crisis and disintegration" of society in the 1970s. Which then in turn allowed for radical change and a rebuilding of traditional society' (2015: 271). He goes on to suggest of Wheatley's film that, 'Its "folk horror" themes have been given a modern cross-genre twist and are framed with a gritty "crime drama" narrative, but it still uses the same social metaphors from the 1970s... Ben Wheatley uses these ideas as metaphors for class struggle in these times of economic uncertainty to great effect' (2015: 278). Class struggle has never seemed as visceral or so uphill as in *Kill List* but it seems to be quite specifically because of how literal the skewing of morality is in 2010s Britain; a rerun of class riots, massive transfers of wealth, recessions, open normalisation of all sorts of xenophobia, public sector cuts, post-factual political debates and revelations about the historical abuse committed by people in positions of power.

Wheatley was only just beginning to tap into Folk Horror ideas as a set of political and cinematic tools. His projects henceforth also bear some of the genre's influence and trademarks. In the black comedy *Sightseers* (2012), a pair of boring caravanning lovers (Alice Lowe and Steve Oram) develop psychopathic tendencies when they go into the English countryside. Clearly channelling Mike Leigh's *Play For Today*, *Nuts In May* (1976), Wheatley and Jump, and screenwriters Lowe and Oram, build upon a mixture of primal violence in dramatic landscapes and humorous detours to the countryside, as envisioned by the National Trust and English Heritage. Also in 2012, Wheatley directed a short instalment in the horror anthology film *The ABCs Of Death*, taking helm for the segment *U Is For Unearthed*. From its title alone, its Folk Horror potential is perceivable, and the vignette follows Wheatley's regular band of performers (including Michael Smiley and Neil Maskell) as they unearth what appears to be some sort of vampiric demon. Shot from the point of view of the monster, the film raises some surprising moral questions about the normalised killing of creatures in horror that is so often taken for granted. Again, the main violence and horror seems to be derived solely from people and Wheatley is a director who often emphasises the link between people and 'folk'; Folk Horror being the true horror of people.

The Folk Horror influence would be most prominent in Wheatley and Jump's most obviously indebted feature film, *A Field in England* (2013); a film that has the visual as well as the thematic hallmarks of a very typical piece of Folk Horror. Set in the same period as *Witchfinder General*, and channelling the influences of *The Blood on Satan's Claw*, *Winstanley* and many others, the film is the ultimate in *homage* to Folk Horror, though detaches itself from its purely referential position and adds intriguing questions about the concepts of the self, class, and identity. Wheatley outlines the film's influences:

> *Witchfinder General* is obviously an influence in terms of it's a film that you have
> to look at if you're making a film about the Civil War. But it's not necessarily
> one that's at the top of my list of general movies that I like. *Winstanley* and Peter

Watkins' *Culloden* are the two movies that we looked at before making *A Field in England*, more specifically. (2013)

A Field in England follows a group of men who are effectively trapped in a strange field during the English Civil War. The assistant of an East Anglian alchemist, Whitehead (Reece Shearsmith), ventures into a field with several deserters from a battle in search of ale. They come across a rope which seems to travel somewhere beyond the field. At the end is tied O'Neill (Michael Smiley), the man whom Whitehead has been searching for as he stole the alchemist's latest research involving the whereabouts of some unknown treasure. O'Neill takes control and forces the group to help him in his search for the treasure, hidden somewhere under the soil. It is revealed after much drama that the treasure the alchemist had researched was in fact a skull and the men fight with each other out of frustration, eventually leaving only Whitehead standing. He buries them in the hole that they have been digging and returns to the battle where he sees a newly formed vision of himself alongside two of his dead colleagues. It is implied earlier in the film that Whitehead had consumed some sort of hallu-cinogenic mushroom, adding further ambiguity to the film's abstraction.

Kim Newman likens Wheatley's film to a mixture of Ingmar Bergman and Piers Haggard, stating that, 'The subject of *A Field in England* is magic, melding, cloak-swishing alchemy with mushroom-based psychedelia... *A Field in England* sometimes seems like Haggard's film put through a blender and transformed into a rustic English take on the earthly symbolic dramas Ingmar Bergman made on his rocky Swedish islands' (2013: 50). The film is clearly channel-ling the more psychedelic-tinged darkness of films produced during the early 1970s, further enhanced by an isolated narrative of recognisable Folk Horror references. Perhaps *A Field in England* would be more fitting an example for the previous section's nostalgia-infused work, but Wheatley and Jump make sure that enough questioning ideas, especially those surrounding power, place and conflict, make it more than simply a hat tip to earlier films. Its mixture of Folk Horror with class conflict is an interesting feature but one that has clear links with the work of Alan Clarke who also straddled the line between these ideas in the 1970s, specifically in *Penda's Fen*. Wheatley even suggests that Clarke's Northern Island military drama for *Screen Two*, *Contact* (1985), is as much of an influence on *A Field in England* as other, more esoteric examples, though it is telling what specific aspect is drawn from such an influence:

Amy and I had talked about doing something that was in a field, or just in a small space. And I'd seen a film years ago called *Contact*, not the one you're thinking of, about soldiers patrolling on the border with Northern Ireland during the Troubles, and it was just these five guys on patrol, dealing with it day to day, never seeing anyone. It's just all fields and stuff. I thought that was kind of interesting, but then this also comes from films like *Dogville*, and then *Lifeboat*, movies that have given themselves a set of parameters. (2013)

This description usefully situates the film in the realm of the Folk Horror Chain, the field itself being the perfect zone to enact its causational happenings. The field is not only rural in its aesthetics but mysteriously isolated by some unknown force. The morals of O'Neill are already skewed enough to begin with, but the happenings in the field speak of the isolation that Wheatley is clearly trying to recreate from *Contact* and other work. The field even provides the literal narrative tools needed in order to skew the perception of even the most moral of characters, in the form of naturally growing drugs, though searching for some vestige of morality in Wheatley's and Jump's characters is an unenviable task. Fittingly, Wheatley and Jump have since moved away from the more overt of Folk Horror influences, adapting J.G. Ballard's novel, *High-Rise* (2015). Yet the director cannot quite switch off the influence of the genre's many traits, with that film again not only examining class through isolating society into a cramped social space, but also deliberately making it a period film set in the 1970s (or rather a Ballardian vision of that decade); the film seems like a rediscovered, digital episode of *Out of the Unknown*'s final season. Wheatley is immersed within the genre and, as O'Neill aptly shouts to Whitehead, 'You cannot escape the field...'.

Wheatley wasn't the only filmmaker making politically conscious statements in Folk Horror cinema during the 2000s. In fact, in the timeline of examples, he comes relatively late to the fold. Neil Marshall's *Dog Soldiers* (2002) is an earlier, excellent example of updating previously failed Folk Horror ideas; specifically, the film reflects a similar narrative to *The Beast in the Cellar* (*sans* Beryl Reid discussing lettuces), as well as bearing a likeness to the television series, *The Nightmare Man*. The film plays with the idea of class and isolation again as a military exercise goes badly wrong thanks to an unforeseen werewolf manifestation. Marshall's next film, *The Descent* (2005), would also involve some vaguely folkloric horror, as a climbing group venture into an underground cave system only to find it inhabited by some unfriendly creatures, not dissimilar to *Death Line*. Marshall's is one of a number of films with this set-up from the period which include *The Cavern* (2005),[22] *The Cave* (2005),[23] and *The Descent*'s 2009 follow up.[24] Most are only fleeting in their relevance to Folk Horror and Marshall's is undoubtedly the strongest, most relevant example.

In 'arthouse' cinema from around the globe, complex and political Folk Horror themes have also been present, albeit in films that again defy genre classification. Tomas Alfredson's *Let The Right One In* (2008) couples urban bullying and dark, Swedish streets with a social vampire theme; Lars von Trier's *Antichrist* (2009) follows an increasingly unhinged couple in mourning for their child through a 'cabin in the woods' isolation, alongside surreal images of talking foxes; Michael Haneke's *The White Ribbon* (2009) depicts a *Village of the Damned*-esque conspiracy in a 1900s German village; and in Cristian Mungiu's *Beyond the Hills* (2012),[25] a Romanian girl visits her ex-lover in a monastery only to become trapped in its social system, which, through overt superstition and an attempted exorcism of her free-will, eventually kills her. British cinema produced a more 'arthouse' leaning Folk Horror film in the form of Paul Wright's incredibly effective, class-conscious parable, *For Those in Peril* (2013). It follows a young man (George MacKay) who becomes determined to find his brother lost in a fishing trawler accident at sea, of which, mysteriously, he was the only survivor. The film mixes social-realist drama with Magic Realist happenings (within a landscape) to great effect. When I interviewed Wright about the film, he suggested a number of key Folk Horror traits within his debut. He wrote specifically of an interesting inversion of isolated communities where the interloper was not a city-dwelling product of modernity, but in fact was someone local but detached from that community instead:

> With the film, what I was most interested in looking at, however, is what happens when one person stands outside this close-knit community and deals with what has happened in the extreme opposite way to everyone else and the conflict that can arise from this decision. (2014)

Of all of the films that channel a sense of modern Folk Horror as such, perhaps the most controversial is outside of 'arthouse' territory altogether; James Watkins' pulp horror, *Eden Lake* (2008). The film is questionable for its problematic relationship to class, arguably playing to the tabloid sensationalism that dominated the first decade of the millennium surrounding young, working-class people, connoted by the sub-culture of the 'Chav'. Newman summarises the film within this context:

> Writer-director James Watkins uses elements from chase-survival horror-in-the-country movies like *Deliverance* and *The Hills Have Eyes* but relocates them to the dark heart of England, and (with either opportunism and insight) relates the clash between upscale, middle-class, good-lucking liberals and the gang to tabloid concerns about 'broken Britain' (keywords: ASBO, hoodie, chav, knife crime). (2011: 476)

The film follows a middle-class couple, Steve (Michael Fassbinder) and Jenny (Kelly Reilly), as they venture into the countryside for a romantic trip, only to be confronted with a violent set of youths from the nearby estate. The violence escalates through a series of encounters, with the group's leader, Brett (Jack O'Connell), tying Steve up and effectively forcing his peers to torture him with a knife. The violence is filmed on mobile phones à la the craze of 'Happy Slapping'. The film never really questions its own portrayal of the working-class, and ends by showing the group's parents to be just as bad, and perhaps responsible for their children's lack of morality. Yet the film does play with a number of Folk Horror elements as Dawn Keetley writes in her essay on the film's place within the genre:

> It is set in a lush natural landscape; Jenny and Steve become isolated, removed from their familiar urban environment; and they soon realize with horror that they are beset by characters whose moral beliefs are at best bewilderingly skewed, at worst entirely absent. (2015)

Keetley is using the Folk Horror Chain to argue for the film's inclusion within the genre, and it is a compelling reasoning, especially as she later affirms that the landscape itself is almost sentient in the film: 'It is also important that landscape in *Eden Lake* is not just present but powerful: it has agency. It doesn't just wait for us to come in; it doesn't just inertly countenance us; it acts on us, sometimes against us, sometimes with us' (ibid.). Owen Jones has condemned the film in his book *Chavs: A Demonization Of the Working Class* (2011), for its apparent adoption of Daily Mail rhetoric in its portrayal of a very middle-class paranoia: 'Here was a film arguing that the middle classes could no longer live alongside the quasi-bestial lower orders' (2011: 131). This is a reading supported by Newman, who suggests the film is 'about as enlightened as the depiction of rural labourers in, say, *The Texas Chainsaw Massacre*' (2011: 476). Though the two films are very different in many ways, it links back to themes of rural vs. urban, the supposed Enlightenment vs. pre-Enlightenment, the old ways vs. the new ways, and now the middle-class vs. the working-class. It is a complex and often illogical mixture.

This ultimately raises the question of Folk Horror's employment of class as a whole; what does the genre ultimately say about class in Britain? Because of its label, the very name of Folk Horror suggests two very different potential readings. The first is one that is built from narratives formed of an oral tradition; one that often has direct links to more working-class narratives anyway because of the transfer of folklore and tales that do not require a written text.

The other is a horror derived from 'folk', the people of general society. In many of the films, both pre- and post-millennium, Folk Horror portrays the working-class as superstitious, easily corruptible and morally dubious; whether it be the workers of the land in *The Blood on Satan's* Claw, the violent henchmen of *Witchfinder General* and *Kill List*, or the needlessly aggressive, almost feral, youths of *Eden Lake*. Though it would be crass to liken this argument either way to any notion of the reality of Britain, there's little doubt that, as one of many genres found in horror cinema as a whole, it is the most earnest and most complex in its politics and class consciousness; where, rightly or wrongly, people themselves become the very source of the horror.

What is Folk Horror?

'If the crops fail, Summerisle, next year your people will kill you on May Day!' – Howie in *The Wicker Man*.

At the heart of this book has been one direct question: what is Folk Horror? Far from providing a straightforward answer, I hope to have demonstrated that the genre resists such a direct question; it is not any one thing but in fact a multitude of creative ideas. It is not just horror media that uses folklore, or an emphasis on the inner evil found in people. It is not simply a few British films and television series from the 1970s, and it is not just a presentation of landscapes imbued with a sense of the eerie; it is all of these things and more. Essentially, even more than just being a genre, the term 'Folk Horror' can be seen as a type of social map that tracks the unconscious ley lines between a huge range of different forms of media in the twentieth century and earlier. It is one that connects the past and the present to create a clash of belief systems and people; modernity and Enlightenment against superstition and faith, the very violence inherent within us as people. It is the evil under the soil, the terror in the backwoods of a forgotten lane, the loneliness in a brutalist tower block, and the ghosts that haunt stones and patches of dark, lonely water. It is both nostalgic for and questioning of days gone by, romantic in its allure of a more open society's ways, but realistic in its honesty surrounding their ultimate prejudice and violence. It is tales of hours dreadful and things strange, a media that requires a literal walking and traversing to fully understand its inner workings.

Something strange occurred during the writing of this book; the near-literal transformation of the UK into 'a local shop for local people'. Immersion in narratives of Martian insect fascism, fear of the outsider and an islander mentality may have meant some projection on my part but all of these traits seemed to gradually manifest in a sizeable chunk of the British populace during the run-up to the referendum on membership of the European Union in June 2016. Far from the 1970s having sole monopoly on real life Folk Horror, there have been few political events in recent years that have resembled the genre in such startling detail. 'Hours dreadful and things strange' is as apt a description of the post-Brexit climate as Folk Horror itself; with its normalisation and spiked increase in xenophobic attacks, a gestalt mentality, any questioning of the result labelled as a heresy by the pro-Brexit tabloids, and a wide-scale embracing of political fantasy and inwardness. Whereas Lord Summerisle controlled his population with the lies and perks of a counter-culture faux-paganism, today the basest of urges and most paranoid of fears have been amplified and satiated, something which simply cannot be explained by a Knealian sense of inherited violent impulses alone. We have burnt our Sgt. Howie in the wicker man, and now wait naively for our apples to grow once more, confident that we have 'taken back control'.

Of course, folkloric material has had a varied and sadly long relationship with such fascist ideals and movements, the irony being how far general folklore and folk aesthetics have been appropriated and removed from their original context by the far right in order to present the required vision of the past that conforms to their needs. This is covered most effectively in Georgina Boyes' *The Imagined Village* (2012), a book that skilfully dismantles such appropriation and cherry-picking of cultural identity and traditions. Aptly, Folk Horror also provides two essential bulwarks against such nostalgia-tinted ideologies. The first is that it blasts apart the romantic visions of an England gone by (or any other western country harkening back to a fictional past, for that matter) through unflinchingly depicting how violent and brutal the past really was. The second is that it often portrays villains who harness similar techniques of indoctrination that contemporary far-right groups and figures use with a pathos that unveils how such power really functions; it regularly shows diegetically how such figures appropriate the same aesthetics and social narratives to control their communities. However, the irony of the far right's appreciation of any sort of Folk Horror or folklore is, like most things, entirely lost upon them.

Folk Horror seems to be so many things inside and outside of reality, so can it really be considered a genre when covering so vast an area of material and themes? In Chapter 2, I introduced the idea of the Folk Horror Chain as one way to highlight and solidify some of these routes and ley lines, sketching out the crossover between certain films and television programs that all draw from the same pool of esoterica. The essence of the landscape, key to the themes enforced by the chain, was used to express different emphases within the ideas of Topography and Rurality of Chapters 3 and 4; further routes beneath the initial paths, the ghost ways and copse roads of a half-remembered popular culture. On the reverse of this, we have seen in Chapter 5 how urban environments and the reality of the recent past has conjured forms that are just as esoteric, occult and 'wyrd' as their rural cousins, whilst in this chapter we have seen the seeds sewn in earlier decades sprout into new nostalgic and political forms; reflecting the 'now' and the 'then'. Folk Horror is all of these things and undoubtedly more. It is the writing of M.R. James, Alan Garner, Susan Cooper and Arthur Machen;[26] it is the television scripts of Nigel Kneale, the films of David Gladwell, *The Blood on Satan's Claw*, the paranoid Public Information Films of the 1970s, the numerous series by HTV, the *Season of the Witch*, The Advisory Circle reminding us to 'Mind how you go!', and a story of two hitmen caught unknowingly in a sadistic, class-saturated ritual. The form's heavily subjectivist approach vouches for its fluctuating canon and ongoing reappraisal, but there is undoubtedly enough solid material for it to now be taken seriously as a form in its own right.

This form is one that is rich and self-reflexive in its own lore. Though the link between folklore itself and the genre as a whole has been little dissected within the chapters of this book, there is clearly further to go in the mapping of its many furrows. Essentially, however, the genre has come full circle, from its early forms in literature and European silent film, to the occult cinema of the US and the UK, and to the full blown Folk Horror film and television of the counter-culture and beyond. Folk Horror's essence is one of an older horror, one – like folklore itself – that has always been here. As long as there are 'folk', there will always be Folk Horror. It will, more accurately, always *be* here. When Howie screams his final, subtle revenge on Lord Summerisle in *The Wicker Man*, the dénouement that implies that the islanders will kill him the following year if the apples fail to grow again, he is laying down the law/lore of Folk Horror; that fear supplanted into communities comes back to haunt those who sowed its first seeds. As the islanders proudly sing 'Sumer-is-icumen-in' while Howie burns to death, we know deep down that the fruit will not grow again no matter how many people are sacrificed to the land. It was an apt foretelling.

Endnotes

1   Its subtitle is 'A New-England Folktale', which should further cement its relevance to us.

2   A period detail reflecting the recent colonialism of the place and era.

3   In Godfrey's article, he says as much: 'Eggers claims not to be a big horror fan, other

than an obsession with *The Shining*, a key inspiration for *The Witch* in terms of tone and atmospherics' (2016).

4   See *Eden Lake* in this chapter's final section.

5   As well as a darker, political nostalgia in the present-day UK with its desire for the mirage-like concept of 'sovereignty' outside of the European Union.

6   For further elucidation, Jamie Sexton provides some context by using the analysis of Jeffery Sconce: 'The name Ghost Box itself is a reference to television and its own uncanny nature, and this is an issue that has accompanied the introduction of many new technologies, as has been illustrated by Jeffrey Sconce, who writes: "Sound and image without material substance, the electronically mediated worlds of telecommunications often evoke the supernatural by creating virtual beings that appear to have no physical form. By bringing this spectral world into the home, the TV set in particular can take on the appearance of a haunted apparatus".' (2012: 17)

7   Jon Brooks.

8   Martin Jenkins.

9   Drew Mulholland.

10   The stage name of Andy Sharp.

11   All of whom create various senses of alternative heritage through re-engaging with darker elements found in the landscape.

12   Directed by James Kent and written by Stephen Greenhorn.

13   Directed by Damon Thomas and written by Simon Tyrrell.

14   Sometimes known under the title of *Altar*.

15   Also of relevance to general modern Folk Horror television are the *Torchwood* episodes *Countrycide* and *Small Worlds*, which, if flawed, do nicely display the split between the simultaneously fantastical and down to earth elements in the genre.

16   Created by Nic Pizzolatto.

17   Directed by David Keating and written by Brendan McCarthy.

18   Sometimes known under the title of *Final Prayer*.

19   Notably, race is still an issue that has yet to be properly addressed in almost any example of Folk Horror film, which perhaps speaks of a still-colonial position to its many guises.

20   Co-written with Robin Hill.

21   Again a familiar theme in the political climate of contemporary Britain.

22   Directed and written by Olatunde Osunsanmi.

23   Directed by Bruce Hunt and written by Tegan West and Michael Steinberg.

24   Directed by Jon Harris with a screenplay by James McCarthy, J. Blakeson and James Watkins.

25   Inspired by accounts written up by Tatiana Niculescu-Bran.

26   The latter two rarely mentioned in the book due to the lack of audio-visual adaptations but certainly both are figures of note in the genre.

Bibliography

Abbott, M., 2014. *Picnic at Hanging Rock: What We See and What We Seem.* [ONLINE] Available at https://www.criterion.com/current/posts/3202-picnic-at-hanging-rock-what-we-see-and-what-we-seem [Accessed 15/04/2016].

Anderson, D., 2014. *The Creeping Terror of Childhood: An Interview with Richard Littler, creator of Scarfolk.* [ONLINE] Available at http://www.humag.co/features/the-creeping-terror-of-childhood [Accessed 16/04/2016].

Ash, R., 1973. *Folklore, myths and legends of Britain.* The Reader's Digest Association Ltd: London.

Baker, B., 2015. *A Night to Kill a King Is This Night.* [ONLINE] Available at http://sciencefiction365.blogspot.co.uk/2015/11/a-night-to-kill-king-is-this-night.html [Accessed 15/04/2016].

Bergom-Larsson, M., 1978. *Film in Sweden: Ingmar Bergman and Society.* The Tantivy Press: London.

Bonner, M., 2013. *'The blood in the earth': an interview with A Field in England director Ben Wheatley.* [ONLINE] Available at http://www.uncut.co.uk/blog/the-view-from-here/the-blood-in-the-earth-an-interview-with-a-field-in-england-director-ben-wheatley-21055 [Accessed 30/03/2016].

Brownlow, K., 1973. *The Parade's Gone By* (1968). Abacus, Sphere Book LTD: London

Campbell, R., 2012. 'Lost Hearts' from *Ghost Stories: Classic adaptations from the BBC Volume 3* DVD Booklet. BFI: London.

Charles, D., 2015. 'An Interview with Kim Newman' from *Folk Horror Revival: Field Studies*. Wyrd Harvest Press: Durham.

Clark, L.G., 2013. *The Christmas Ghost Stories of Lawrence Gordon Clark* (ed. Tony Earnshaw). Spectral Press: Milton Keynes.

Cooper, I., 2011. *Witchfinder General*. Auteur (Devil's Advocates): Leighton Buzzard.

Coulthart, J., 2015. 'Sacred Demons: The Dramatic Art of David Rudkin', from *Folk Horror Revival: Field Notes*. Wyrd Harvest Press: Durham.

Cowie, P., 1966. *Swedish Cinema*. A. Zwemmer Limited, London.

Cummings, D., 2007. 'Shindo's Onibaba', from *Onibaba* DVD Booklet. Eureka (Masters of Cinema): London.

Cummings, D., 2009. 'Shindo's Kuroneko', from *Kuroneko* DVD Booklet. Eureka (Masters of Cinema): London.

Deen, A., 2013. *An Interview with Robin Hardy (The Wicker Man) by Andy Deen*. [ONLINE] Available at http://www.ukhorrorscene.com/an-interview-with-robin-hardy-the-wicker-man-by-andy-deen/ [Accessed 21/05/2016].

Derrida, J., 1976. *Of Grammatology*. The John Hopkins University Press: Baltimore and London.

Easterbrook, A., 2012. 'A Warning to the Curious' from *A Warning to the Curious* DVD Booklet. BFI: London.

Ebert, R., 2012. *Wake in Fright*. [ONLINE] Available at http://www.rogerebert.com/reviews/wake-in-fright-2012 [Accessed 15/04/2016].

Evans, G, E., 1966. *The Pattern under the Plough*. Faber & Faber: London.

Evans, G., and Fowler, W., 2014. 'The Edge is Where the Centre is: David Rudkin and Penda's Fen' from *The Edge is Where the Centre is: David Rudkin and Penda's Fen: A Conversation*. Texte und Töne with the Colloquium for Unpopular Culture: New York.

Fischer, R., 2014. *Film Interview: 'A Field in England' Director Ben Wheatley*. [ONLINE] Available at http://www.slashfilm.com/film-interview-a-field-in-england-director-ben-wheatley/ [Accessed 30/03/2016].

Fisher, M., 2012. 'Old Haunts: The Landscapes of MR James', from *Whistle and I'll Come to You* DVD Booklet. BFI: London.

Fisher, M., 2014. *Ghosts of My Life: Writings on Depression, Hauntology and Lost Futures*. Zero Books: Winchester.

Farber, S., 1972. *'Deliverance', How it Delivers*. [ONLINE] Available at https://www.nytimes.com/books/98/08/30/specials/dickey-delivers.html [Accessed 15/04/2016].

Foucault, M., 1984. *The Foucault Reader: An Introduction to Foucault's Thought* (ed. Paul Rabinow). Penguin Books: London.

Frazer, J., 1993. *The Golden Bough* (1912). Wordsworth Editions: Hertfordshire.

Garner, A., 1988. *The Owl Service* (1967). William Collins Son and Co. Ltd: Glasgow.

Garner, A., 1972. *One Pair of Eyes: All Systems Go - Alan Garner*. BBC Television, 2 February.

Garner, A., 1975. *Red Shift* (1973). William Collins Sons and Co. Ltd: Glasgow.

Garner, A., 1980. *The Edge of The Ceiling (Celebration)*. ITV, 5 June.

Garner, A., 1997. *The Voice That Thunders*. Vintage: London.

Garner, A., 2014. 'A note on *Red Shift*' from *Red Shift* DVD Booklet. BFI: London.

Gatiss, M., 2010. *A History of Horror: Home County Horrors*. BBC 4 Television, 18 October.

Gatiss, M., 2013. *M.R. James: Ghost Writer*. BBC 4 Television, 25 December.

Gatiss, M., 2013. 'Foreword' from *The Christmas Ghost Stories of Lawrence Gordon Clark* (ed. Tony Earnshaw). Spectral Press: Milton Keynes.

Godfrey, A., 2016. *The Witch: 'Good horror is taking a look at what's dark in humanity'*. [ONLINE] Available at http://www.theguardian.com/film/2016/mar/07/17th-century-horror-drama-the-witch [Accessed 04/04/2016].

Hames, P., 2008. 'Valerie and Her Week of Wonders', from *Valerie and Her Week of Wonders* DVD Booklet. Second Run DVD: London.

Harrigan, J., 2015. 'The Sacred Theatre of Summerisle', from *Folk Horror Revival: Field Studies*. Wyrd Harvest Press: Durham.

Heaney, S., 1999. *Beowulf.* Faber & Faber: London.

Hearn, M, and Barnes, A., 2007. *The Hammer Story: The Authorised History of Hammer Films* (1997). Titan Books: London.

Hills, G., 2008. 'Owl Service Memories', from *The Owl Service* DVD Booklet. Network: London.

Hughes, T., 2016. *Evil of English Villages...* [ONLINE] Available at http://www.dailymail.co.uk/news/article-3829968/Evil-English-villages-Midsomer-Murders-writer-Anthony-Horowitz-says-mistrust-suspicion-bitterness-make-perfect-setting-mysteries.html [Accessed 10/10/2016].

Hutchings, P. 2016. '10 great British Rural Horror films' [ONLINE] Available at http://www.bfi.org.uk/news/10-great-british-rural-horror-films [Accessed 28/03/2017].

Hutchings, P., 2004. 'Uncanny Landscapes in British Film and Television', from *Visual Culture of Britain.* Manchester University Press: Manchester.

James, M.R., 1930. *Suffolk and Norfolk: A Perambulation of the Two Counties with Notices of Their History and Their Ancient Buildings.* J.M. Dent & Sons: London and Toronto.

James, M.R., 1961. *The Collected Ghost Stories of M.R. James* (1931). Edward Arnold: London.

James, M.R., 2013. *The Christmas Ghost Stories of Lawrence Gordon Clark* (ed. Tony Earnshaw). Spectral Press: Milton Keynes.

Jolly, A., 2015. 'Kill Lists: The occult, paganism and sacrifice in cinema as an analogy for political upheaval in the 1970s and the 2010s', from *Folk Horror Revival: Field Studies.* Wyrd Harvest Press: Durham.

Jones, O., 2011. *Chavs: The Demonization of The Working Class.* Verso: London.

Keetley, D., 2015. 'Eden Lake (2008): Folk Horror for a Disenchanted World.' [ONLINE] Available at http://www.horrorhomeroom.com/eden-lake-2008-folk-horror-for-a-disenchanted-world/ [Accessed 31/03/2015].

Kennedy, J., 2013. 'Terror in the Terroir: Resisting the Rebranding of the Countryside', *The Quietus.* [ONLINE] Available at http://thequietus.com/articles/14114-country-life-british-politics-uncanny-music-art [Accessed 20/10/2016].

Kerrigan, L., *Dead of Night* from *Dead of Night: The Surviving Episodes from the Classic Series* DVD Booklet. BFI: London.

Kneale, N., 1979. *Quatermass II* (1960). Arrow Book Ltd: London.

Koven, M, J., 2008. *Film, Folklore, And Urban Legends*. The Scarecrow Press: Plymouth & Toronto.

Kristeva, J., 1982. *Powers of Horror: An Essay In Abjection*. Columbia University Press: New York.

Larkin, P., 2003. *Collected Poems*. Faber & Faber: London.

Lee, B., 2016. 'The Witch review: an eerie campfire tale that gets under your skin', *The Guardian*. [ONLINE] Available at http://www.theguardian.com/film/2016/mar/10/the-witch-review-a-eerie-campfire-tale-that-gets-under-your-skin [Accessed 04/04/2016].

Leith, D, P., 1966. *Season of the Witch*. Epic Records, California.

Macfarlane, R., 2015. *The Eeriness of the English Countryside*. [ONLINE] Available at http://www.theguardian.com/books/2015/apr/10/eeriness-english-countryside-robert-macfarlane [Accessed 15/04/2015].

Malkin, G., 2015. *Public Information Films: Playing Safe* from *Folk Horror Revival: Fields Studies*. Wyrd Harvest Press: Durham.

McCallum, S., 2012. 'A View from a Hill', from *Ghost Stories: Classic adaptations from the BBC Volume 5* DVD Booklet. BFI: London.

McKay, S., 2008. 'The Owl Service: The Legend Unravelled', from *The Owl Service* DVD booklet. Network: London.

Murray, A., 2006. 'Animal Magic: A BEASTS overview', from *Beasts* DVD booklet. Network: London.

Negarestani, R., 2008. *Cyclonopedia: Complicity with Anonymous Materials*. Re-Press: Victoria (Australia).

Newland, C., 2013. 'Screen Woman: The Chauvinist Male Fantasy of Straw Dogs.' [ONLINE] Available at https://kubrickontheguillotine.com/2013/09/06/screen-women-the-male-chauvinist-fantasy-of-straw-dogs/ [Accessed 27/04/2016].

Newman, K., 2007. 'The Sound of Fear: The Influences and Production of "The Shout"' from *The Shout* DVD Booklet. Network: London.

Newman, K., 2008. 'The Owl Service: Unexplained Mysteries', from *The Owl Service* DVD Booklet. Network: London.

Newman, K., 2011. *Nightmare Movies: Horror on Screen Since the 1960s* (1988). Bloomsbury: London.

Newman, K., 2013. 'This Spectred Isle', from *Sight & Sound, July 2013*. BFI: London.

Oliver, R., 2012. 'MR James' Oh, Whistle, and I'll Come to You, My Lad', from *Whistle And I'll Come To You* DVD Booklet. BFI: London.

Owens, R., 2017. *Macbeth*. Auteur (Devil's Advocates): Leighton Buzzard.

Paciorek, A., 2015. 'Folk Horror: From the Forests, Fields and Furrows. An Introduction' from *Folk Horror Revival: Field Notes*. Wyrd Harvest Press: Durham.

Paciorek, A., 2015. 'An Arthurian Antichrist: Alternative Readings of Kill List', from *Folk Horror Revival: Field Studies*. Wyrd Harvest Press: Durham.

Picard, A., 2012. 'A Man Apart', from *Sight & Sound, May 2012*. BFI: London.

Poe, E, A., 1968. *Tales of Mystery and Imagination* (Everyman Library, 1908). J.M. Dent & Sons: London.

Pratt, V., 2013. 'Long Arm of the Lore', from *Sight & Sound, October 2013*. BFI: London.

Pratt, V., 2013. 'Hunting for Sherds: Robin Redbreast', from *Robin Redbreast* DVD Booklet. BFI: London.

Rafferty, T., 2010. 'Holy Terror', from *The Night of the Hunter* DVD Booklet. Criterion: New York.

Rattigan, D, L., 2012. 'Robert Fuest's And Soon The Darkness (1970).' [ONLINE] Available at http://diaboliquemagazine.com/robert-fuests-and-soon-the-darkness-1970/ [Accessed 27/04/2016].

Richards, A., 2016. 'Hippies and the Counterculture: Origins, Beliefs and Legacy.' [ONLINE] Available at http://study.com/academy/lesson/hippies-and-the-counterculture-origins-beliefs-and-legacy.html#courseInfo [Accessed 04/10/2016].

Rolinson, D., 2014. 'The Boundary's Undefined: Red Shift', from *Red Shift* DVD Booklet. BFI: London.

Russell, P., 2013. 'Searching', from *Captured* DVD booklet. BFI: London.

Sandhu, S., 2016. *Penda's Fen* DVD Booklet. BFI: London.

Scovell, A., 2012. 'Interview with Ben Rivers.' [ONLINE] Available at https://celluloidwickerman.com/2012/11/30/interview-with-ben-rivers/ [Accessed 25/04/2016].

Scovell, A., 2013. 'Interview with Digby Rumsey (BFI Flipside, The Pledge).' [ONLINE] Available at https://celluloidwickerman.com/2013/11/04/interview-with-digby-rumsey-bfi-flipside-the-pledge/ [Accessed 26/04/2016].

Scovell, A., 2014. 'Interview with Paul Wright (For Those in Peril).' [ONLINE] Available at https://celluloidwickerman.com/2014/04/14/interview-with-paul-wright-for-those-in-peril/ [Accessed 18/05/2016].

Scovell, A., 2015. 'Interview with Jeremy Burnham - Children of The Stones (1977).' [ONLINE] Available at https://celluloidwickerman.com/2015/03/02/interview-with-jeremy-burnham-children-of-the-stones-1977/ [Accessed 22/04/2016].

Scovell, A., 2015. 'Interview with David Gladwell (Requiem for a Village).' [ONLINE] Available at http://liverpoolsmallcinema.org.uk/cinema/interview-with-david-gladwell-requiem-for-a-village [Accessed 24/04/2016].

Sexton, J., 2012. *Weird Britain in Exile: Ghost Box, Hauntology, and Alternative Heritage* from *Popular Music and Society*. Routledge: London.

Shakespeare, W., 2007. *Macbeth* (1611) from *The Complete Works of William Shakespeare*. Wordsworth Library Collection: Hertfordshire.

Shimon, D, D., 2010. *That Old Black Park Magic: The Strange Story of Blood On Satan's Claw*. Odeon Entertainment: London.

Simpson, M.J., 2003. 'Interview: Piers Haggard.' [ONLINE] Available at http://mjsimpson-films.blogspot.co.uk/2013/11/interview-piers-haggard.html [Accessed 16/05/2016].

Sinclair, I., 1998. *Lights Out for the Territory*. Granta: London.

Skakov, N., 2012. *The Cinema of Tarkovsky: Labyrinths of Space and Time*. I.B. Tauris: London.

Stephens, G., 2009. 'Confining Nature: Rites of Passage, Eco-Indigenes and the Uses of Meat in Walkabout.' [ONLINE] Available at http://sensesofcinema.com/2009/towards-an-ecology-of-cinema/walkabout/ [Accessed 15/04/2016].

Sussex, E., 2011. 'Requiem for a Village - a contemporary review', in *Sight & Sound, vol 45 no1, 1975/76)* from *Requiem For A Village* DVD Booklet. BFI: London.

Sweet, M., 2015. *Black Aquarius*. BBC Radio 4, April 25th (20:00).

Thompson, D., 2011. 'Jerzy Skolimowski: The Fugitive', from *Sight & Sound, April 2011*. BFI: London.

Thrower, S., 2013. 'The Finishing Line', from *Captured* DVD booklet. BFI: London.

Trubshaw, B., 2010. *Exploring Folklore*. Heart of Albion Press: Wiltshire.

Twitchwell, J, B., 1997. *The Living Dead: A Study of the Vampire in Romantic Literature* (1981). Duke University Press: Durham, N.C.

Ward, M., 2014. 'Careful with that axe, Eugene: Sex, drugs and mind-swapping in seventies suburbia', from *Out Of The Unknown* DVD Booklet. BFI: London.

Wheatley, H., 2012. 'Stigma', from *Ghost Stories: Classic adaptations from the BBC Volume 4* DVD Booklet. BFI: London.

Worthington, T., 2011. 'Completing the Circle: A Retrospective of HTV's Cult Children's Programming', from *Children of the Stones* DVD Booklet. Network: London.

Wright, P., 1998. 'A conversation between Patrick Wright and Patrick Keiller', from *London and Robinson in Space* DVD Booklet. BFI: London.

Wynn Westcott, W., 1890/2000. 'Numbers: Their Occult Power and Mystic Virtues.' [ONLINE] Available at: http://www.hermetics.org/pdf/gd/Numbers__Their_Occult_Power_and_Mystic_Virtues_by_W._Wynn_Westcott.pdf [Accessed 13 April 2016].

Young, R., 2010. 'The Pattern Under the Plough: The Films Of Old, Weird Britain', from *Sight & Sound, August 2010*. BFI Publishing, London.

Young, R., 2011. *Electric Eden: Unearthing Britain's Visionary Music*. Faber & Faber: London.

Selected Filmography

Cinema

Akenfield (1974). Directed by Peter Hall. Written and based on a novel by Ronald Blythe.

An American Werewolf in London (1981). Directed and written by John Landis.

Andrei Rublev (1966). Directed by Andrei Tarkovsky. Written by Andrey Konchalovskiy.

And Soon the Darkness (1970). Directed by Robert Fuest. Written by Terry Nation and Brian Clements.

Antichrist (2009). Directed and written by Lars von Trier.

The Beast in The Cellar (1970). Directed and written by James Kelley.

Beyond the Hills (2012). Directed and written by Cristian Mungiu.

Blackwood (2012). Directed by Adam Wimpenny. Written by J.S. Hill.

Black Sunday (1960). Directed by Mario Bava. Written by Ennio De Concini and Mario Serandrei, based on a story by Nikolai Gogol.

The Blair Witch Project (1999). Directed and written by Daniel Myrick and Eduardo Sánchez.

The Blood-Beast Terror (1968). Directed by Vernon Sewell. Written by Peter Bryan.

The Blood on Satan's Claw (1971). Directed by Piers Haggard. Written by Piers Haggard and Robert Wynne-Simmons.

Blood Orgy of the She-Devils (1973). Directed and written by Ted V. Mikels.

The Borderlands (2013). Directed and written by Elliot Goldner.

By Our Selves (2015). Directed by Andrew Kötting.

A Canterbury Tale (1944). Directed by Michael Powell. Written by Emeric Pressburger.

Celia (1989). Directed and written by Ann Turner.

Children of the Corn (1984). Directed by Fritz Kiersch. Written by George Goldsmith, based on a story by Stephen King.

The City of the Dead (1960). Directed by John Llewellyn Moxey. Written by George Baxt, based on a story by Milton Subotsky.

The Conjuring (2013). Directed by James Wan. Written by Chad Hayes and Carey Hayes.

Creep (2004). Directed and written by Christopher Smith.

The Crimson Blade (1963). Directed and written by John Gilling.

Cromwell (1970). Directed and written by Ken Hughes.

Crucible of Terror (1971). Directed by Ted Hooker. Written by Tom Parkinson.

Cry of the Banshee (1970). Directed by Gordon Hessler. Written by Tim Kelly and Christopher Wicking.

Cul-De-Sac (1966). Directed by Roman Polanski. Written by Gerard Brach and Roman Polanski.

The Curse of the Crimson Altar (1968). Directed by Vernon Sewell. Written by Mervyn Haisman and Henry Lincoln.

The Damned (1963). Directed by Joseph Losey. Written by Evan Jones, based on a novel by H.L. Lawrence.

Daughters of Satan (1972). Directed by Hollingsworth Morse. Written by John C. Higgins, based on a story by John A. Bushelman.

Death Line (1972). Directed by Gary Sherman. Written by Ceri Jones.

Deliverance (1972). Directed by John Boorman. Written and based on a novel by James Dickey.

The Descent (2005). Directed and written by Neil Marshall.

The Devil (1972). Directed and written by Andrzej Żuławski.

The Devil Rides Out (1968). Directed by Terence Fisher. Written by Richard Matheson, based on a novel by Dennis Wheatley.

The Devil's Hand (1961). Directed by William J. Hole Jr. Written by Jo Heims.

The Devil's Rain (1975). Directed by Robert Fuest. Written by Gabe Essoe, James Aston and Gerald Hopman.

The Devil's Widow (1970). Directed by Roddy McDowall. Written by William Spier.

The Devils (1971). Directed and written by Ken Russell, based on a play by John Whiting and a novel by Aldous Huxley.

Devils of Darkness (1965). Directed by Lance Comfort. Written by Lyn Fairhurst.

Dog Soldiers (2002). Directed and written by Neil Marshall.

Don't Deliver Us from Evil (1971). Directed and written by Joël Séria.

Doomwatch (1972). Directed by Peter Sasdy. Written by Clive Exton.

Dracula A.D. 1972 (1972). Directed by Alan Gibson. Written by Don Houghton.

Drowning by Numbers (1988). Directed and written by Peter Greenaway.

The Dunwich Horror (1970). Directed by Daniel Heller. Written by Curtis Hanson and Henry Rosenbaum, based on a story by H.P. Lovecraft.

Eden Lake (2008). Directed and written by James Watkins.

The Edge of The World (1937). Directed and written by Michael Powell.

The Exorcist (1973). Directed and written by William Friedkin, based on a novel by William Peter Blatty.

Eye of the Devil (1967). Directed by J. Lee Thompson. Written by Robin Estridge, based on a novel by Dennis Murphy.

The Falling (2014). Directed and written by Carol Morley.

A Field in England (2013). Directed by Ben Wheatley. Written by Amy Jump.

This Filthy Earth (2001). Directed by Andrew Kötting. Written by Sean Lock, based on a novel by Émile Zola.

For Those in Peril (2013). Directed and written by Paul Wright.

Fright (1971). Directed by Peter Collinson. Written by Tudor Gates.

Frightmare (1974). Directed by Pete Walker. Written by David McGillivray.

The Go-Between (1971). Directed by Joseph Losey. Written by Harold Pinter, based on a novel by L.P. Hartley.

The Golem (1920). Directed Paul Wegener. Written by Henrik Galeen and Paul Wegener.

Gone to Earth (1950). Directed by Michael Powell. Written by Emeric Pressburger.

The Hallow (2015). Directed by Corin Hardy. Written by Corin Hardy, Tom de Ville and Felipe Marino.

Häxan: Witchcraft Through the Ages (1922). Directed and written by Benjamin Christensen.

The Hills Have Eyes (1977). Directed and written by Wes Craven.

The Hound of The Baskervilles (1959). Directed by Terence Fisher. Written by Peter Bryan, based on a novel by Arthur Conan Doyle.

Hour of the Wolf (1968). Directed and written by Ingmar Bergman.

'I Know Where I'm Going!' (1945). Directed by Michael Powell. Written by Emeric Pressburger.

I Walked with a Zombie (1943). Directed by Jacques Tourneur. Adapted by Curt Siadmak and Ardel Wray, based on a story by Inez Wallace.

Images (1972). Directed by Robert Altman. Written by Susannah York and Robert Altman.

Island of Terror (1966). Directed by Terence Fisher. Written by Edward Mann and Al Ramsen.

A Journey to Avebury (1970). Directed by Derek Jarman.

Kill List (2011). Directed by Ben Wheatley. Written by Ben Wheatley and Amy Jump.

Kwaidan (1964). Directed by Masaki Kobayashi. Written by Yôko Mizuki, based on a story by Lafcadio Hearn.

The Lair of the White Worm (1988). Directed and written by Ken Russell, based on a novel by Bram Stoker.

The Last House on the Left (1972). Directed and written by Wes Craven.

Leaves from Satan's Book (1920). Directed by Carl T. Dreyer. Written by Edgar Høyer, based on a novel by Marie Corelli.

Legend of the Witches (1970). Directed and written by Malcolm Leigh.

Let the Right One In (2008). Directed by Tomas Alfredson. Written and based on a novel by John Ajvide Lindqvist.

Long Weekend (1978). Directed by Colin Eggleston. Written by Everett De Roche.

Long Weekend (2008). Directed by Jamie Banks. Written by Everett De Roche.

Macbeth (2015). Directed by Justin Kruzel. Written by Jacob Koskoff, Michael Lesslie and Todd Louiso, based on a play by William Shakespeare.

Mark of the Devil (1970). Directed by Michael Armstrong. Written by Adrian Hoven.

Mark of the Witch (1970). Directed by Tom Moore. Written by Mary Davis and Martha Peters.

Marketa Lazarová (1967). Directed by Frantisek Vlácil. Written by Frantisek Vlácil and Frantisek Pavlícek, based on a novel by Vladislav Vancura.

Messiah of Evil (1973). Directed by Willard Huyck. Written by Gloria Katz and Willard Huyck.

Morgiana (1972). Directed by Juraj Herz. Written by Vladimír Bor and Juraj Herz, based on a story by Alexander Grin.

Neither the Sea Nor the Sand (1972). Directed by Fred Burnley. Written by Gordon Honeycomb.

Night Creatures (Captain Clegg) (1962). Directed by Peter Graham-Scott. Written by Anthony Hinds.

Night of the Demon (1957). Directed by Jacques Tourneur. Adapted by Charles Bennett and Hal. E. Chester, based on a story by M.R. James.

Night of the Eagle (1962). Directed by Sidney Hayers. Written by Charles Beaumont and Richard Matheson, based on a novel by Fritz Leiber Jr.

The Night of the Hunter (1955). Directed by Charles Laughton. Written by James Agee, based on a novel by Davis Grubb.

Nosferatu (1922). Directed by F.W. Murnau. Written by Henrik Galeen, based on a novel by Bram Stoker.

The Omen (1976). Directed by Richard Donner. Written by David Seltzer.

Onibaba (1964). Directed and written by Kaneto Shindô.

The Others (2001). Directed and written by Alejandro Amenábar.

Paranoiac (1963). Directed by Freddie Francis. Written by Jimmy Sangster.

Penny Journey (1938). Directed by Humphrey Jennings.

The Phantom Carriage (1921). Directed and written by Victor Sjöström, based on a novel by Selma Lagerlöf.

Picnic at Hanging Rock (1975). Directed by Peter Weir. Written by Cliff Green, based on a novel by Joan Lindsay.

The Plague of the Zombies (1966). Directed by John Gilling. Written by Peter Bryan.

The Pledge (1981). Directed and written by Digby Rumsey, based on a story by Lord Dunsany.

Puffball: The Devil's Eyeball (2007). Directed by Nicolas Roeg. Written by Dan Weldon, based on a novel by Fay Weldon.

Psychomania (1973). Directed by Don Sharp. Written by Julian Zimet and Arnaud d'Usseau.

Quatermass II (1957). Directed by Val Guest. Written by Nigel Kneale.

Quatermass and the Pit (1967). Directed by Roy Ward Baker. Written by Nigel Kneale.

The Quiet Ones (2013). Directed by John Pogue. Written by Craig Rosenberg and Oren Moverman.

Race with the Devil (1975). Directed by Jack Starrett. Written by Lee Frost and Wes Bishop.

Rawhead Rex (1986). Directed by George Pavlou. Written by Clive Barker.

The Reptile (1966). Directed by John Gilling. Written by Anthony Hinds.

Requiem for a Village (1975). Directed and written by David Gladwell.

Rituals (1977). Directed by Peter Carter. Written by Ian Sutherland.

Rosemary's Baby (1968). Directed and written by Roman Polanski, based on a novel by Ira Levin.

The Sacrifice (1986). Directed and written by Andrei Tarkovsky.

Satan's Slave (1976). Directed by Norman J. Warren. Written by David McGillivray.

Satanic Pandemonium (1975). Directed and written by Gilberto Martínez Solares, based on a story by Jorge Barragán.

The Satanic Rites of Dracula (1973). Directed by Alan Gibson. Written by Don Houghton.

Season of the Witch (Hungry Wives) (1972). Directed and written by George A. Romero.

The Seventh Seal (1957). Directed and written by Ingmar Bergman.

The Seventh Victim (1943). Directed by Mark Robson. Written by Charles O'Neal and DeWitt Bodeen.

The She Beast (1966). Directed and written by Michael Reeves.

The Shout (1978). Directed by Jerzy Skolimowski. Written by Michael Austin and Jerzy Skolimowski, based on a story by Robert Graves.

The Shuttered Room (1967). Directed by David Greene. Written by Nat Tanchuck and D.B. Ledrov, based on a story by H.P. Lovecraft.

Sightseers (2012). Directed by Ben Wheatley. Written by Steve Oram and Alice Lowe, with additional material by Amy Jump.

Something Weird (1967). Directed by Herschell Gordon Lewis. Written by James F. Hurley.

The Sorcerers (1967). Directed by Michael Reeves. Written by Tom Baker and John Burke.

Straw Dogs (1971). Directed by Sam Peckinpah. Written by David Zelag Goodman and Sam Peckinpah, based on a novel by Gordon Williams.

Tales That Witness Madness (1973). Directed by Freddie Francis. Written by Jennifer Jayne.

The Texas Chainsaw Massacre (1974). Directed by Tobe Hooper. Written by Kim Henkel and Tobe Hooper.

To the Devil a Daughter (1976). Directed by Peter Sykes. Written by Christopher Wicking and John Peacock, based on a novel by Dennis Wheatley.

The Tomb of Ligeia (1966). Directed by Roger Corman. Written by Robert Towne, based on a story by Edgar Allan Poe.

Tower of Evil (1972). Directed and written by Jim O'Connolly, based on a story by George Baxt.

The Undead (1957). Directed by Roger Corman. Written by Charles B Griffith and Mark Hanna.

Valerie and Her Week of Wonders (1970). Directed by Jaromil Jires. Written by Ester Krumbachová and Jaromil Jires, based on a novel by Vítezslav Nezval.

The Virgin Spring (1960). Directed by Ingmar Bergman. Written by Ulla Isaksson.

Viy (1967). Directed by Konstantin Ershov and Georgiy Kropachyov. Written by Aleksandr Ptushko, Konstantin Ershov and Georgiy Kropachyov, based on a novel by Nikolai Gogol.

Wake in Fright (1971). Directed by Ted Kotcheff. Written by Evan Jones, based on a novel by Kenneth Cook.

Walkabout (1971). Directed by Nicolas Roeg. Written by Edward Bond, based on a novel by James Vance Marshall.

Warlock Moon (1973). Directed and written by Bill Herbert.

Watership Down (1978). Directed and written by Martin Rosen, based on the novel by Richard Adams.

The White Reindeer (1952). Directed by Erik Blomberg. Written by Erik Blomberg and Mirjami Kuosmanen.

The Wicker Man (1973). Directed by Robin Hardy. Written by Anthony Schaffer, based on a novel by David Penner.

The Wicker Man (2006). Directed and written by Neil LaBute, based on a screenplay by Anthony Shaffer.

The Wicker Tree (2011). Directed and written by Robin Hardy.

Winstanley (1975). Directed and written by Kevin Brownlow and Andrew Mollo, based on a novel by David Caute.

The Witch (2015). Directed and written by Robert Eggers.

Witchcraft '70 (1970). Directed and written by Luigi Sacttini.

Witchcraft (1964). Directed by Don Sharp. Written by Harry Spalding

Witchhammer (1970). Directed by Otakar Vávra. Written by Ester Krumbachová and Otakar Vávra, based on a novel by Václav Kaplický.

The Witches (1966). Directed by Cyril Frankel. Written by Nigel Kneale, based on a novel by Norah Lofts.

Witchfinder General (1968). Directed by Michael Reeves. Written by Tom Baker and Michael Reeves, based on a novel by Roland Bassett and a poem by Edgar Allan Poe.

The Witchmaker (1969). Directed and written by William O. Brown.

Withnail & I (1987). Directed and written by Bruce Robinson.

Wolf Creek (2005). Directed and written by Greg McLean.

The Woman In Black (2012). Directed by James Watkins. Written by Jane Goldmam, based on a novel by Susan Hill.

Television

Note: For individual episodes and standalone dramas mentioned, the director and writing credits are listed. For whole series, the series producer is mentioned alongside directorial and writing duties when only a singular person is responsible. For the sake of simplicity, productions for ITV through their various past companies such as Granada, ATV, HTV, etc. are simply accredited to ITV.

The Village of Evil (1966), *Adam Adamant Lives!* (BBC). Directed by Anthea Browne-Wilkinson. Written by Vince Powell and Harry Driver.

Murrain (1975), *Against the Crowd* (ITV). Directed by John Cooper. Written by Nigel Kneale.

Apaches (1977) (Public Information Film). Directed by John Mackenzie. Written by Neville Smith.

Arthur of the Britons (1972–1973) (ITV). Produced by Patrick Dromgoole and Peter Miller.

The Ash Tree (1975) (BBC). Directed by Lawrence Gordon Clark. Adapted by David Rudkin, based on a story by M.R. James.

Murdersville (1968), *The Avengers* (ITV). Directed by Robert Asher. Written by Brian Clements.

Beasts (1976) (ITV). Produced by Nicholas Palmer. Written by Nigel Kneale.

The Box of Delights (1984) (BBC). Directed by Renny Rye. Adapted by Alan Seymour, based on the novel by John Masefield.

Look to the Lady (1989), *Campion* (BBC). Directed by Martyn Friend. Written by Alan Plater, based on a story by Margaret Alingham.

The Changes (1975) (BBC). Directed by John Prowse. Written by Peter Dickinson and Anna Home.

A Child's Voice (1978) (BBC). Directed by Kieran Hickey. Written by David Thompson.

The Children of Green Knowe (1986) (BBC). Directed by Colin Cant. Adapted by John Stadelman, based on the novel by Lucy M. Boston.

Children of the Stones (1977) (ITV). Directed by Peter Graham-Scott. Written by Trevor Ray and Jeremy Burnham.

Classic Ghost Stories of M.R. James (1986) (BBC). Produced by Angela Beeching. Directed by David Bell. Based on stories by M.R. James.

The Clifton House Mystery (1978) (ITV). Produced by Leonard White and Patrick Dromgoole. Written by Daniel Farson and Harry Moore.

Crooked House (2008) (BBC). Directed by Damon Thomas. Written by Mark Gatiss.

The Exorcism (1972), *Dead of Night* (BBC). Directed and written by Don Taylor.

A Woman Sobbing (1972), *Dead of Night* (BBC). Directed by Paul Ciappessoni. Written by John Bowen.

The Android Invasion (1975), *Doctor Who* (BBC). Directed by Barry Letts. Written by Terry Nation.

The Awakening (1984), *Doctor Who* (BBC). Directed by Michael Owen Morris. Written by Eric Pringle.

The Curse of Fenric (1989), *Doctor Who* (BBC). Directed by Nicholas Mallett. Written by Ian Briggs.

The Daemons (1971), *Doctor Who* (BBC). Directed by Christopher Barry. Written by Barry Letts and Robert Sloman.

Doctor Who and the Silurians (1970), *Doctor Who* (BBC). Directed by Timothy Combe. Written by Malcolm Hulke.

Hide (2013), *Doctor Who* (BBC). Directed by Jamie Payne. Written by Neil Cross.

The Green Death (1973), *Doctor Who* (BBC). Directed by Michael E. Briant. Written by Robert Sloman.

Image of the Fendhal (1977), *Doctor Who* (BBC). Directed by George Spenton-Foster. Written by Christopher Boucher.

The Sea Devils (1972), *Doctor Who* (BBC). Directed by Michael E. Briant. Written by Malcolm Hulke.

The Stones of Blood (1978), *Doctor Who* (BBC). Directed by Darrol Blake. Written by David Fisher.

Terror of the Zygons (1975), *Doctor Who* (BBC). Directed by Douglas Camfield. Written by Robert Banks Stewart.

The Visitation (1982), *Doctor Who* (BBC). Directed by Peter Moffat. Written by Eric Saward.

Elidor (1995) (BBC). Directed by John Reardon. Adapted by Alan Garner and Don Webb, based on a novel by Alan Garner.

The Enfield Haunting (2015) (Sky). Directed by Kristoffer Nyholm. Written by Guy Lyon Playfair and Joshua St. Johnston.

The Finishing Line (1977) (Public Information Film). Directed by John Krish. Written by John Krish and Michael Gilmour.

Ghost Stories for Christmas (2000) (BBC). Produced by Richard Downes. Directed by Eleanor Yule. Adapted by Ronald Frame, based on stories by M.R. James.

The Haunting of Radcliffe House (2014) (Channel 5). Directed and written by Nick Willing.

The Ice House (1978) (BBC). Directed by Derek Lister. Written by John Bowen.

Into the Labyrinth (1981–1982) (ITV). Produced by Patrick Dromgoole and Peter Graham-Scott.

Casting the Runes (1979), *ITV Playhouse* (ITV). Directed by Lawrence Gordon Clark. Adapted by Clive Exton, based on a story by M.R. James.

K-9 & Company: A Girl's Best Friend (1981). Directed by John Black. Written by Terence Dudley.

King of the Castle (1977) (ITV). Produced by Leonard White and Patrick Dromgoole. Written by Bob Baker and Dave Martin.

The Living Grave (1980), *A Leap in the Dark* (BBC). Directed by Colin Rose. Written by David Rudkin.

To Kill a King (1980), *A Leap In the Dark* (BBC). Produced by Michael Croucher. Written by Alan Garner.

The Lost Will of Dr. Rant (1951), *Lights Out!* (NBC). Directed by Lawrence Schwab Jr. Adapted by Doris Halman, based on a story by M.R. James.

Lost Hearts (1973) (BBC). Directed by Lawrence Gordon Clark. Adapted by Robin Chapman, based on a story by M.R. James.

Moondial (1988) (BBC). Directed by Colin Cant. Written by Helen Cresswell.

The Nightmare Man (1981) (BBC). Directed by Douglas Camfield. Adapted by Robert Holmes, based on a novel by David Wiltshire.

Number 13 (2006) (BBC). Directed by Pier Wilkie. Adapted by Justin Hopper, based on a story by M.R. James.

The Omega Factor (1979) (BBC). Produced by George Gallaccio.

Whistle and I'll Come to You (1968), *Omnibus* (BBC). Directed and adapted by Jonathan Miller, based on a story by M.R. James.

Deathday (1971), *Out of the Unknown* (BBC). Directed by Raymond Menmuir. Written by Brian Hayles, based on a novel by Angus Hall.

This Body Is Mine (1971), *Out of the Unknown* (BBC). Directed by Eric Hills. Written by John Tulley.

To Lay a Ghost (1971), *Out of the Unknown* (BBC). Directed by Ken Hannam. Written by Michael J. Bird.

Welcome Home (1971), *Out of the Unknown* (BBC). Directed by Eric Hills. Written by Moris Farhi.

The Owl Service (1969) (ITV). Produced and directed by Peter Plummer. Adapted and based on a novel by Alan Garner.

Nuts in May (1976), *Play for Today* (BBC). Directed and written by Mike Leigh.

Penda's Fen (1974), *Play for Today* (BBC). Directed by Alan Clarke. Written by David Rudkin.

A Photograph (1977), *Play for Today* (BBC). Directed by John Glenister. Written by John Bowen.

Red Shift (1978), *Play for Today* (BBC). Directed by John Mackenzie. Adapted and based on a novel by Alan Garner.

Robin Redbreast (1970), *Play for Today* (BBC). Directed by James MacTaggart. Written by John Bowen.

The Season of the Witch (1970), *Play for Today* (BBC). Directed by Desmond McCarthy. Written by Johnny Byrne.

Play Safe (1978) (Public Information Film). Directed and written by David Eady.

Power of the Witch: Real Or Imaginary (1971) (BBC). Produced by Oliver Hunkin. Written by Michael Bakewell.

A Home of One's Own (1971), *The Persuaders!* (ITV). Directed by James Hill. Written by Terry Nation.

Quatermass II (BBC). Directed by Rudolph Cartier. Written by Nigel Kneale.

Quatermass (aka *The Quatermass Conclusion*) (1979) (ITV). Directed by Piers Haggard. Written by Nigel Kneale.

Raven (1977) (ITV). Directed by Michael Hart. Written by Trevor Ray and Jeremy Burnham.

Remember Me (2014) (BBC). Directed by Ashley Pearce. Written by Gwyneth Hughes.

Rogue Male (1977) (BBC). Directed by Clive Donner. Written by Frederic Raphael, based on a novel by Geoffrey Household.

Sapphire and Steel (1979-1982). Produced by Shaun O'Riordan and David Reid. Created and part written by Peter Hammond.

The Secret of Crickley Hall (2012) (BBC). Directed and written by Joe Ahearne, based on a novel by James Herbet.

The Signalman (1976) (BBC). Directed by Lawrence Gordon Clark. Adapted by Andrew Davies, based on a story by Charles Dickens.

Sky (1975) (ITV). Produced by Leonard White and Patrick Dromgoole. Written by Bob Baker and Dave Martin.

Spine Chillers (1980) (BBC). Produced by Angela Beeching.

The Stalls of Barchester (1971) (BBC). Directed and adapted by Lawrence Gordon Clark, based on a story by M.R. James.

Stigma (1977) (BBC). Directed by Lawrence Gordon Clark. Written by Clive Exton.

The Stone Tape (1972) (BBC). Directed by Peter Sasdy. Written by Nigel Kneale.

The Tractate Middoth (2013) (BBC). Directed and adapted by Mark Gatiss, based on a story by M.R. James.

The Treasure of Abbott Thomas (1974) (BBC). Directed by Lawrence Gordon Clark. Adapted by John Bowen, based on a story by M.R. James.

True Detective (2014–) (HBO). Created by Nic Pizzolatto.

The View from a Hill (2005) (BBC). Directed by Luke Watson. Adapted by Peter Harness, based on a story by M.R. James.

A Warning to the Curious (1972) (BBC). Directed and adapted by Lawrence Gordon Clark, based on a story by M.R. James.

Whistle and I'll Come to You (2010) (BBC). Directed by Andy de Emmony. Adapted by Neil Cross, based on a story by M.R. James.

The Woman in Black (1989) (ITV). Directed by Herbert Wise. Adapted by Nigel Kneale, based on a novel by Susan Hill.

The Witches and the Grinnygogg (1983) (ITV). Directed by Diarmuid Lawrence. Adapted by Roy Russell, based on a novel by Dorothy Edwards.

The Witches of Pendle (1977). Directed by Anthea Browne-Wilkinson. Written by Barry Collins.

Acknowledgements

My thanks firstly go to my parents, Jan and Keith, for their constant support of my work. Without the freedom they afforded me during my Masters degree especially, I wouldn't have been able to explore many of the ideas which would finally make up this book. It is to them that this book is dedicated.

Thanks as well to Lauren Burke for being there during the early stages of this book whilst it was driving me totally mad. I'd have probably gone loopy (a lot more quickly...) without your support. You're in these pages too.

Folk Horror has become a huge beast in the last few years and this has been down to a number of key figures, all of which deserve thanks for various reasons. Thank you to my fellow Folk Horror Revival administrators, especially Andy Paciorek, Darren Charles, Jim Peters, Grey Malkin and John Pilgrim. My thanks to the organisers of the many conferences and events which have allowed me to explore several of the ideas in this book including: Eamon Byers and Craig Wallace for 'A Fiend in the Furrows', James Riley and Yvonne Salmon for 'The Alchemical Landscape', John Reppion and Leah Moore for 'Spirits of Place', Jen Wood and Erin Lafford for 'Spectral Landscapes' and Jim Peters for 'Otherworldly' at the British Museum.

My thanks in particular to Dr. Robert Macfarlane for his constant and much appreciated academic support and friendship throughout everything I do. His words are a constant inspiration and played heavily on several chapters in this book. Thanks as well to Dr. Holly Rogers, Dr. Giles Hooper and Dr. John McGrath for keeping me on the straight and narrow with my *actual* PhD research and work.

Thank you to 92 Degrees Coffee and Unit 51 in Liverpool for copious caffeine during the writing of this book and thanks to Volcano Coffee and The Rosendale in Dulwich for the coffee and alcohol during its editing.

I would not have got this far with my work without the support and help of many people in my digital life. My thanks to John Atkinson at Auteur, Dr. Brian Baker, Jeff Barrett at *Caught by the River*, George Bickers, Gary Budden, Arianne Churchman, Peter Guy at Get Into This, Justin Hopper, James Jackson at *The Times*, Sharron Kraus, Eddie Proctor, Laura and Mike Robertson at *The Double Negative*, Dr. Katy Soar, David Southwell, Sam Wigley at the BFI, all of the team at Small Cinema Liverpool and the many other people who have supported, shared and got my work out there in the last few years.

Index

Also available

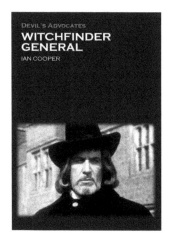

Witchfinder General
Ian Cooper

'I enjoyed it very much; it sets out all the various influences, both before and after the film, and indeed the essence of the film itself, very well indeed. It's great to see the film celebrated and dissected at such length.' Jonathan Rigby, author of *English Gothic*

Frightmares A History of British Horror Cinema
Ian Cooper

' . . . a witty, affectionate yet highly perceptive whistle-stop tour of Britain's genre legacy. . . Eminently readable and flab-free, *Frightmares* is among the most enjoyable studies of Brit horror to date.' *Frightfest*

Macbeth
Rebekah Owens

This is the first, serious attempt to regard Polanski's *Macbeth* as a horror film in its own right, and not exclusively as one of a multitude of ongoing Shakespeare film adaptations.

.

www.ingramcontent.com/pod-product-compliance
Ingram Content Group UK Ltd.
Pitfield, Milton Keynes, MK11 3LW, UK
UKHW021943260225
455626UK00010B/79